VIOLENT CHILDREN

A Reference Handbook

VIOLENT CHILDREN

A Reference Handbook

Karen L. Kinnear

**CONTEMPORARY
WORLD ISSUES**

ABC-CLIO

Santa Barbara, California
Denver, Colorado
Oxford, England

Library of Congress Cataloging-in-Publication Data

Kinnear, Karen L.
    Violent Children : a research handbook / Karen L. Kinnear.
        p. cm. — (Contemporary world issues)
    Includes bibliographical references and index.
    1. Violence in children—United States.   2. Violence in children—United States—Societies, etc.—Directories.   3. Violence in children—United States—Bibliography.   4. Juvenile delinquents—United States.   5. Juvenile delinquency—United States.   I. Title.
II. Series.
    HQ784.V55K56   1995   305.23—dc20   95-6457

ISBN 0-87436-786-7

02 01 00 99 98 97 96 95   10 9 8 7 6 5 4 3 2 1

ABC-CLIO, Inc.
130 Cremona Drive, P.O. Box 1911
Santa Barbara, California 93116-1911

This book is printed on acid-free paper ⊗.
Manufactured in the United States of America

To Carol—who helps bring out the gentle child in me

Contents

Preface

The purpose of this book is to provide a survey of the available literature and other resources on the topic of violent children and to provide sources for further research. The literature and resources available offer a variety of theories for the recent growth in violent acts committed by children, including biological, psychological, environmental, and societal causes. Researchers have examined this topic from a variety of aspects and opinions differ on what can be done to turn children away from violence and to protect them from becoming victims of violence. Theories vary from blaming television for dulling children's emotions by exposing them to hours of violent shows to believing the competitive nature of American society is responsible for the increasing levels of violence in this country, especially among children. Because there is no simple reason for what causes violence, there is also no easy solution to this problem. Today, many programs are trying various methods for reducing violence among our young people; several of these programs are succeeding.

This book, like other books in the Contemporary World Issues series, provides a balanced survey of the resources available and a guide to further research on the topic of violent children. Chapter 2 provides a chronology of the significant events relevant to issues surrounding violent children. Chapter 3 offers biographical sketches of individuals who have played or are currently playing key roles in the area of child violence. Chapter 4 provides statistical information on the extent of violent acts committed by children, discusses the results of research conducted on the causes and reasons for children becoming violent, and describes the various treatment options being explored today. Chapter 5 provides a directory of private and public organizations, associations, and government agencies involved in treating violent children as well as trying to prevent children from becoming violent. In Chapter 6, books, handbooks, manuals, and periodicals focusing on the causes of and recommended solutions to violent children are annotated; the literature varies from popular accounts to primary research carried out and provides a wide perspective on this problem. Chapter 7 includes an annotated list of nonprint resources including films and videocassettes.

Introduction 1

Attorney General Janet Reno has called youth violence "the greatest single crime problem in America today." According to the *Uniform Crime Reports*, published by the Federal Bureau of Investigation, the number of juveniles arrested for committing a serious violent crime, including murder, rape, robbery, and aggravated assault, increased by 50 percent between 1987 and 1991. During this same period, there was an 85 percent increase in the number of juveniles arrested for murder (Federal Bureau of Investigation 1989, 1991, 1993).

Throughout history, children have caused trouble, played pranks on each other, and fought with each other and with adults. However, today's violence among children seems more hostile, more vindictive, more violent. Acts of violence committed by children seem to be on the rise. Many studies have been conducted on adults who commit violent acts, and we know many of the reasons, or underlying causes, for these acts, including alcoholism, poverty, abusive childhoods, and dysfunctional families. It is harder for many people to understand how a child can murder another child, pull a gun and shoot someone, or commit countless other horrendous crimes. Childhood should be innocent, fun, and full of play. We find it hard to believe that children are capable of killing.

Attention has been drawn to violent children in recent years, with the kidnapping and murder of James Bulger by two ten-year-old boys in England in 1993 and incidents of violence within many of our local communities. We used to think that children committing violent acts were a commonplace occurrence in the inner cities of our country, but not in our "nicer," middle-class communities. This type of violence can now be found in communities all across the United States. Gangs are being blamed for introducing violence to many areas, but there is more to the story than this; gangs cannot be blamed for all the violent acts committed by children today.

Sociologists, psychologists, criminologists, and other experts have explored a wide variety of theories on what causes the violence that makes people want to hurt other people. They have identified several factors that may play a role in aggressive and violent behavior. These include: (1) biological factors, such as high testosterone levels in boys, learning disabilities, fetal alcohol syndrome, and attention deficit disorder; (2) psychological factors, such as low self-esteem, the influence of alcohol and drug use, and personality disorders; (3) environmental and situational factors, such as living in an urban area, growing up in a violent home, growing up in a single-parent family, having easy accessibility to guns, and the extent of television viewing; and (4) societal factors, such as growing up in a society that values competition, being male in a society that often glorifies violence, and living in a violent or peaceful culture.

Most American families today are under more stress than families years ago. The pressures are heavy to excel at work, buy the big, beautiful house in the suburbs, send the children to the best schools, and keep up with the Joneses. We are bombarded with television programs and commercials admonishing us to look our best, entertain with charm and excess, own the fastest cars, and provide our children with the best of everything.

Throughout the literature on violent children, theories suggesting the causes or reasons for this violence center around three major themes: poverty and social class and all the problems associated with poverty, our competitive American society, and children growing up unattached to others and without empathy for others.

In the Inner Cities

We are all familiar with the problems of the inner cities: poverty, alcoholism, racism, single-parent families, hopelessness, and a vast array of other maladies. When stories appear about children acting violently in the inner cities, we shake our heads, knowing that these children are our future criminals. Given the conditions under which they grow up—often with no positive role models and no hope for an improved future—we are seldom surprised when these children don't grow up to be positive, productive adults. What is surprising is how young many of these children are when they turn to violence.

Many of these young children are jaded by the time they are adolescents; they have already lived through so much that they may be old before their time. These children often view life and death from a different perspective than most middle-class, suburban children.

> In the most fearsome youths such a cavalier attitude toward death grows out of a very limited view of life. Many are uncertain about how long they are going to live and believe they could die violently at any time. They accept this fate; they live on the edge. Their manner conveys the message that nothing intimidates them; whatever turn the encounter takes, they maintain their attack—rather like a pit bull, whose spirit many such boys admire. The demonstration of such tenacity "shows heart" and earns their respect.
>
> This fearlessness has implications for law enforcement. Many street-oriented boys are much more concerned about the threat of "justice" at the hands of a peer than at the hands of the police. Moreover, many feel not only that they have little to lose by going to prison but that they have something to gain. The toughening-up one experiences in prison can actually enhance one's reputation on the streets. Hence the system loses influence over the hard core who are without jobs and with little perceptible stake in the system. If mainstream society has done nothing for them, they counter by making sure it can do nothing to them. (Anderson 1994, 94)

Socioeconomic status also plays a role in whether or not a

child is at high risk for violent behavior. Low socioeconomic status is a critical factor in predicting later violent behavior. For example, homicide rates rise significantly for both whites and blacks as their socioeconomic status declines (Wintemute et al. 1992, 81).

Single-parent families are often blamed for raising children who get into trouble at some time in their lives. Often led by women, these families may have trouble making ends meet. The mother may work long hours to help put food on the table and a roof over her children's heads, there may be no positive male role model at home, and a variety of other problems may also exist. Teenage pregnancies may add to the problems of an already troubled teenager. Some researchers believe that police play an important part in providing positive role models for children and helping them learn right from wrong. Others believe that the police presence in the inner cities only helps perpetuate the problems of youth in these areas.

> The police are the major representatives of societal authority within the inner city; with their uniforms, guns, and cars, they present an image of power and control; and they are the most visible governmental response to specific incidents of violence. Police officers have daily encounters with children and families in crisis—those involved in family violence, witnessing crimes, or suffering as victims of aggression—and increasingly are confronted by very young children who are the perpetrators or victims of aggression.
>
> At their best, police can provide children and families a sense of security and safety through rapid, authoritative, and effective responses at times of difficulty. All too often, however, children's contacts with police officers arouse far less comforting and more negative feelings. In the psychological lives of inner-city children, the appearance of police officers in the context of aggression makes them the objects for displacement of both children's and their families' rage; their arrival "after the fact" strengthens children's view of society as unprotective, and the role of police as symbols of the dominant culture may shape children's views of them as representatives of an alien, uncaring outside world. In fact, the contacts between police and children are sometimes harsh and police

officers, especially in the midst of a crisis, may not have time to be considerate to, or may be thoughtless about, children's emotional needs. Negative encounters may further reinforce a child's view of society as uncaring and aggressive. Thus, these experiences may strengthen a child's concept that hostile behavior—being rough and tough, bullying, acting strong—is not only appropriate and reasonable in certain situations but is the normative mode of adult behavior. There are often too few countervailing models of social authority available in an inner-city child's world. (Marans and Cohen 1993, 283)

Helping children in the inner cities escape the violence and grow into productive adults may go a long way toward reducing violence among these children. However, there are additional reasons why children behave violently.

Competitive Society

We live in a competitive society—American culture tends to be more competitive than many other cultures; Americans tend to focus on success, on winning. We teach our children to want to be the best, to get the highest grades, win the most games, and outperform everyone else. Parents teach their children that they must be competitive in order to survive and prosper in today's society and that it is an inevitable part of life. They must learn to compete in order to get into the best colleges, to get the best jobs, and to attract the best mate, all in the quest to be successful. Many of our school systems foster competitive, rather than co-operative, learning. Students compete against each other for the best grades, the most recognition, and the best positions on the sports teams. There is always a winner and a loser. America's focus on success leaves many children out; those children who are failures in school, believe their home lives are a failure, or have trouble with friendships are not considered successful by most of society.

The way we participate in sports activities also emphasizes the importance we place on competition. Several researchers believe that participating in sports teaches boys to be aggressive, which can lead to violent behavior, while others contend that even watching sports can lead to violent behavior. Some researchers have found that boys involved in youth sports activities demonstrate less sportsmanship than boys not involved in sports; others have found that the people who participate in sports on a regular basis value winning over fairness and justice. While many Americans believe that, by participating in sports, boys learn valuable lessons for later in life, such as teamwork and cooperation, much of the research on sports and violence leads to a very different conclusion. Also, while these findings apply specifically to boys, even girls may be exposed to similar teachings as opportunities expand for them in the sports world.

The importance of high self-esteem and its frequent absence in many children with aggressive or violent behavior may also be a factor in children becoming violent. Michael Novak writes that "a game tests, somehow, one's entire life," suggesting that losing at games impacts people psychologically and may lower their self-esteem (Novak 1976). The relationship between self-esteem, competition, and violent behavior needs to be studied in-depth.

Lack of Empathy

Children today may also be at higher risk for becoming aggressive and violent because they have not become attached, either to their families or to people in general. Some researchers believe that if children do not bond properly and early with their parents, especially their mothers, they will not be able to trust others or develop a conscience (Magid and McKelvey 1987). Many reasons exist for this lack of attachment and lack of caring for others. Working mothers have less time for their children: many mothers are forced, by financial reasons or maternity leave policies, to return to work before properly bonding with their children, and more parents are forced to place their children in day care because both must work. Even television has been blamed for creating children lacking in empathy. Many studies have found that children who watch violence on television are more aggressive than others, less likely to cooperate and share possessions with others, more afraid of the real world, and less likely to help victims of real-life violence. The federal government concluded in 1982 that excessive levels of television violence lead to aggressive, violent behavior in children (National Institute of Mental Health 1982).

Other researchers have examined the reasons why some children get into trouble while others stay out of trouble, no matter what their home environment is like. Stanton Samenow believes "that children become antisocial by choice: lying, fighting, stealing, and other forms of destructive behavior are willful acts" (Samenow 1989, 3). He believes that the environment in which a child grows up is less important than the child's reaction to that environment.

Why Do Children Murder?

To the casual observer, most violent acts committed by children seem to have been committed for no apparent reason—they seem senseless. However, many of the children involved in violent acts believe they have plenty of reasons. Children who murder their parents may be motivated by the actions of one or both parents, including physical abuse or sexual abuse perpetrated against the other parent or one or more of the children. Children who murder strangers may be doing so for several reasons. They may have intended only to rob a victim, but decided at the last minute to murder the victim when they realized that they could be identified. For many children, what they have done may seem logical and acceptable to them.

Who are the victims of these violent juveniles? Cornell and his colleagues studied 72 juveniles who committed murder and found that 15 killed family members, 34 killed friends or acquaintances, and the remaining 23 killed strangers (Cornell, Benedek, and Benedek 1987). Cormier and Markus studied the cases of 29 juvenile killers and found that 6 killed parents and 23 killed acquaintances or strangers (Cormier and Markus 1980). Other studies have focused exclusively on children who kill their parents. No statistics have been developed to show the distribution of all juvenile murder victims, although most researchers estimate that less than 20 percent of the victims are family members.

Charles Patrick Ewing believes that in addition to the types of murder described above,

> there are, however, many juvenile homicides that can only be described as senseless. While it is obvious that senseless killings are extremely deviant acts, it does not necessarily follow that youths who commit such acts are seriously disturbed or otherwise significantly abnormal. Indeed, in many cases, senseless, even brutal and bizarre, killings are committed by relatively normal juveniles acting on impulse—often in conjunction

with or under the influence of other juveniles. Some of these youths are disturbed, some even appear to be sociopathic, but very few show signs of gross psychological or psychiatric disturbance, most have functioned at home, at school, and in the community prior to the killing . . . very few juveniles who kill are psychotic. (Ewing 1990, 63)

The following sections explore the theories and thoughts of many researchers and experts in the field of children and violence.

Causes

In the past, many researchers believed that violence was caused by biological factors, i.e., that it was genetically determined and a person had no control over whether or not he was violent. Some believed that the tendency toward violent behavior was genetic, but that people did have some control over whether or not violent behavior actually occurred. Others believed that certain environmental factors, such as how a child was raised or whether the child had an extended family available, were the primary factors in determining violent behavior. Today, many scholars who study criminal behavior believe that no theory of the causes of crime exists to explain every criminal act; a complex interaction of influences determines whether or not a child becomes violent.

For example, Roth believes that

every violent event is a chance occurrence, in the sense that no human characteristic, set of circumstances, or chain of events makes violence inevitable. It seems reasonable to assume that some intervention might have prevented each violent event, but the correct intervention cannot be known in advance for every individual case. As starting points for exploring prevention, there are well-documented risk factors, which increase the odds that violence will occur. Some risk factors can be modified to reduce those odds. There is always a chance, however, that violence will occur in a low-risk setting or fail to occur in a very high-risk setting. (Roth 1994b, 5)

Dryfoos, synthesizing research in this field, identified seven major predictors of delinquency, teenage pregnancy, juvenile delinquency, and failure in school. These included early signs of aggressive or violent behavior; failing in school or expecting to fail in school; impulsive behavior, avoiding school, and antisocial tendencies; failing to resist peer pressure; lack of bonding to parents and poor relationships with parents; living in poverty; and not attending church (Dryfoos 1990).

The following section explores theories of the causes of violent behavior, organizing these theories into four basic categories: biological, psychological/psychosocial, environmental, and societal. The reader should keep in mind, however, that most authorities believe that violent behavior is often caused by a complex interplay among many factors.

1. Biological—The theories included here emphasize the importance of the interactions of chemical, electrical, and hormonal influences, primarily in the brain, which form the basis of all human behavior. The role of genetics is often mentioned as a causal factor in violent criminal behavior. Many researchers believe that the tendency toward aggressive behavior will be as easily measured in the future as IQ is today. Factors included in this category include genetic predispositions to aggressive behavior, the effect of diet on violent behavior, chemical imbalances in the brain, the presence of learning disabilities, high levels of testosterone, psychomotor epilepsy, severe head injuries, mental retardation, and attention-deficit disorder (ADD).

2. Psychological—Theories in this category focus on individual characteristics that influence our interactions with each other. Learned ways of behaving, such as how we are taught to deal with anger, and how we behave when under stress, under the influence of alcohol or drugs, and in awkward situations, as well as low self-esteem, personality disorders, and how we have learned to make choices in our lives, are included here.

3. Environmental/Situational—In this category we find the characteristics of people encountering other people, that is, how we react when we meet other people: do we exchange insults, have a weapon available, have group support through gang membership, go to church, or have a strong extended family? Many theories of what causes children to become violent fall into this category.

Risk factors that are environmental include living in an urban area; growing up in a violent home or one lacking appropriate affection and care; coming from a single-parent family, a family in which both parents work or in which neither parent works; lacking a strong social support network (or looking to gangs for that support); having easy access to weapons; being victimized by others; and the extent of television viewing.

4. Societal—Poverty, lack of economic opportunities, multicultural influences, sex-role socialization and stereotypes, and other overall societal forces that we have little or no control over are factors considered here to contribute to delinquency and violent behavior. Being male in a society that often tends to glorify violence, being a minority, being homosexual, living in a competitive society, and living in a passive or violent culture are some of the factors considered here.

Biological Factors

Sigmund Freud, the founder of psychoanalysis, believed in the role of the sexual drive in motivating individuals to behave in a variety of ways; he was convinced that evil was an essential part of human nature. He also wrote about his belief in the existence of a "death instinct":

Men are not gentle friendly creatures wishing for love. . . . A powerful measure of desire for aggression has to be reckoned as a part of their instinctual endowment. . . . *Homo homini lupus*: who has the courage to dispute it in the face of all the evidence in his own life and in history? This aggressive cruelty usually lies in wait for some provocation, or else it steps into the service of some other purpose, the aim of which might well have been achieved by milder measures. In circumstances that favor it, when those forces in the mind which ordinarily inhibit it cease to operate, it also manifests itself spontaneously and reveals men as savage beasts to whom the thought of sparing their own kind is alien. Anyone who calls to mind the atrocities of the early migrations, of the invasions by the Huns or by the so-called Mongols under Genghis Khan and Tamerlane, of the sack of Jerusalem by the pious Crusaders, even indeed of the horrors of the last world war, will have to bow his head before the truth of this view of man. (Freud 1930, 86)

Other researchers over the years, including Konrad Lorenz, Desmond Morris, Raymond Dart, Robert Ardrey, Anthony Storr, and Niko Tinbergen, have proposed that aggression is innate. However, few experts today believe that aggressive behavior is totally genetic; most believe that a general tendency for aggressive behavior may be genetic, but environmental factors play a significant role in the expression of aggressive behavior.

According to Roth, current research indicates that

> violent behavior may be associated with certain relatively permanent conditions and temporary states of the nervous system. These possibilities relate to the following processes: the functioning in the brain of certain hormones and other body chemicals called neurotransmitters; certain physical abnormalities in the brain, which could be present at birth or develop as a result of brain injuries or maturation; certain abnormal brain wave responses to outside stress; brain dysfunctions that, by interfering with communication and thought processes, lead to school failure and other childhood problems that are well-known precursors of violent behavior; and temporary effects of drinking alcohol, perhaps heightened by hypoglycemia or other health problems. (Roth 1994b, 7–8)

Many studies of genetic influences on behavior indicate that individual characteristics such as impulsiveness, thrill seeking, and the inclination to attack are inherited characteristics (Cairns, Gariepy, and Hood 1990). Studies in neurobiology have shown that neurotransmitters play a role in impulsive violence (Linnoila et al. 1983, 2609–2614). While these biological influences are demonstrated in several studies, they are also influenced by the physical, family, and social environments to which each person is exposed, especially at an early age.

Lewis and her colleagues studied 14 male juveniles who were awaiting execution in 4 states for violent crimes; they were estimated to be 40 percent of all juveniles on death row (35) in the United States. They found that 8 boys had suffered head injuries that were severe enough to require hospitalization, 9 boys had abnormal EEGs which indicated neurological dysfunction, and 12 boys had an IQ of less than 90 (Lewis et al. 1988, 584–589). In another study, Lewis and her colleagues studied 97 juvenile delinquents who were incarcerated for displaying varying degrees of violent behavior. They found significant differences between the violent juveniles and the nonviolent or less violent juveniles: the violent juveniles were more likely to exhibit paranoid symptoms, rambling speech patterns, and poor mental functioning. Although not statistically significant, the researchers also found that the violent boys experienced hallucinations and exhibited major neurological problems (Lewis et al. 1980, 591–603).

Testosterone

Many scientists have examined the link between high levels of testosterone and violent behavior in boys. Dan Olweus, a Norwegian psychologist, and his colleagues conducted a study of adolescent males to determine the effect that varying levels of testosterone had on their behavior, specifically antisocial and violent behavior. They found that boys with high levels of testosterone were more likely to become frustrated, more impatient, and more irritable than other boys (Olweus, Block, and Radke-Yarrow 1986). They referred to these displays of aggressiveness as "testosterone poisoning" but were unsure whether higher levels of testosterone increased aggressive behavior or whether aggressive behavior increased levels of testosterone. These higher levels may increase the likelihood of boys displaying aggressive or violent behavior at some point in their lives. Higher levels of testosterone in boys may also explain why boys tend to exhibit more violent behavior than girls do, although some researchers believe that this difference is primarily a function of socialization—boys are socialized to be aggressive and violent, while girls are taught to be gentle and passive.

Two psychologists, Eleanor Maccoby and Carol Jacklin, studied the psychological aspects of differences between the sexes. They found that aggression was one of the few characteristics that were indeed different between the sexes. In general, they found that males, as a group, tend to become more easily frustrated than females and to act more impulsively (Maccoby and Jacklin 1974). This difference may be explained by biological factors such as higher levels of testosterone, but there could also be other factors involved, including socialization practices.

Studies in this area suggest that when looking for a biological basis for male behavior, characteristics such as an increased tendency toward frustration, irritability, and impulsiveness should be taken into account. Another factor to be considered here is the way in which boys are raised. Edward O. Wilson, a sociobiologist, while arguing that biology is the basis of human behavior, underscores the important role of culture and the interaction of biology and culture (Wilson 1982).

Learning Disabilities

Children who are learning disabled, i.e., slower to think about and react to information and various situations, also may be at higher risk for violent behavior. However, the U.S. Department of Justice reviewed many research studies on the relationship between learning disabilities and criminal behavior and concluded that the "existence of a causal relationship between learning disabilities and delinquency has not been established; the evidence for a causal link is feeble" (U.S. Department of Justice 1976, 2). On the other hand, other researchers have found that learning disabilities are often found in greater proportion in the juvenile and adult jail populations. Miedzian reports that estimates have been made that "approximately 32 percent of delinquent boys and 40 percent of the jail population in the United States suffer from learning disability" (Miedzian 1991, 67).

Attention Deficit Disorder

Several researchers believe that children with attention deficit disorder are more likely to engage in aggressive, even violent, behavior; because they are unable to stay focused on anything, these children may be more likely to become frustrated and angry and always need some excitement in their lives. Miedzian suggests that boys with ADDH (attention-deficit disorder with hyperactivity) may be more prone to aggressive or violent behavior. She also believes that ADDH is a predisposing factor for developing an antisocial personality disorder in later childhood or as an adult (Miedzian 1991).

Fetal Alcohol Syndrome

What a woman does while she is pregnant also may influence her child's behavior. Jeffrey Roth describes research that demonstrates that pregnant women who use psychoactive drugs, including alcohol, interfere with their child's development. These children often exhibit learning and communication problems (Roth 1994a).

Psychological/Psychosocial Factors

Wilson and Herrnstein suggest that we look at crime from the perspective of the forces that control individual behavior. While many factors can contribute to crime, including the breakdown of the family, the ready availability of drugs, the failure of public schools, and the state of the economy, Wilson and Herrnstein believe that these factors must somehow affect the behavior of individuals in deciding whether or not to commit a crime. Their theory states that "whatever people choose to do, they choose it because they prefer it. . . . All we mean is that their behavior is determined by its consequences. A person will do that thing the consequences of which are perceived by him or her to be preferable to the consequences of doing something else" (Wilson and Herrnstein 1985, 43). Every behavior or action has a consequence associated with it; if the result (reward) is greater than the punishment, as perceived by the individual, a crime will likely be committed.

Stanton Samenow looked for explanations as to why some children get into trouble while others stay out of trouble, no matter what their background or upbringing. He believes that children choose to become antisocial; when children lie, steal, or fight they have made a conscious choice to behave in this way (Samenow 1989, 3). Many therapists believe that the environment does play a role in shaping a child, that parents are responsible for their child's behavior, and that bad parenting is a major cause of a child's problems. Samenow believes otherwise; he believes that the "environment from which a person comes is less crucial than the choice the individual makes as he responds to that environment" (Samenow 1989, 18). He goes on to say that

> yet while currently much is said about holding people accountable for their behavior, whenever one reads about antisocial conduct, the inclination still is to place the locus of responsibility outside the individual. My objective in clinical work has been to help the antisocial individual change the way he thinks so that he will change the way he behaves. . . . In no sense do I move away from my findings that irresponsible and criminal behavior are the results of choice. I do not blame parents for "producing" criminals because they may be deficient as parents. But I do recognize that there are errors parents make that could be avoided as they try to help their children become responsible

citizens, errors that may in fact reinforce the behavior they wish to inhibit. (Samenow 1989, 23)

Samenow sees the antisocial child as refusing to become a responsible and caring human being; instead, this child expects people to act as if he is the center of attention, always wanting things done his way.

> The antisocial youngster knows right from wrong. In his mind, however, he can cloak wrongdoing in righteousness because it is what he wants to do at the time. Because he wants to do it, it is right; if someone else does the same thing, then it is wrong. The second point is that, after the fact, the antisocial youngster still does not think about the harm he has done. He is concerned about saving his own skin. He finds the best defense is to go on the offensive and blame others. . . . Third, the antisocial youngster can thoroughly confuse others and sometimes gain sympathy by emphasizing how good his intentions were. He expects that focusing on his good intentions will obscure or at least mitigate the harmfulness of whatever he did. (Samenow 1989, 57–58)

Antisocial children are usually bored with school and socially acceptable hobbies. They find little reason to spend time doing things that other children consider normal; they are looking for excitement that no school can provide. They refuse to be held accountable for their actions; whatever happens is always someone else's fault. They have no connection to others, no empathy with others, and use relationships with others only for their own gain (Samenow 1989). This reasoning may explain why some children claim that they committed a crime because they were bored and they wanted to find something exciting to do.

Other researchers also believe that children make choices according to the perceived rewards. Lawrence Kohlberg, a psychologist, examined moral judgment in children. He described six stages in developing morals that are universal across cultures; in early stages, whether an act is good or bad is determined by the consequences of that act. In the final stages, the individual develops ethical and moral principles (Kohlberg 1971). Normally, children progress through all stages; however, some children appear to get caught at one stage and are not able to develop further.

Lefkowitz, Eron, Walder, and Heusmann studied children's aggressive behavior over 20 years and found that the presence of aggressive behavior in an 8-year-old is the best predictor for aggressive behavior at age 19; other factors such as social class, IQ, and aggression levels and behavior in parents have little influence. Children who display aggressive behavior are more likely than other children to continue aggressive actions into adulthood and may even exhibit violent behavior (Lefkowitz et al. 1977).

Individual Psychological Factors

Rollo May believed that violence occurs when people feel powerless.

> Violence, or acts close to it, gives one a sense of counting, of mattering, of power. . . . This in turn gives the individual a sense of significance. . . . It is the lack of this sense of significance, and the struggle for it, that underlies much violence. (May 1972, 36–37)

He suggests that American children are taught that aggression and violence are wrong, but television shows and movies have been created that teach aggressive behavior to children and show them that aggressive, even violent, behavior is acceptable. The messages conveyed are confusing and children do not know whether aggression is right or wrong. This confusion adds to a child's feeling of impotence and frustration.

May also talks about parents' love for their children. If parents do not love their children and demonstrate that love, the children will grow up with an underlying desire to seek revenge, to destroy others in the same way that their world was destroyed. When people feel insignificant and unimportant, May believes that they will look for ways in which they can gain that feeling of being significant and important through any means available to them. Often, aggressive and destructive behavior is the means by which significance is achieved. When feelings of aggression build up in an individual, violence often results. The ways in which an individual understands and interprets his environment are critical to the ways he responds to that environment. For example, if a child feels victimized by those around him, with no way to control what happens to him, he will feel powerless and will likely lash out in some aggressive and violent way to gain back some feeling of power and control (May 1972).

Many researchers believe that children who are emotionally

neglected, humiliated, or physically abused while very young are more likely than other children to become violent in later life. Heinz Kohut believes that the likelihood of violent behavior increases if a child's parents or guardians ignore the child, neglect the child's physical and/or emotional needs, or fail to praise the child. All children need recognition, love, and admiration, referred to as "narcissistic" needs by Kohut, and when these needs are not met, children feel a "narcissistic rage" in later life. This rage can take many forms, but no matter what the form, feelings of revenge and desires to fix the hurt are always evident (Kohut 1989). These feelings can often lead to violent behavior.

Alice Miller, a Swiss psychoanalyst, suggests that fulfilling children's emotional needs when they are young is critical to avoiding violent behavior in later life. She examines German child-rearing practices and their effects on the growth of Nazism and concludes that the German practices of breaking a child's will early in life through physical punishment, repression of spontaneity, and demanding unquestioned obedience to authority contributed to the growth of Nazism. Children lack empathy and are emotionally detached when raised in this way. Humiliation and rage are the primary emotions these children feel, which can lead to aggressive and violent behavior in later life (Miller 1983).

Unattachment/Lack of Bonding

Magid and McKelvey believe that "what happens, right or wrong, in the critical first two years of a baby's life will imprint that child as an adult. A complex set of events must occur in infancy to assure a future of trust and love. If the proper bonding and subsequent attachment does not occur—usually between the child and the mother—the child will develop mistrust and a deep-seated rage. He becomes a child without a conscience" (Magid and McKelvey 1987, 3). They believe that while all unattached children do not become criminals, some psychological damage does occur and may manifest itself in various ways. However, unattached children can suffer from antisocial personality disorder (APD), also known as "psychopathology," and after committing a violent crime will feel no remorse or guilt. They believe that there are many reasons that infants do not become attached to their mothers; these include "high divorce rates, day-care problems, lack of a national parental leave policy, epidemic teenage pregnancies, too-late adoptions, the foster care system, absence of mother and/or father during critical periods, postpartum depression, infant medical problems, abuse and neglect and infant unresponsiveness" (Magid and McKelvey 1987, 4).

Magid and McKelvey believe that society must give working mothers more time with their infants and fatherhood must be encouraged and made easier for working fathers. Day-care opportunities must be increased and the quality of day care must be improved, parental leaves must be encouraged, and foster care must be improved. Teenage pregnancies must be discouraged, but when they occur, society must improve treatment and services, both prenatal and after the baby is born. Abuse and neglect of children must stop. If these problems are addressed and resolved, far fewer unattached children will exist and the incidence of violent crime committed by children, as well as by adults, will be decreased (Magid and McKelvey 1987).

According to Foster Cline, an authority on unattached children, children are becoming increasingly violent in today's society as a result of faulty attachment while young, but because these children often appear as friendly, outgoing, bright, and loving, therapists often are fooled into thinking that the parents are responsible for the trouble these children are in. He cites the following characteristics of the unattached, disturbed child:

1. Lack of ability to give and receive affection
2. Self-destructive behavior
3. Cruelty to others
4. Phoniness
5. Severe problems with stealing, hoarding, and gorging on food
6. Speech pathology
7. Marked control problems
8. Lack of long-term friends
9. Abnormalities in eye contact
10. Parents appear angry and hostile
11. Preoccupation with fire, blood or gore
12. Superficial attractiveness and friendliness with strangers
13. Various types of learning disorders
14. A particular pathological type of lying—"primary process lying" (Magid and McKelvey 1987, 13–14)

Martin Lazarus has worked with 50 children who display characteristics of unattached children and have severe character disorders. He believes that if children, as well as adults, can maintain attachments to people, they are less likely to kill other people; unattached children have no connection to other people and therefore feel nothing toward others, do not feel their humanity, and can kill without remorse or guilt (Magid and McKelvey 1987). These children are the ones who are most likely to have no emotion and no reaction to the murders they commit. They continue on as if nothing had happened. Ewing reports the case of one such youngster:

> A fifteen-year-old boy rapes, sodomizes, and bludgeons a thirteen-year-old girl from his neighborhood. He then drags her facedown across the street and several hundred feet through the woods before dumping her into a swamp, where she drowns. After the incident, the boy goes home, cleans up, and attends a birthday party for a girl he has been dating. (Ewing 1990, xiv)

Mary Ainsworth is a leading authority on separation anxiety. She developed a scale for measuring separation anxiety that has become a well-known and often used instrument in testing for separation anxiety in infants and toddlers. Ainsworth believes that people respond automatically with fear when faced with unfamiliar, unexpected circumstances. Once a child has developed trust in other people, has bonded with others, he or she may feel an initial separation anxiety but will be able to work through it; this does not happen with unattached children (Ainsworth 1978). Unattached children are not able to trust other people and are prime candidates for committing violent crimes at some point in their lives.

Many authors cite the fact that mothers are forced to return to work too soon after giving birth as a major reason for unattached, troubled children; they believe that the United States needs a parental leave policy that will allow mothers as well as fathers time to bond with their newborn. For example, T. Berry Brazelton believes that this issue must be addressed. He recognizes critical stages in a baby's development and strongly believes that each stage must include critical, quality time together for the mother and infant (Brazelton 1985). He also believes that competent, unbiased research must be conducted on the relationship between day care and its effects on children.

Self-Esteem

The importance of high self-esteem and its absence in many children with aggressive or violent behavior has been the subject of a great deal of research. Ruth Rubenstein, a sociologist, found that children attending a noncompetitive summer camp increased their levels of self-esteem, while these levels did not change significantly in children attending a competitive summer camp (Rubenstein 1977, 55–57). Contrary to popular opinion, Rubenstein found that children do not increase their self-esteem by participating in competitive activities. Richard Eggerman agrees, suggesting that children with low self-esteem may be more likely to be harmed by competition than children with high self-esteem, in part because they are more sensitive to their position relative to other children. These children are more sensitive to losing than other children and they may feel they have lost more than just a game; competitive activities increase their feelings of inadequacy and insecurity (Eggerman 1982, 48–51).

Michael Novak writes about the psychological impact of losing, noting what it does to one's self-esteem. He believes that a game is a test of a person's life (Novak 1976, 47). Even though winning isn't everything, not losing is important to many people's self-esteem. For people with low self-esteem, competition may make them feel worse, less capable, and unable to cope with losing. For them, winning may be everything. Psychologist Karen Horney examined neuroses and defined them as the absence of "basic confidence" in oneself (Horney 1950, 86). Harry Stack Sullivan and Abraham Maslow also emphasized the importance of self-esteem to a person's healthy growth (Maslow 1970).

Carole Ames, in examining how children behave in competitive situations, found that children often believe they cannot control competitive situations or what happens to them. When they fail at any competitive event, they lose confidence in their ability and in themselves, which often lowers their self-esteem (Ames 1978).

Substance Abuse

According to a report from the National Institute of Justice, research has shown that women who use psychoactive drugs during their pregnancy are harming their child's development. Their children are more likely than other children to develop learning and communication problems which increase the risk of failure in school, one factor that can lead to aggressive, violent behavior (Roth 1994a). Both animal and human research findings indicate "that patterns of substance abuse and aggressive behavior reinforce each other. It cannot be said that one 'causes' the other" (Roth 1994a, 4). These patterns often develop during childhood.

> Research suggests at least four possible explanations for the link between substance abuse and violent behavior in adolescents. First, adolescents may chronically use psychoactive substances to help them temporarily escape from such feelings as rage, guilt, worthlessness, or depression—emotions that often precede aggressive behavior. Second, repeated family arguments over teenage substance abuse may eventually take on a violent character. Next, underlying family problems or socially expected responses may lead some adolescent males to patterns of heavy drinking and fighting as ways to demonstrate their masculinity. Last, boys who regularly observe older males fighting while drinking may learn to expect that violent behavior accompanies alcohol use. All of these processes may be at work, but their roles, interactions, and importance as explanations have not yet been sorted out. (Roth 1994a, 4–5)

Research into the relationship between substance abuse and aggressive or violent behavior suggests a relationship does exist. For example, Malmquist studied 20 juveniles who had committed murder and found that 5 of those 20 had abused some type of drug just before committing the murder (Malmquist 1971, 461–462). In a later study, Corder and his colleagues studied 30 juvenile killers and found that 6 of them had histories of alcohol or drug abuse, indicating that alcohol and/or drug abuse may play a role in aggressive behavior (Corder et al. 1976, 957). Cornell and his colleagues studied 72 juveniles involved in killing someone and found that 38 of them were intoxicated when they committed the murder. Twenty-four of the juveniles used alcohol regularly and heavily, and 29 were regular or heavy users of drugs (Cornell, Benedek, and Benedek 1987, 15–16).

Environmental Factors

Many theories focus on environmental factors that may contribute to aggressive, violent behavior in children.

Kent E. Hayes, a juvenile criminologist, believes that parental neglect is the primary cause of disturbed children. He believes that the rules for parenting and the pressures put on parents have changed drastically from years ago—today most parents do not have an extended family surrounding them to support, help, and teach them the ways of parenting; more mothers are working than ever before and must place their children in day care with strangers or leave them home alone; and parents often do not have time to spend with their children, getting to know them. Hayes believes that learning to be a good parent does not come naturally but must be learned. Good parents know how to teach their children not to be selfish or self-centered but to understand the value of delayed gratification; parents do not help their children by giving them everything they want whenever they want it. Good parents also know how to provide structure, which teaches children responsibility. Good parents know their child because they are actively involved in the child's activities; they know their child's interests and can anticipate and understand their child's needs. They also know how to communicate with their child and work hard at developing communication skills. Good parents also know how to discipline their children, be consistent with punishment as well as rewards, and teach their children self-discipline. Good parents help their child develop a positive self-image, by focusing on their child's behavior as being good or bad; they do not tell the child that he or she is bad, but only that his or her behavior is unacceptable. Finally, good parents are not angry or depressed—they know how to laugh, are nurturing, and provide their children with good social skills and the understanding that they are part of a larger community and are responsible for their behavior in that community (Hayes 1989).

In some instances, children experience emotional and even physical abuse from single mothers who don't have a strong emotional support network and are overwhelmed by their situation. These children often become more aggressive than other children and have the potential to become violent (Willock 1986, 65). Some mothers may be unable to raise children without a strong positive father figure, although some research also shows that fathers must not only be present but must also be nurturing, loving fathers in order for their children, especially boys, to be empathic without being violent. Many fathers continue to believe that their sons must be tough, manly, and show no emotions; the presence of this kind of father in the house does not help teach children to be nonviolent.

Television

As early as 1954, congressional studies were authorized to study the effects of television on human behavior. In the 1960s and early 1970s, the focus of those concerned with delinquent and violent behavior among young people turned to the effects of television watching on children and the relationship of television viewing to aggressive or violent behavior. Action for Children's Television (ACT) was started in Boston in 1968 by a group of mothers who were concerned with the amount of television their children were watching, with the violent content of many of these shows, and with the commercials that turned their children into unthinking consumers. Dr. Anne Somers reported in 1976 that the average American child between the ages of 5 and 15 watched 13,000 people being killed on television. By the time these children reach the age of 18, they will have witnessed over 200,000 violent acts while spending over 15,000 hours watching television (Somers 1976, 811–817).

Many people believe that children who watch violence on television are more aggressive than others, less likely to cooperate with others, less likely to help victims of real-life violence, and more afraid of the world outside of their own homes. Marie Winn believes that television, by blocking out the real world, induces a "pleasurable and passive" state of mind.

> The worries and anxieties of reality are as effectively deferred by becoming absorbed in a television program as by going on a "trip" induced by drugs or alcohol. And just as alcoholics are only vaguely aware of their addiction, feeling that they control their drinking more than they really do . . . people similarly overestimate their control over television watching. Even as they put off other activities to spend hour after hour watching television, they feel they could easily resume living in a different, less passive style. But somehow or other, while the television set is present in their homes, the click doesn't sound. With television pleasures available, those other experiences seem less attractive, more difficult somehow. (Winn 1985, 24–25)

Leonard Eron is another researcher who has studied children and aggression. Using long-term studies, he and his colleagues followed hundreds of young people beginning at age 8 over 30 years, at 10-year intervals. One of their major findings was that aggression is usually established early in a child's life and continues unless and until some type of intervention occurs. Eron and his colleagues also demonstrated a relationship between television viewing and aggression in children. They found that boys who preferred watching violent shows on television were more likely to display aggressive or violent behavior in real life. They determined that a preference for watching violent shows on television was a valid predictor of later aggressive behavior. They also discovered that young, aggressive children who attended church were less likely to grow up as aggressive children and to get into trouble with the police (Eron et al. 1987).

In 1982 the federal government updated the 1972 surgeon general's report on the effects of television on social behavior, concluding that excessive levels of television violence lead to aggressive, even violent behavior in children (National Institute of Mental Health 1982). However, many people find it hard to believe that children who watch violence on television will go out and assault or murder someone. Some experts, including Selma Fraiberg, believe that violence on television by itself will not turn children into killers, that television's influence is much more subtle, that parents are responsible for helping their children develop a conscience, and that children with a strong relationship with their parents will not ignore all that they have learned or turn their backs on their parents (Fraiberg 1961). It is more likely that children who are emotionally detached, who can rape, assault, or murder without feeling any emotion or without seeing the victim as a human being, may be reinforced by passively watching violence on television. Fraiberg continues:

> These bondless men, women, and children constitute one of the largest aberrant populations in the world today, contributing far beyond their numbers to social disease and disorder. These are the people who are unable to fulfill the most ordinary human obligations in work, in friendship, in marriage, and in child-rearing. The condition of non-attachment leaves a void in the personality where conscience should be. Where there are no human attachments, there can be no conscience. As a consequence, the hollow men and women contribute very largely to the criminal population. It is this group, too, that produces a particular kind of criminal, whose crimes, whether they be petty or atrocious, are always characterized by indifference. The potential for violence and destructive acts is far greater among these bondless men and women; the

absence of human bonds leaves a free "unbound" aggression to pursue its erratic course. (Fraiberg 1977, as
quoted in Kramer 1988, 217)

Winn also believes that television affects antisocial children
more than "normal" children.

But the five, six, or seven hours a day that troubled
children spend watching television, more hours than
they spend at any real-life activity, is a distinctly new
phenomenon. Is it possible that all these hours disturbed children spend involved in an experience that
dulls the boundaries between the real and the unreal,
that projects human images and the illusion of human
feelings, while requiring no human responses from
the viewer, encourages them to detach themselves
from their antisocial acts in a new and horrible way?
If it is, then the total banishment of violence from the
television screen will not mitigate the dehumanizing effects of long periods of television viewing upon emotionally disturbed children. For the problem is not that
they learn how to commit violence from watching violence on television (although perhaps they sometimes
do) but that television conditions them to deal with real
people as if they were on a television screen. Thus they
are able to "turn them off," quite simply, with a knife or
a gun or a chain, with as little remorse as if they were
turning off a television set. (Winn 1985, 109–110)

Thus we can understand the stories in the newspapers and
news magazines that describe apathetic children committing violent acts. For example, one juvenile who was charged with
killing an elderly woman and a six-year-old girl claimed, "I don't
know the girl so why should I have any feelings about what happened to her?" ("Tale of a Young Mugger" 1976).
The people who want the television networks to reduce violence on television appear to be fighting a losing battle. Many researchers believe that most people want to see violence and
action on television, primarily because watching television is a
purely passive activity. Many people want action on television
because they believe it will compensate for their inactivity and
their own passivity (Winn 1985).

Some researchers believe that television has lowered our ability to empathize with others and our respect for life. If our ability to respect the lives of others is lessened, our feelings for others will also be lessened, resulting in feelings of indifference to other people. Denise Shine, a psychoanalyst, believes three elements can be found in the personality of teenage violent offenders who feel no remorse for any crimes they have committed. These elements are lack of respect, the inability to notice or understand the experiences of another person, and impatience. Shine believes that this shows "a total lack of guilt and respect for life. To them another person is a thing. They are wild organisms who cannot allow anything to stand in their way" (Morgan 1975, 15).

William Belson, a British psychologist, studied the relationship between violence and television viewing among 1,565 teenage boys living in London over a six-year period. He found that television viewing had a disinhibiting effect, that is, every time a child saw someone shot or killed on television, he lost a bit of his inhibitions, became a bit less caring of others. Belson referred to this as the "battering ram effect," as each violent act on television is imprinted in the child's brain, and the effect is cumulative; over time, Belson found the boys displayed a range of aggressive acts, including swearing, threatening other boys with violence, painting graffiti, breaking windows, and aggressive play. One of the more important of Belson's findings was that actions involving breaking bonds between people—arguments between husbands and wives or between friends or lovers—had a more serious negative effect than physically aggressive, violent acts on television. These acts demonstrated a loss of caring and concern for each other, which was carried over into real life, alienating people from one another (Belson 1978).

Albert Bandura and George Gerbner have also demonstrated scientifically that television has a negative effect on human relationships. It alienates us from each other, showing a lack of respect for human life, and socializes children with moral and ethical values that are inconsistent with the principles that most of us were taught. Gerbner and Larry Gross, professors at the Annenberg School of Communications at the University of Pennsylvania, studied the effects of television on people's perception of reality. They surveyed light and heavy television viewers to see what their perceptions were of the real world. The multiple-choice answers they provided reflected differing perceptions of reality between the two groups. They found that heavy viewers of television were more likely to choose answers that mirrored television reality rather than the real world. For example, heavy viewers rated their own chances of seeing or experiencing violence much higher than light television viewers; heavy viewers guessed their chances at 50 percent or 10 to 1, while light viewers chose the answer more likely in reality, that is, 100 to 1 (Gross 1974).

Many researchers believe that by watching violence on television and in films, children would get most of their aggression "out of their system," that this expression would not carry over into their daily lives. However, George Comstock, a leading authority on the effects of violence in television and film, reviewed the literature in the field and found that watching television did not have this cathartic effect. A majority of the studies he reviewed found that watching violence on television increased children's level of aggressive, violent behavior (Comstock 1988). A 1982 National Institute of Mental Health (NIMH) report on television and behavior found that "children who watch a lot of violence on television may come to accept violence as normal behavior" (National Institute of Mental Health 1982, 6).

Several researchers in this field argue that the profit motive is the major incentive behind the networks' emphasis on violence in programming. Some researchers claim that networks do not care about the effects of watching violence on children; they provide what the public wants to see (as determined through their advertising dollars). Miedzian confirmed this in an interview with Arthur Taylor, president of CBS from 1972 to 1976:

> When I interviewed him in 1989, Taylor pointed out that while Peggy Charren and other reformers were deeply concerned with the quality of programming, this was not a significant concern for broadcasters. For them "the most important part of broadcasting is the size of the audience. . . . It really had to do with 'Did it sell? Did the sponsor like it? Did it produce the size and definition of audience that was required?'" Taylor does not deny that some people in broadcasting are concerned about TV violence, but he adds they are not concerned enough to risk losing six-figure salaries. (Miedzian 1991, 210)

Violence can also be found in films and videos, including "slasher" films. Edward Donnerstein and his colleagues studied the desensitizing effects of slasher films. They chose 52 men out of a larger group because the authors believed that these men were less likely than the others to be desensitized after watching one slasher film per day for five days. After viewing these films, the authors found that the men displayed an increasing acceptance of violent behavior and found these films less violent, degrading, and offensive than they had earlier thought. After viewing violence against women, they believed that assaulted and raped women were less injured than other men in a control group believed. After viewing the violence in the films, the exposed men became less likely to empathize with the victims and less likely to be sensitive to others (Donnerstein, Linz, and Penrod 1987). What happens when children and teenagers view these kinds of films? Many researchers believe the same thing happens to them.

Music lyrics have also been thought to influence levels of aggression and the incidence of violent acts among listeners. In 1985, the Parents' Music Resource Center was started in order to publicize the excesses in song lyrics and videos and to create a grass-roots, consumer movement to pressure the music and video industry into placing warning labels on their products so that parents could monitor what their children were listening to and watching.

Toys, Video Games, and Other Amusements

Toys have also been linked to aggressive and violent behavior by many authors. Miedzian, for example, believes that

> 1. Not only are boys encouraged to play with violent toys, but TV, films, and VCRs provide them with an endless series of violent heroes and scenarios to emulate. . . . 2. Toy manufacturers now often provide a violent story line or characterization that goes along with their toy. The story line sometimes has political content. . . . 3. Video games represent a new area of toy violence. . . . 4. Many men who reminisce about their own childhood war play will talk about playing cowboys and Indians, or cops and robbers, or some other version of the triumph of good over evil. Many of these games reinforced xenophobia, racial prejudices, and a narrow American perspective on the sociopolitical world. . . . 5. Today's toy manufacturers are not content to exploit traditional forms of violence in

boy's toys—soldiers, military weapons, cowboy and Indian outfits. They have widened their horizons considerably. A large number of toys involve interplanetary violence that often has a military quality. (Miedzian 1991, 262–265)

However, there are other researchers who have a different view of war toys and war play. Carlsson-Paige and Levin believe that war play is not necessarily bad. They discuss the purposes of play: that it is critical to healthy development, that children use play to work through current issues or things that are bothering them, that children use play to figure out some of the experiences they have, and that children learn things through play. They believe that war play helps children work through and understand the violence that they see in the mass media and that they experience in their environment (Carlsson-Paige and Levin 1990).

Carlsson-Paige and Levin do, however, see a challenge to raising children today:

For children growing up in the current political climate and using their war play to develop views of war and peace, there is a two-pronged challenge. First, probably now more than ever before, they need to achieve the quality of play which will help them construct their own meaning of the ideas which bombard them. For without a lot of high-quality play, children will run the risk of just mimicking the messages they hear without ever establishing a foundation for their own political ideas which can expand and develop over time.

Second, children will need to be confronted with ideas and experiences which challenge the simplistic and violent political themes in their play. For without this challenge, they can easily remain stuck with the militaristic thinking promoted by media and toys. (Carlsson-Paige and Levin 1990, 115)

Day Care

Day care also may be an important factor in whether or not a child becomes delinquent or violent. Today, in the United States, we often pay more for people to clean our houses than we do for people to take care of our children. Many parents will agree that day care in this country must be improved. Belsky examined the effects of day care on infants by asking parents to evaluate their day-care situations and measured their satisfaction with current day-care opportunities. He found that babies who are in day care away from their mothers for 20 hours or more each week are more likely to become insecure than other infants, are more aggressive than other children, or experience withdrawal during their preschool and early school years. He believes that research has shown a relationship between insecure infants and troubled children (Belsky 1986).

Teenage Pregnancy

The increase in teenage pregnancies also has been connected to aggressive and violent behavior in children. Many sociologists have studied the "feminization of poverty," which includes the fact that so many teenage girls are having babies and are not able to care for them financially as well as emotionally. "So many can't rise above it to go back to school or get job skills," says Lucille Dismukes of the Council on Maternal and Child Health in Atlanta (Wallis 1985, 84). Teenage parents often are not prepared to raise a child, what with all the other pressures of growing up that an average teenager faces.

Divorce

Many studies have been conducted on the relationship between divorce and troubled children. Divorce can affect children in many ways, including producing feelings of depression, guilt, denial, anger, insecurity, and aggression. The percentage of children from broken homes who display violent tendencies is higher than that of children with both parents living at home. For example, Petti and Davidman studied nine homicidal juveniles and found that seven of them came from broken homes (Petti and Davidman 1981). Rosner and his colleagues studied 45 juveniles who had committed murder and found that 33 of the 45 (73 percent) were from broken homes (Rosner et al. 1978, 342–346). Other researchers have found similar family situations among violent youth. Children not actively raised by both parents are at higher risk for aggressive, violent behavior than children raised by both parents.

Troubled Families

There are a variety of ways in which families can be troubled without being affected by divorce. Alcohol abuse and emotional instability or mental illness also can contribute to a child becoming violent. The 9 violent children studied by Petti and Davidman had a total of 6 mothers and 3 fathers who had a history of psychiatric problems and treatment (Petti and Davidman 1981). Sorrells studied 31 juveniles who murdered someone and determined that 5 fathers and 5 mothers were alcoholic, and 9 fathers and 10 mothers were emotionally unstable (Sorrells 1977, 312, 316). Children who come from violent homes, in which one or both of the parents are physically abusive to each other and/or to the children, may also be more likely to become violent (see separate section below on child abuse).

James Dobson, head of Focus on the Family, and Gary Bauer, head of the Family Research Council, believe that broken homes, primarily resulting from current societal trends, cause many of today's problems, including violence.

> On many inner-city street corners, gangs of taunting teenage thugs harass women and children. They are products of a society where intact families are now the exception. The glib chatter of amateur sociologists on TV talk shows, the research papers of liberal academics, the social engineering of liberal judges, and the legislating of government bureaucrats have all sown seeds that have now grown into a twisted harvest of broken lives and crushed spirits. (Dobson and Bauer 1990, 168)

Dobson and Bauer believe that the absence of the father in the home has contributed to troubled, often aggressive children:

> Nowhere is the flight from fatherhood more apparent than in the inner cities of our nation. There the full effect of the anti-family, "liberation" philosophy is painfully apparent. . . . Men enticed by drugs, easy sex, and the other temptations of urban life have abandoned the responsibility of parenting and husbanding. These bad choices have been made more likely by a culture that mocks traditional values and by government policies that many times discourage family formation.
>
> Our current welfare system, for example, encourages the formation of "the mother-state-child family." Uncle Sam has become a marriage partner and "father" of last resort. The results are predictable—no bureaucrat, however well meaning, can substitute for a father.

> Studies show that the absence of the father ex-
> presses itself in male children in two very different
> ways: it is linked to increased aggressiveness on one
> hand, and greater manifestations of effeminacy on the
> other. (Dobson and Bauer 1990, 167)

Deborah Prothrow-Stith also believes that violence begins at
home.

> That's the conclusion that nearly all the specialists
> who address the issue of violence in our society come
> to sooner or later. . . . The destructive lessons parents
> teach when they are physically and psychologically
> abusive to their children and when they allow their
> children to be physically and psychologically abusive
> to others, in conjunction with our society's glorifica-
> tion of violence, the ready availability of guns, and the
> drug culture are an explosive combination that set our
> children up to be the perpetrators and the victims of
> violence. (Prothrow-Stith 1991, 145)

Prothrow-Stith continues her discussion of family dynamics
by mentioning the work done by psychologists and family therapists led by Gerald Patterson at the Oregon Social Learning
Center (OSLC).

> In the past twenty years, Patterson and his colleagues
> at OSLC have penetrated some of the mysteries of
> family life. Their work is based on social learning the-
> ory, which states that children learn how to behave by
> imitating role models. What children learn this way is
> then "reinforced" by other people. Behavior that is
> positively reinforced will be repeated often and added
> to a child's normal repertoire. Behavior that is not re-
> inforced will disappear.
> By minutely studying the interactions of parents
> and children in troubled and untroubled families, the
> Patterson team concluded that the parents of untrou-
> bled kids have certain skills that enabled them to
> "control" their children's behavior most of the time
> without excessive screaming or hitting. They knew in-
> tuitively how to positively reinforce desirable behav-
> ior. The parents of troubled kids were not necessarily

bad, or neurotic, but they lacked these crucial parenting skills. They did not know how to get their children to comply with their requests. They did not know how to reinforce good behavior; without intending to, they reinforced undesirable traits. (Prothrow-Stith 1991, 147)

Child Abuse

The connection between child abuse and aggression and violence in children has also been well documented. According to Garbarino and Groninger, 97 percent of serious delinquents have come from a violent home in which physical assaults were common (Garbarino and Groninger 1983).

Research has shown that children who have been abused often become abusers themselves. Several studies have also shown that children who have been abused also become violent, either as children or later as adults. Maurer studied violent inmates at San Quentin and found that all of them had been severely abused between the ages of one and ten (Maurer 1976). Ralph Welsh, a psychologist, found that all of the violent children he has worked with came from a violent home environment. Even if the child experienced no violence after the age of four years, he still was likely to become a violent juvenile (Welsh 1976, 17–21). Straus, Gelles, and Steinmetz believe that evidence points to the fact that the main causes of violence in society today are the home environment and methods of child-rearing. Research findings suggest that "each generation learns to be violent by being a participant in a violent family" (Straus, Gelles, and Steinmetz 1980, 122).

Vissing, Straus, Gelles, and Harrop studied data from a sample of 3,346 parents of children under the age of 18 living at home. The authors found that 63 percent of the children had been sworn at or insulted, which the authors defined as verbal aggression. Children who had been frequent victims of this verbal aggression were more likely than the other children to be physically aggressive, delinquent, and display interpersonal problems. Children who were victims of both verbal and severe physical violence had the highest rates of physical aggression and delinquency (Vissing, Straus, Gelles, and Harrop 1991, 223–238).

Garbarino and Groninger believe that families in which abuse and delinquency are both found are very negative environments. They found that the "fathers of aggressive boys are typically hostile to and rejecting of their sons, express little warmth for them, and spend little time interacting with them during their childhood" (Garbarino and Groninger 1983, 3). Parents in these environments were also found to discipline their children erratically—"fathers of delinquents are cruel, neglectful, and often absent, and the mothers cruel, neglectful, and passively helpless" (Garbarino and Groninger 1983, 4).

The National Institute of Justice conducted a study on the relationship between child abuse and later violent behavior. After following 1,575 children from early childhood through young adulthood, one of the primary findings was that "childhood abuse increased the odds of future delinquency and adult criminality overall by 40 percent" (Widom 1992, 1). The study also found that children who had been neglected, but not abused, were also more likely to display violent criminal behavior later in life. Other findings were that girls who had been abused or neglected as children were more likely to be arrested for juvenile crime than those not abused or neglected; white children who had been abused or neglected were not more likely to be arrested than white children not abused or neglected, while abused or neglected black children were much more likely to be arrested than black children not abused or neglected. "Previously abused or neglected persons were at higher risk of beginning a life of crime, at a younger age, with more significant and repeated criminal involvement. Notably, however, among those arrested as juveniles, abused or neglected persons were no more likely to continue a life of crime than other children" (3). The study concluded that early intervention was critical in preventing later violent behavior; that policies must be developed that recognize neglect as a risk factor, in addition to abuse; and that policies that remove abused and neglected children from their homes must be reexamined to determine whether in-home intervention services are more appropriate than locking these children up in juvenile facilities.

Dating violence and abuse also occur among children and young adults. The majority of such violence is perpetrated by boys against girls, although it has been found that teenage girls tend to fight back more against this type of violence than adult women in abusive situations.

Availability of Guns

According to the American Psychological Association's Commission on Violence and Youth, "children can buy handguns on street corners in many communities. In part because of this ready availability of firearms, guns are involved in more than 75 percent of adolescent killings" (American Psychological Association 1993, 12). Many experts believe that this ready availability of guns has helped contribute to the rising number of juveniles who commit some type of violent crime, especially murder.

According to a report from the National Institute of Justice, a study of gun possession by juveniles wanted to determine where they obtained guns, why they thought they needed them, how they got them, and what types of weapons they had. The study included 835 male juveniles detained for serious crimes in six different juvenile correctional facilities and 758 male high-school students in inner cities near the correctional facilities. The researchers found that 83 percent of the inmates and 22 percent of the high-school students possessed guns; that favorite weapons were high-quality, powerful revolvers, while next favorite on the list were handguns; and that the primary reason for carrying a gun was for protection. Of the inmates, 55 percent of them had carried a gun all or most of the time before they were jailed and 12 percent of the students carried guns all or most of the time, while 23 percent of the students carried them occasionally. Forty-five percent of the inmates and 53 percent of the students said they could borrow a gun from family members or friends and 37 percent said they could get one off the street. Of the inmates, 45 percent would borrow one from family or friends and 54 percent would get one off the street (Sheley and Wright 1993).

Deborah Prothrow-Stith, a physician and public health official, has found that

> in many of our nation's cities, carrying a weapon has come to be defined as "normal" behavior for adults and especially for kids. Guns are not just for drug dealers and gang members. "Good" kids as well as "bad" feel compelled to protect themselves with a firearm. In a survey of high-school students conducted by a Boston commission to study school safety, 37 percent of boys and 17 percent of girls reported carrying a weapon to school at least once. These figures may be inflated, but the mere fact that a child would brag about carrying a weapon to school is reason enough for alarm. A national student health survey conducted in 1987 among eighth- and tenth-grade students in twenty states found that nearly 2 percent of the 11,000 students asked had carried a handgun to

school at least once in the previous year. Extrapolating nationally from the survey results, that would add up to 338,000 armed students, a third of whom report carrying a handgun every day. Eight times as many students reported carrying knives. (Prothrow-Stith 1991, 19)

The Centers for Disease Control and Prevention (CDC) conducted a study in 1991 that found four percent of high-school students carry a gun (Carnegie Corporation 1994b, 2–5).

Access to firearms by adolescents is not always or even typically illegal. Laws that pertain to gun ownership vary markedly across the nation. The primary laws concern the sale and transfer of ownership of guns and ammunition as opposed to their possession and use. In this regard, the Bureau of Alcohol, Tobacco, and Firearms stipulates that retail dealers cannot sell handguns to persons who are less than 21 years of age, and they cannot sell rifles or shotguns to persons who are less than 18 years of age. But there are significant loopholes in the laws concerning the transfer of ownership or making the firearms available to persons who are younger than the age limits stipulated in the law. Gifts of guns, for example, are illegal in North Carolina for children only if they are under 12 years of age. (Earls, Cairns, and Mercy 1993, 293)

Children may have settled fights in the past with fists, but now that guns are readily available, they have become the more "popular" means of settling disagreements. For example,

three twelve-year-old boys were lifting weights in one boy's bedroom. When they left the room, heading for a video arcade, one of the visiting boys picked up a baseball belonging to the boy in whose room the three had been playing. When the visitor refused to give the ball back, the boy picked up a nearby semiautomatic rifle and shot the visiting boy, who was hit at least fifteen times and suffered twenty-two entrance and exit wounds. Charged with murder, the boy offered no defense and was sentenced to the California Youth

Authority for an indeterminate term not to exceed his twenty-fifth birthday. The boy's attorney noted that this youngster had no history of violent behavior, had never been in trouble before, and had never before fired a gun. Explaining how and why the killing occurred, the attorney said, "He was basically taunted into doing it." (Ewing 1990, from Palermo 1986)

Physical Punishment

Related to child abuse is the role that physical punishment plays in leading to aggressive and violent children. Physical punishment is often believed to lead to aggressive behavior and delinquency (Wilson and Herrnstein 1985). Slaby and Roedell have shown that "one of the most reliable predictors of children's level of aggression is the heavy use by parents of harsh, punitive discipline and physical punishment." They found that "parental punishment is one important aspect of a general pattern of interrelated parental behaviors that influence the child's aggression. This pattern includes such additional factors as parental permissiveness for aggression, negativism or lack of warmth, low use of reasoning, and inconsistent application of discipline" (Slaby and Roedell 1982, 106–107).

Sheldon and Eleanor Glueck conducted a long-term study of the causes of delinquency, starting in 1940, by comparing delinquent and nondelinquent boys from English, Irish, and Italian families living in poor urban areas. While many of their findings have since been challenged by other scholars, their fundamental finding that the causes of delinquency are found in early childhood experiences is still confirmed by many researchers; important contributing factors include discipline and family life (Glueck and Glueck 1964).

Philip Greven looked at the roots of physical punishment in the Judeo-Christian tradition. He believes that physical punishment is actually a continuum of violence that must be analyzed, understood, and then abandoned in today's society. He argues that the consequences of physical punishment include aggression, buried anger, depression, sadomasochism, and family violence. He urges parents, educators, clergy, and others to understand the consequences of physical punishment and to resort to only nonviolent means to correct children's behavior (Greven 1990).

Beverly La Haye, arguing for the other side, urges parents to spank their children as often as they believe is necessary to correct and control their behavior; parents should teach their children that feelings of anger or rage resulting from this punishment are wrong. She believes breaking a child's will is of utmost importance (La Haye 1977). Many mainstream Christians disagree with this philosophy; they often see extreme physical punishment as excessive, undesirable, and deplorable (Greven 1990).

Cults

In recent years, as interest in the occult has grown, researchers and law enforcement agencies have seen increased participation of adolescents and youth in cults and cult-related activity. Many law enforcement agencies have observed an increase in ritual crimes, usually associated with cult activity. Musical groups and others with influence over adolescents and teenagers can sometimes be observed wearing satanic symbols and having anti-Christian messages in their lyrics.

In Nebraska, a father, Michael Ryan, and his 16-year-old son, Dennis, were convicted of murdering James Thimm in a cult-related killing. The father was the self-declared head of a survivalist cult, consisting of approximately 20 adults and children, organized in military fashion. The father received his orders from God and was the "king," and the son was the "prince."

> At some point, Michael Ryan decided that Thimm was to be demoted to the rank of "slave." As a result, for the month prior to his death, Thimm was kept chained to a post at night but allowed to work around the farm during the day. A month or so before Thimm's death, the younger Ryan shot him in the face. Thimm recovered from the wound without medical attention, but the day before his death, Michael Ryan, Dennis Ryan, and three other followers took turns torturing Thimm. . . . The next day, just before Thimm died, the same group, including Dennis Ryan, again inflicted fifteen lashes each and were each directed by Michael Ryan to shoot one of Thimm's fingers. (Ewing 1990, 70)

In a case in Missouri, three 17-year-old members of a satanic cult, using baseball bats, beat another teenager to death, tied a large rock to his body, and dumped his body down a well. The boys admitted that they murdered the boy as a human sacrifice to Satan. All three were convicted of murder and sentenced to life in prison without parole (Ewing 1990).

While it appears that most juveniles who are involved in satanic murders are psychologically impaired in some way, little evidence exists to suggest that they are psychotic. In some cases there is little or no evidence that they are involved in a formal satanic organization. Some may be fascinated by the satanic rituals and Satanism. Some juveniles will kill themselves after they have murdered someone else. Fantasy games, such as "Dungeons and Dragons," have been suggested as encouraging adolescents and teenagers to learn more about satanic cults, rituals, sacrifice, witchcraft, and murder. While it is difficult to estimate the number of children influenced by this game, children have committed murder as a result of playing these types of games.

> In Alabama, for example, three boys—two seventeen-year-olds and a fourteen-year-old—were charged with capital murder in the killing of a convenience store clerk. All three, described by teachers and others as "bright, popular, all-American youths," were frequent players of a fantasy game called "Top Secret."
>
> On the day of the killing, two of the boys agreed to play out their respective roles in the fantasy game and then commit suicide. In playing out their fantasy game roles, they stole guns, drove to the convenience store, shot and killed the clerk, and then took $700 in cash. The third youth alerted the police of the impending suicide. When the two boys were captured by police, they were holding cocked guns to their heads. (Ewing 1990, 75)

Juvenile Justice System

The juvenile justice system has come under fire in the past several years for the ways it deals with juveniles. Hearings in juvenile court are held behind closed doors and the public is not allowed in the courtroom. Records are sealed—from the public, from adult courts, and from anyone else who wants to know what a child has done. Rita Kramer, who was allowed unprecedented access to the juvenile justice system in New York City and studied it for three years, believes that

> opening the court to public scrutiny, identifying the repeat violent criminals, and making their records

available to an adult system that functions in continuity with the family court or juvenile court would provide a more effective means of prevention of violent crime, control of the criminal, and protection of the community. . . .

The policy that bars juveniles' criminal proceedings from public scrutiny and results in their criminal records being sealed and expunged from the public record may have made more sense in the past, when juveniles committed delinquencies rather than felonies, when the community was capable of invoking meaningful sanctions, and when shame and remorse could be an expectable reaction on the part of a youngster. Today many of the teenagers arrested actually flaunt their criminal acts in their communities. Arraignment in Family Court becomes a rite of passage, a sign of having arrived as a leader among peers. (Kramer 1988, 223–226)

Kramer reports that many of the youth looked forward to being sent to Family Court because they gained new respect in the eyes of their peers, and often young men over the age of 21 would then use these youth in criminal activity so if anyone got caught, the youth would serve less time than the young adults would. Many of these juveniles and young adults had the juvenile justice system figured out and used it to their advantage (Kramer 1988).

Falcon Baker believes that the juvenile justice system has failed to rehabilitate these young criminal offenders. He believes that the only way to help these children is to make them accountable for their behavior while at the same time making society accountable for the conditions that contribute to the juveniles' delinquent behavior. The current system slaps these juveniles on the wrist; the current emphasis on trying serious offenders as adults misses the point—that treating these kids as adults after years of slapping them on the wrist, putting them on probation, or releasing them will do nothing to rehabilitate them. By then, it's too late. Society must make them immediately responsible for what they have done and make them pay the consequences. Baker believes that "most delinquent youths grow out of their antisocial behavior—provided nothing disturbs that natural process" (Baker 1991, 38). He believes that delinquents will change their delinquent behavior when they realize that they will have a better life if they change their ways. But they need to see the possibility of a better life. Society must look at ways of reaching children when they are still young, restructuring schools to help these children, offering alternative schools that fight illiteracy and delinquency, helping to provide jobs for teenagers, winning the war on drugs, and improving the juvenile justice system (Baker 1991).

Finally, Ashley Montagu, the noted anthropologist, sees the environment as a major force in contributing to the delinquency of youth.

> We find no juvenile delinquents in "primitive" societies simply because the conditions for producing them are absent in such communities, whereas in civilized societies, especially in our large cities, those conditions abound. The juvenile delinquent is the product of a delinquent society, in which parents, teachers, and the community have forgotten, if they have ever known, what it is to be human and what the needs of a growing human being are, the need, especially, for love. No child who was ever adequately loved ever became a delinquent or a murderer. Aggressive behavior is frequently the response to the frustration of the need for love, as well as a means of compelling attention to that need. Thus, aggression is often a signal, even at its most violent, of the need for love. But the varieties of aggression are many, and not all of them, by any means, are to be interpreted as such signals. However, in human beings, children in particular, aggressive behavior frequently constitutes such a signal. More often than not it is either misunderstood or ignored, or both, and the victim—for that is what he or she is—feels more abandoned than ever. Under such conditions, as a juvenile, the individual is likely to look for support to those who, like himself, have also been failed in their need for recognition, for love. In the cities especially, among the impoverished such support is most likely to be found among one's peers in the street gang.
>
> . . . the birthright of every child is growth and development free from physical and mental handicap. The most important of the requirements for the achievement of such growth and development is the satisfaction of the need for love. Love frustrated leads

to maldevelopment, an inability to love, and aggression. Love satisfied leads to healthy development, the ability to love, and cooperativeness. (Montagu 1976, 323–324)

Societal Factors

Many theories about delinquency usually have a social class component. Some argue that life chances are determined by class position and that the lower the class, the higher the rate of delinquency. Others believe that lifestyles are different for members of each class and that these lifestyles affect each person's propensity toward delinquency and other deviant behaviors (Richards, Berk, and Forster 1979). Socioeconomic status also plays a role in whether or not a child is at high risk for violent behavior.

> Low socioeconomic status is a far more potent risk factor for violence than is generally recognized. For example, homicide rates rise dramatically—by a factor of four or more—among both whites and blacks as socioeconomic status declines. With few exceptions, this variation is greater than that between whites and blacks at the same socioeconomic level. Homicide rates among poor whites may thus be substantially higher than those for more affluent blacks. Our present understanding of violence as fundamentally a race-related phenomenon is at least in part the result of our data collecting practices. Information on race is routinely collected on police reports and death certificates; socioeconomic data are not. (Wintemute et al. 1992, 81)

Myriam Miedzian believes that boys are being raised in a violent society today and that the masculine mystique results in boys proving their manhood by committing dangerous, often violent, acts. A young black male growing up in poverty may feel compelled to commit robbery, assault, or murder to prove he is a man and gain acceptance into his peer group. For a boy in a middle- or upper-class neighborhood, proving his manhood may require raping someone or stealing a car and going for a joy ride. Miedzian believes that many men have the potential to become violent and society must encourage behaviors and qualities, such as empathy, that are contrary to violence. Studies indicating that environmental factors such as child abuse, drug abuse, poverty, broken homes, and use of day care contribute to aggressive, violent behavior in children also point out that girls growing up in the identical environment do not become violent to the same extent that boys do. Therefore, Miedzian argues, boys are socialized into romanticizing war and glorifying winning at all costs; they are told "don't cry" and "take it like a man." This results in a lack of empathy, an inability to understand and sympathize with others, and can lead to aggressive behavior. Society's reliance on sex-role stereotypes in managing the behavior of individuals within the society encourages the image of strong men who do not show any signs of weakness and therefore are often unable to empathize, to understand and care about others. Society must continue to work on ridding itself of such strong stereotypes and continue to encourage and allow men to learn to feel their emotions, empathize with others, and understand the need for everyone to be more caring and mindful toward each other.

Maccoby believes that male peer groups have a greater influence on the behavior of young males than their families have. However, she believes that dysfunctional patterns in family life predispose a boy to greater aggression (Maccoby 1980, 964–980).

Joseph Pleck, a sociologist, reviewed theories of masculinity and hypermasculinity which argue that the traditional sex-role dichotomy is valid and that if boys have a father at home providing a positive male role model, then they will not become delinquent. Pleck believes that these theories are wrong. He argues that rigid sex-role stereotypes contribute to delinquency and that if boys were not forced into a masculine, macho role, they would not become violent. He believes that boys will often act aggressively to show off, to prove that they are masculine (Pleck 1983). Sociologist Warren Miller suggests that boys, especially in lower-class culture and without a consistent father figure to help provide a model for their behavior, are obsessively concerned with being masculine. Miller also believes that it is this obsessive attention to being macho that creates opportunities for violent behavior (Miller 1962).

Boys who have the opportunity to identify with their fathers at an early age, and thus grow up with a positive role model, are less likely to need to prove themselves to others or to themselves. With a nurturing, loving father, boys will not feel the need to deny their relationship with their mother and her feminine qualities. Studies show that when there is an increase in empathy, there is a corresponding decrease in violence (Feshbach 1982; Hoffman 1978, 169–218). Miedzian explains that empathy is a more highly valued quality in girls than in boys, and that empathy, like any other emotion, is more easily displayed by someone who has experienced similar emotions. Boys are generally taught to not show emotions, weakness, and vulnerability; therefore, their emotional experience is usually much more limited than girls, who are usually allowed, even encouraged, to show emotions, weakness, and vulnerability (Miedzian 1991).

Many parents fear that if they teach their sons to be empathic, caring, and sensitive as well as to avoid playing with guns and other war-type toys, their sons will become homosexual. Most parents would rather have a tough, strong son than one who is homosexual. Research findings don't support these fears. For example, Socarides, a psychoanalyst who focuses his research on homosexuality, found that for most homosexual or prehomosexual children he studied, the fathers were emotionally unavailable to them. Nurturing, caring fathers are not believed to be the cause of male homosexuality (Socarides 1982).

Dorothy Dinnerstein also has found that most boys believe that they must deny any identification with their mothers and their feminine qualities in order to be considered "men." Instead of learning to understand their feminine side and acknowledge and enjoy a positive relationship with their mothers, boys believe that they will not be considered tough and be rejected by their friends if they identify with their mothers (Dinnerstein 1977).

Hamburg sees the many changes in American culture as contributing to children being forced to become adults, to mature too soon. Included in these historical changes

> is the difficulty adolescents now have foreseeing the years ahead. In premodern times, children were regarded as small, inexperienced adults whose sole task was preparation for adult life. They had abundant opportunity to observe and imitate their parents and other adults performing the roles that they would one day occupy. Career options were limited. Strong social-support networks provided predictability, guidance, and strong coping resources in established, small societies. In today's highly technological and rapidly changing world, such direct modeling is much less widely available. Most societies are too large and their economies too complex to permit children and adolescents much direct observation of adult roles, especially occupational ones. Many jobs change so fast

that skills needed today are obsolete fifteen years from now. Moreover, traditional social-support networks have been disrupted. Science and technology have liberated adolescents from the drudgery experienced by their predecessors but, as a paradox of success, have made it harder for them to view the future. What is the adult world, anyway? Is it really what you see on television? (Hamburg 1992, 182)

Hamburg also believes that the easy availability of alcohol and drugs, earlier onset of puberty, and even poor nutrition abetted by the popularity of junk food, all add to the stresses on youth today. He sees a history of family violence, weak parental bonding, loose ties to schools and other social institutions, "personal beliefs that justify crime and violence under a wide range of circumstances, and involvement in peer groups that encourage these behaviors" as risk factors for serious juvenile violence (Hamburg 1992, 192). The availability of guns only increases the seriousness of these violent actions.

Sports

Sports is another area that has been linked to violent behavior among youth. Some people argue that participating in sports teaches boys to be aggressive which can lead to violent behavior, while others contend that even watching sports can lead to violent behavior. Girls also may be affected by participating in team sports, but little research has been conducted on the effects of this participation.

Gary Fine, a sociologist, studied Little League Baseball and found that private youth leagues were started because public educators and recreation personnel in the 1930s believed that competitive sports were harmful to young boys and their proper development (Fine 1987). Today, many parents and professionals involved in youth sports believe that these activities are harmful only when coaches and other adults place the emphasis on competitiveness and winning. Otherwise, they believe that young people involved in team sports can learn a great deal about cooperation and teamwork and have a good time just playing certain sports. Fine found that while coaches emphasized the importance of moral factors early in the season, later competition and winning were the only factors they emphasized (Fine 1987).

George Sage reviewed six studies that were conducted to examine the effect of organized sports on levels of sportsmanship.

Three of these studies demonstrated that those boys not involved in youth sports demonstrated a greater amount of sportsmanship than those involved in group sports. Another study found that children initially value fun and fairness when participating in sports, but as they grow older, they focus on winning and increased skill levels as being most important (Sage 1978, 18–22).

Brenda Jo Bredemeier also examined the link between sports and values. She looked at college students' views on morality and how their thinking affected moral judgment and behavior; she found that game morality and morality in life were clearly seen as different by college athletes (Bredemeier 1983; Bredemeier and Shields 1985). It appears that a distinct difference exists between sports and life. However, violence in sports does spill over into violence in life. David Phillips studied the relationship between violence in sports and in daily life, examining U.S. heavyweight boxing fights and homicide rates. He found that directly after heavyweight championship fights homicides increased by 12.5 percent. He argues that there is a direct relationship between violence shown in the mass media and violence in real life (Phillips 1983).

Watching sports on television can also lead to violence. According to David Klatell,

> Even in legitimate sports such as football, ice hockey, and tennis, dangerous or obsessive behavior can be learned from television. Many parents and high school coaches have remarked on the upsurge in violence, hostility, and rule breaking among youngsters in local sports down to the peewee level. It often seems that they are imitating the roughest, toughest, most contentious players instead of the most skilled. Perhaps it is because television tends to focus on—and replay—winning and losing, personal competition and confrontation, dramatic moments, highly charged emotions, and distinctive personalities. These are the elemental building blocks for almost all types of television entertainment formats, and sports are just that—entertainment. (Klatell 1982, 28)

Klatell has several suggestions for emphasizing the positive aspects of televised sports. These include

> 1.) De-emphasize the thrill of victory and the agony of defeat. Emphasize the thrill of participation.

2.) Reduce the dramatic nature of some personality conflicts and athletic competitions.

3.) Increase the instructional content of programs.

4.) Integrate sports into other entertainment formats such as the after-school specials, situation comedies, and family dramas in which adolescents are featured characters. Raise some relevant sports issues.

5.) Feature more women prominently.

6.) Show minorities in roles other than that of the great athlete. De-emphasize the notion that all black athletes have come from wretched backgrounds and that they can achieve success only through sports.

7.) Place more ordinary, everyday, achievable sports on the air, such as jogging, racquetball, soccer and bicycle racing.

8.) Made-for-TV events such as the "Battle of the Network Stars" and "Challenge of the Sexes" should emphasize events that are commonly practiced by the general public. (Schwartz 1982, 29–30)

Children exposed to sports may learn that it doesn't matter what it takes to win, because winning is everything. As two researchers have concluded, the "evidence [suggests] that regular sport participants become more committed to winning at any cost and less committed to values of fairness and justice as their competitive experience increases" (Johnson and Johnson 1985, 27).

Competitive Society

The nature and characteristics of competition in U.S. society may also contribute to aggressive and violent behavior in children. Alfie Kohn examines competition, distinguishing between

structural competition and intentional competition. The former refers to a situation; the latter, to an attitude. Whereas structural competition has to do with the win/lose framework, which is external, intentional competition is internal; it concerns the desire on the part of an individual to be number one. (Kohn 1986, 4)

He dispels the myths of competition—that it is inevitable, motivational, enjoyable, and that it builds character. Children are taught early on that there is a winner and loser in all games and, by extension, in all situations in life. They are taught to be the best, get the best grades, win the most games, and beat the competition. Parents often teach their children that they must be competitive in order to survive in society and that it's an inevitable part of life. "By teaching children to act in a way that is said to be inevitable, we make the practice inevitable and so make the proposition true. This may well be the heart of the socialization process" (Kohn 1986, 29).

The ways in which parents reinforce their children's behavior play a major role in how competitive they become. American culture tends to be more competitive than many others. For example, in one study on competition, Nelson and Kagan found that "rural Mexican mothers tend to reinforce their children noncontingently, rewarding them whether they succeed or fail, whereas Anglo-American mothers tend to reinforce their children as a rigid function of the child's achievement" (Nelson and Kagan 1972, 90–91). Other cross-cultural research has revealed similar findings. Margaret Mead, in her research, has found that the levels of cooperation and competition in a society reflect that society's total social emphasis and that members will work toward goals that are culturally determined and defined (Mead 1961).

Sissela Bok analyzed lying as a moral choice and found that a vicious cycle is created by the pressure we feel to win at any cost—we believe that others are cheating and playing dirty, which allows us to play dirty. If we don't play dirty, others will take advantage of us and we will lose (Bok 1979).

Kohn argues that the American educational system is highly individualistic, with an evaluation method that also is highly competitive (Kohn 1986). Children who do not or cannot perform well under pressure in order to be better than everyone else will not do well in school. Does this experience set them up for failure, does it result in aggressive behavior toward others, especially against those who do compete well? First-grade teachers rated their students' competitiveness for a study by Barnett, Matthews, and Howard, who also administered a test to measure empathy levels in the students. They found that "children rated as highly competitive were found to have lower empathy scores than children rated as relatively less competitive" (Barnett, Matthews, and Howard 1979, 221–222).

Ewing recalls the murder of a seven-year-old girl by a nine-year-old boy in Pennsylvania, possibly because the girl claimed she was better at playing video games than he was:

> A nine-year-old Pennsylvania boy shot and killed a
> seven-year-old neighbor girl with his father's hunting

rifle. The boy, an honor student and Cub Scout, entered his parents' bedroom, took the key to his father's gun cabinet, unlocked the cabinet, removed and loaded the gun, and then went outside where the victim and other children were snowmobiling. After shooting the girl in the back, the boy removed the spent cartridge, hid it, and then put the gun back and relocked the cabinet.

The boy claimed that he had been playing "hunter" and accidentally fired the gun. According to the prosecutor, however, the killing was deliberate, perhaps in reaction to the girl's bragging that she was better than the boy at playing video games. In any event, a ballistics expert testified at a pretrial hearing that the rifle could not have been discharged accidentally unless struck with a severe blow forcing the hammer to hit the firing pin. (Ewing 1990, 99, from DePalma 1989, 6)

Kohn suggests "that we compete to overcome fundamental doubts about our capabilities and, finally, to compensate for low self-esteem" (Kohn 1986, 99). Schools often foster competitive rather than cooperative learning. Students compete against each other for the best grades, the most recognition, and the best positions, or any position, on the sports teams. Morton Deutsch suggests ways that schools can encourage cooperative learning by teaching students how to develop values, attitudes, and knowledge that lead to constructive behavior. He believes that in the many movements founded to teach some type of constructive, positive learning, four key components are found: "cooperative learning, conflict resolution training, the constructive use of controversy in teaching subject matters, and the creation of dispute resolution centers in the schools" (Deutsch 1993, 510).

Cooperative learning consists of five basic elements, including positive interdependence, face-to-face interaction, individual accountability, interpersonal and small group skills, and processing skills. Students must be taught that "it is to their advantage if other students learn well and that it is to their disadvantage if others do poorly" (Deutsch 1993, 510). Students must also be able to interact with other students constructively in order to learn cooperatively. Each student must be accountable to all other students for his learning the material and be able to support and assist others. All students need appropriate intergroup skills in order to work together in small groups and be successful. Finally, students must be able to process information and determine how successful their learning groups are in working together and meeting goals (Deutsch 1993).

Kvaraceus examined the cultural roots and influences of delinquency. He believes that solving personal problems through violence is one influence and television reinforces this behavior. American society has become self-indulgent and impatient—people want everything right away. We are no longer content to save our money to buy something special or to put an item on layaway; we pull out the credit card and gain immediate possession of the desired item. Americans also have become more play-oriented rather than work-oriented; the number of toys for adults has grown dramatically over the number available several years ago. Modern society has fewer roots than years ago; this rootlessness may leave a child unattached and less caring about the rights and property of others. Today's adult attitudes toward youth see children as a surplus commodity, separate from the mainstream of life. Children respond to the way adults expect them to behave; adults must show more trust in youth's abilities, maturity, and potential for good. Today's society values social acceptance and popularity. America's emphasis on success leaves many children out; those who are failures in school, believe their home life is a failure, or have trouble with friendships are not considered successful by most of society. They may turn to aggressive or violent behavior to gain attention and prove their worth (Kvaraceus 1966).

Michael Nagler believes that human beings are joined together as one system, one organism made up of many parts. He believes that we will not get rid of violence until we realize that violence results from a breakdown in human relationships and is carried out by people who are alienated from others and who violate "the natural spirit of cooperation" (Nagler 1982, 13).

> What is eating away at our ability to tolerate frustration, making ever greater numbers of ordinary people into killers? In the simplest terms it is a gradual erosion of respect for life. As our collective capacity to respect the lives of others rises or falls, we can expect a corresponding fall or rise in the physical expressions of indifference—not only in matters such as assault or murder but also in the routine events of everyday life. . . .
>
> It is no mystery how this "new breed" of remorseless youth has sprung up in our midst; as James

Baldwin says, they are simply "imitating our disrespect" for the feelings of other people. You could say that a particular murder is caused on one level by a tendency toward aggression that all human beings inherit. On other levels it is caused by the artificial arousal of that tendency, for example, through violent entertainment; by the inability to relate to others as fellow human beings; by the availability of a "Saturday night special"; by someone who annoys a potential murderer once too often. But it is useful to remember that all these factors have to do with our respect for life. (Nagler 1982, 38–40)

Treatment

Many researchers disagree about the most effective ways of treating violent children. The publication of *Deadly Consequences,* by Deborah Prothrow-Stith, has led to renewed interest in violent children from experts in many fields. As a physician and public health official, Prothrow-Stith focuses on the public health aspects of violent crime committed by adolescents and teenagers, believing that if violence was viewed as a public health problem, solutions could be developed to help reduce this violence (Prothrow-Stith, 1991). She has developed a violence prevention curriculum, in cooperation with the Education Development Center, that teaches youth nonviolent alternatives to violence.

Other researchers are focusing on conflict resolution training to help children learn how to resolve conflicts peacefully, without violence. They believe that if children can learn how to resolve their problems without resorting to violence, there will be fewer instances in which children become violent.

Most experts agree that a multifaceted approach has the best chance of success. Families, schools, and communities must be involved in helping children avoid violent confrontations, and early intervention offers the best chance to reach these children before they become violent. All agree that prevention offers the best chance for success.

Experts disagree, however, on the best ways to treat violent children. Options include rehabilitation, boot camps, adult prisons, or conflict resolution training—preferably before children get into trouble.

Rehabilitation

Today, the question often arises as to whether rehabilitation really works or whether we as a society should just build more prisons and lock up criminals. Several studies indicate that juveniles do not have high rates of recidivism, that is, they do not often violate the laws a second time. An early study conducted on juvenile recidivism rates by Marvin Wolfgang and his colleagues found that only 18 percent of juveniles arrested for delinquent behavior continued that behavior. Most juveniles do not repeat delinquent behavior (Wolfgang, Figlio, and Sellin 1972). Another study conducted by Howard Snyder had similar results. He studied youth in the state of Utah and Maricopa County, Arizona, which includes Phoenix, born between 1962 and 1965. Only 34 percent had at least one referral to juvenile court before they turned 18, 59 percent of those who had a court referral had only one court referral, and 84 percent who had had at least one court referral were not referred to juvenile court more than three times. That means that 64 percent of these adolescents were never referred to juvenile court and that only 16 percent had more than three referrals. Therefore, many juveniles get into trouble, testing the limits of parental and societal discipline, but once they get into trouble decide that the consequences are not worth the experience (Snyder 1993).

Boot Camps

The National Guard operates ten ChalleNGe programs, also known as boot camps, around the country. These programs usually offer general equivalency diplomas (GEDs) and other types of motivational programs to school dropouts. They are usually not part of a state's juvenile justice system. One camp operated by the Connecticut National Guard was closed down by the governor because the program was not able to guarantee the safety of members and staff; infiltration by gang members, gambling, drug use, code of conduct violations, and other problems were uncovered. Many experts believe that boot camps are not the best method of intervening in the lives of juvenile delinquents. Some believe that putting delinquents with other delinquents only provides more opportunities to learn negative, often illegal, behavior and encourages that behavior. Others believe that a military-style environment may control aggressive behavior on the surface, but does not get to the causes of this behavior, and therefore does not have much success in rehabilitating these juveniles.

The Office of Juvenile Justice and Delinquency Prevention (National Institute of Justice) has funded three boot camps as demonstration projects; these sites are in Denver, Colorado; Mobile, Alabama; and Cuyahoga County, Ohio. They are currently in the process of being evaluated for their potential for successful rehabilitation.

Most boot camps are not set up for violent juveniles; nonviolent juveniles, drug offenders, and first-time offenders are usually the target group. Many people believe that they are promising alternatives for high-risk youth and that they have the potential to prevent violent activity. They are all operated in a military style—drill instructors yell directions at the "recruits" and use calisthenics, insults, and anything else necessary to instill discipline in the juveniles.

Adult Prisons

Many juvenile facilities are not set up to deal with violent youth, while at the same time more and more jurisdictions are charging teenagers who commit murder as adults. Juveniles charged as adults in criminal courts are treated much more severely than those in juvenile courts (Ewing 1990). Cormier and Markus studied 41 cases of juveniles charged with murder or manslaughter in either juvenile courts (25) or charged as adults (16). They found that of those tried in juvenile court, 24 were sent to state facilities until they turned 21, and 1 was placed in his family's custody. Of those tried as adults, "one was acquitted, nine were sentenced to life imprisonment, one was sentenced to 30 years, one was sentenced to two years, one received a ten-year suspended sentence, two were found not guilty by reason of insanity, and one was found unfit to stand trial" (Cormier and Markus 1980, 245).

Prevention

The Office of Juvenile Justice and Delinquency Prevention in the U.S. Department of Justice believes that in order to prevent juvenile delinquency and violent acts by children, six principles must be followed. First, families must be strengthened, taught how to provide guidance and discipline, and must teach positive values to their children. Basic social institutions, including schools, churches, and community-based organizations, must be supported in their efforts to identify at-risk youth and alleviate the pressures that lead these children to become at risk for aggressive and violent behavior. Prevention strategies that "reduce the impact of negative risk factors and enhance protective factors" should be promoted (Allen-Hagen and Sickmund 1993, 4). Once a delinquent act has occurred, intervention must be immediate. Sanctions that emphasize accountability and services must be available and appropriate to the needs of each delinquent juvenile. Finally, methods must be developed to identify those juveniles who are chronic, serious, and violent offenders (Allen-Hagen and Sickmund 1993).

Many programs believe that prevention programs must incorporate many ideas and practices in order to be successful. For example, violent behavior is a health issue and can be prevented. Males are involved in most violent incidents and must be included in solutions. Developing solutions to violence must include children and their families. Training children in conflict resolution is essential. Interagency cooperation is important. Understanding the relationship between alcohol and drugs and violence is necessary. Current violence prevention strategies must be studied and evaluated to learn the best ways to combat violence in society. Parenting skills must be taught before children are born or at least before they reach adolescence. Positive daily behavior must be reinforced in students.

According to Dr. Dennis Embry, the president of Heartsprings, a Tucson-based program teaching children nonviolent intervention skills, early intervention is critical in preventing future violent behavior (Embry 1994). He believes that early intervention is more important than teaching conflict resolution skills to older children, because the earlier children are reached, the less likely they are to resort to violent behavior.

Dr. Deborah Prothrow-Stith, a physician and public health official, focuses on the public health aspects of violent crime committed by young people. When she first proposed that violent children were a public health problem, she found that "many of my colleagues, though respectful, thought I was misguided. They saw violence as a regrettable inevitability of human life, like taxes or old age. I was told again and again that as violence was not a disease, medicine could not cure it" (Prothrow-Stith 1991, 135). However, she pursued her belief that, if violence was viewed as a public health problem, solutions could be developed to help reduce this violence. She has developed a violence prevention curriculum, in cooperation with the Education Development Center, that teaches youth nonviolent alternatives to violence. She believes that violent acts committed by children are a public health problem, one that requires public health strategies to reduce violent crime. She advocates health education in schools and through the mass media, community awareness activities, hospital screening to identify at-risk children, and parent training. From her experience, she has realized that classroom intervention is not enough to completely prevent violence; communities as a whole must be included in these efforts.

Public health models for designing preventive strategies focus on the "host," the "agent," and "environmental factors," in which the host is the person at risk for injury, the agent is the means of inflicting injury and can include guns, knives, or fists, and the environment is the setting in which the violence occurs, such as the home, neighborhood, school, or workplace. The social environment in which all this occurs is influenced by poverty, racism, joblessness, alcohol and other drugs, the family environment, and the media. Using this model, a variety of intervention and prevention strategies can be developed. Possible intervention strategies that can be applied to the host include training in self-defense or conflict resolution, encouraging local businesses to help mentor students, and providing parenting skills training to families with children. Intervention strategies applied to the agent of injury might include developing public policies to prevent injuries by firearms, offering firearm safety courses, and encouraging the media to reduce the portrayal of guns and violence as something desired. Strategies for making the environment safe might include providing better day-care facilities, improving facilities and services for battered women, developing policies to ensure the safety of the school environment, and restricting the availability of alcohol. Social environment strategies could include providing job-training programs for the hard-to-employ, providing leadership training for local community leaders and advocates, and encouraging the local communities to develop and promote prevention activities.

The public health approach to preventing violence has gained popularity in recent years. It applies epidemiological techniques to the study of violence in society; uses surveillance systems and other data collection methods to gather information about the characteristics of violent offenders, victims, and acts of violence; develops and implements prevention programs; and addresses the basic social norms in American society.

The Centers for Disease Control suggest that any program developed to prevent violence should have five essential components: they should target high-risk populations, apply surveillance systems to track data, empower local communities to help prevent violence, train professionals in all fields of violence prevention, and evaluate prevention programs to learn what approaches work in preventing violence (Centers for Disease Control 1992).

The American Psychological Association's Commission on Violence and Youth also studied the characteristics of effective programs to curb youth violence. They found that successful programs have two qualities in common: "they draw on the understanding of developmental and sociocultural risk factors leading to antisocial behavior, and . . . they use theory-based intervention strategies with known efficacy in changing behavior, tested program designs, and validated, objective measurement techniques to assess outcomes" (American Psychological Association 1993, 53–54). Other important characteristics include early intervention; treatment of aggression as one part of antisocial behavior; inclusion of multiple components, such as family, school, peer groups, and the community; and the use of transitional periods in children's lives, such as starting school, as "windows of opportunity" to improve children's lives (American Psychological Association 1993, 54). In their review of the literature, they found evidence that programs to divert high-risk juveniles from the juvenile justice system are likely to have a positive effect on rates of recidivism. Problem-solving skills training, parenting training for parents (including anger management, negotiating skills, and providing positive reinforcement), and school and community intervention are promising techniques for treating children who are already displaying aggressive or violent tendencies. They found that prevention programs that meet specific needs of the target group are the most successful. They also caution that intervention programs and policies will only be successful if society stops accepting aggression and violence in certain contexts (American Psychological Association 1993).

Conflict Resolution Training

Introduced in 1972 in New York City schools, conflict resolution programs are now offered in over 2,000 schools across the country. Ann Arbor, Michigan, schools have trained 14,000 people in conflict resolution. Approximately 30,000 students in over 100 schools in New Mexico have been trained. In Chicago, all students are trained in conflict resolution. "Preliminary evaluations by 200 teachers using the [Morton] Deutsch program show that within a year it reduced the number of fights in 71 percent of the classrooms and also reduced the incidence of verbal putdowns and name calling by 66 percent" (Carnegie Corporation 1994a).

Morton Deutsch emphasizes teaching children conflict resolution skills, showing them that violence produces more violence, teaching them positive ways to express anger, and providing them with nonviolent ways to deal with conflict (Carnegie Corporation 1994b, 2–5).

One problem with teaching children violence prevention and conflict resolution skills is that schools are the best environments for teaching these skills. The addition of teaching conflict resolution skills adds to the pressure on many teachers to cram more information into an already crowded school day. Dryfoos suggests that schools should expand their traditional hours and become all-day community centers, focusing on the mental, physical, and emotional needs of the students (Dryfoos 1994). Others suggest that middle schools be set up to accommodate 150 children, with teachers working together in teams to assure the students' academic and personal progress. Experience with this approach indicates that violence among children is reduced, almost eliminated, in large part because each student has at least one adult who is available for advice and support (Carnegie Corporation 1993).

Mediation

Mediation is also being used in many areas to resolve disputes. The "mediation process allows people to resolve conflicts in a nonthreatening and nonpunitive atmosphere through the use of effective communication and problem-solving skills. Mediators are third-party neutrals who help people in a dispute express their points of view, vent their feelings, clarify needs and issues, and negotiate satisfactory agreements" (Smith 1991, 7). Many researchers and program officials believe that the mediation process can be applied successfully to solving juvenile conflicts because the current juvenile justice system is not always an appropriate environment for resolving conflicts and juveniles can learn nonviolent ways of resolving their conflicts from the process. Most mediation programs help students improve their communication and problem-solving skills, improve family dynamics, improve the school environment, prevent youthful aggressive and violent behavior, and improve community relations.

One type of mediation program that is growing in popularity is the victim-juvenile offender program in which juveniles who commit crimes against individuals are forced to face the victim and negotiate restitution. These programs are unusual in the sense that in the juvenile justice system, as well as the adult criminal justice system, "offenders are not held directly accountable for their actions against their victims. Because of this, offenders often fail to understand the human impact of their actions, especially the emotional repercussions of victimization. In fact, offenders themselves can feel victimized by the system and emerge from it rationalizing their delinquent behavior" (Smith 1991, 9). By facing their victims, juvenile offenders and their victims discuss the incident, their feelings during and after it, and its emotional impact, and they are then able to negotiate restitution. The offender is held responsible for his action in a more proactive and positive way and is more likely to learn from this experience. As of 1991, over 100 victim-juvenile offender programs were in place in the United States (Smith 1991).

Mediation programs in juvenile correctional facilities have been started recently. The New Mexico Center for Dispute Resolution has developed a program that has been implemented in several facilities. This New Mexico model is based on three goals: to improve the communication and problem-solving skills of staff and inmates, to improve the quality of life within the institution, and to provide the juveniles with a positive way of resolving conflicts once they leave the institution. The program has three components: a conflict resolution curriculum, mediation training for both staff and juveniles, and training for juveniles and their parents to establish rules and expectations for the time when the juveniles will return home.

Some states are beginning to apply the mediation process to disputes between gangs. The New Mexico Center for Dispute Resolution has participated in mediating these types of conflicts. For example, three gangs were involved in a dispute over territory and complaints about the actions of school administrators at a middle school, guns and knives were found daily, and students and teachers were worried about getting caught in the crossfire. Mediators from the New Mexico Center for Dispute Resolution worked to resolve the issues. After negotiating for three months, all three gangs signed an agreement that resolved their differences peacefully; this agreement was still being honored two years after it was signed (Smith 1991).

In addition to all the above prevention efforts, the National Council of Juvenile and Family Court Judges believes that additional steps must be taken to protect the public safety when dealing with violent juvenile offenders. These include holding violent juveniles accountable for their crimes and providing punishment appropriate to the crime; providing the juvenile courts with adequate resources to assess the violent juveniles and their behavior, and develop appropriate treatment and punishment alternatives; making a commitment to rehabilitation, always with public safety in mind; passing legislation that will transfer these violent juveniles to adult criminal court; allowing police and criminal courts access to juvenile court records; allowing public access to juvenile court; expanding community resources to help these juveniles and their families; providing adequate funding for existing juvenile programs; developing more effective re-entry programs; and expanding training opportunities for juvenile justice professionals (National Council of Juvenile and Family Court Judges 1994).

Notes

Ainsworth, M.D.S. 1978. *Patterns of Attachment.* Hillsdale, NJ: Lawrence Erlbaum Associates.

Allen-Hagen, Barbara, and Melissa Sickmund. 1993. *Juveniles and Violence: Juvenile Offending and Victimization Fact Sheet #3* (July). Washington, DC: Office of Juvenile Justice and Delinquency Prevention.

American Psychological Association. 1993. *Violence and Youth: Psychology's Response, Volume I: Summary Report of the American Psychological Association Commission on Violence and Youth.* Washington, DC: American Psychological Association.

Ames, Carole. 1978. "Children's Achievement Attributions and Self-Reinforcement: Effects of Self-Concept and Competitive Reward Structure." *Journal of Educational Psychology* 70:345–355.

Anderson, Elijah. 1994. "The Code of the Streets." *Atlantic Monthly* 273 (May):80–94.

Baker, Falcon. 1991. *Saving Our Kids from Delinquency, Drugs, and Despair.* New York: Cornelia and Michael Bessie Books.

Barnett, Mark A., Karen A. Matthews, and Jeffrey A. Howard. 1979. "Relationship between Competitiveness and Empathy in 6- and 7-Year-Olds." *Developmental Psychology* 15:221–222.

Belsky, J. 1986. "Infant Day Care: A Cause for Concern?" *Zero to Three* (Bulletin of the National Center for Clinical Infant Programs, Washington, DC) 6, no. 5 (September).

Belson, William. 1978. *Television Violence and the Adolescent Boy.* Lexington, MA: Lexington Books.

Bok, Sissela. 1979. *Lying: Moral Choice in Public and Private Life.* New York: Vintage.

Brazelton, T. Berry. 1985. *Working and Caring.* Reading, MA: Addison-Wesley.

Bredemeier, Brenda Jo. 1983. "Athletic Aggression: A Moral Concern." In *Sports Violence*, ed. J. H. Goldstein. New York: Springer-Verlag.

Bredemeier, Brenda Jo, and David L. Shields. 1985. "Values and Violence in Sports Today." *Psychology Today* 19 (October):22–25.

Cairns, R. B., J. L. Gariepy, and K. E. Hood. 1990. "Development, Microevolution, and Social Behavior." *Psychological Review* 97:49–65.

Carlsson-Paige, Nancy, and Diane E. Levin. 1990. *Who's Calling the Shots? How To Respond to Children's Fascination with War Play and War Toys.* Santa Cruz, CA: New Society Publishers.

Carnegie Corporation. 1993. "Turning Points Revisited." *Carnegie Quarterly* 39, no. 1 (Winter).

———. 1994a. "Charting New Paths to Safety." *Carnegie Quarterly* 38, no. 2 (Spring).

———. 1994b. "Saving Youth from Violence." *Carnegie Quarterly* 39, no. 1 (Winter):2–5.

Centers for Disease Control. 1992. "An Agenda for Violence Prevention: Where We Are, Where We Want To Be, and How We Get There." In *Position Papers from the Third National Injury Control Conference Setting the National Agenda for Injury Control in the 1990s.* Atlanta: Centers for Disease Control.

Cline, Foster. 1979. *Understanding and Treating the Severely Disturbed Child.* Evergreen, CO: Evergreen Consultants in Human Behavior.

Comstock, George. 1988. "Television Violence and Antisocial and Aggressive Behavior." Paper prepared for Television and Teens: Health Implications, a conference sponsored by the Kaiser Foundation, Los Angeles (June 22–24).

Corder, Billie, et al. 1976. "Adolescent Parricide: A Comparison with Other Adolescent Murder." *American Journal of Psychiatry* 133:957–961.

Cormier, Bruno, and Baila Markus. 1980. "A Longitudinal Study of Adolescent Murderers." *Bulletin of the American Academy of Psychiatry and Law* 8.

Cornell, Dewey, and Elissa Benedek. 1987. "Characteristics of Adolescents Charged with Homicide: Review of 72 Cases." *Behavioral Sciences and the Law* 5, no. 11:15–16.

DePalma, Brett. 1989. "Ten-Year-Old Boy Is Charged as Adult in Fatal Shooting of Seven-Year-Old Girl." *New York Times*, 26 August.

Deutsch, Morton. 1993. "Educating for a Peaceful World." *American Psychologist* 48, no. 5 (May):510–517.

Dinnerstein, Dorothy. 1977. *The Mermaid and the Minotaur: Sexual Arrangements and Human Malaise.* New York: Harper and Row.

Dobson, James, and Gary L. Bauer. 1990. *Children at Risk: The Battle for the Hearts and Minds of Our Kids.* Dallas: Word Publishing.

Donnerstein, Edward, Daniel Linz, and Steven Penrod. 1987. *The Question of Pornography: Research Findings and Policy Implications.* New York: Free Press.

Dryfoos, Joy G. 1990. *Adolescents at Risk: Prevalence and Prevention.* New York: Oxford University Press.

———. 1994. *Full-Service Schools: A Revolution in Health and Social Services for Children, Youth, and Families.* San Francisco: Jossey-Bass Publishers.

Earls, Felton, Robert B. Cairns, and James A. Mercy. 1993. "The Control of Violence and the Promotion of Nonviolence in Adolescents." In *Promoting the Health of Adolescents: New Directions for the Twenty-First Century,* ed. Anne C. Petersen and Elena O. Nightingale. Washington, DC: Carnegie Council on Adolescent Development.

Eggerman, Richard W. 1982. "Competition as a Mixed Good." *The Humanist* 42 (July/August):48–51.

Embry, Dennis. 1994. Telephone conversation with author (July).

Eron, Leonard D., Rowell L. Heusmann, et al. 1987. "Aggression and Its Correlates over 22 Years." In *Childhood Aggression and Violence,* ed. David Crowell, Ian M. Evans, and Clifford R. O'Donnell. New York: Plenum.

Ewing, Charles Patrick. 1990. *When Children Kill: The Dynamics of Juvenile Homicide.* Lexington, MA: Lexington Books.

Federal Bureau of Investigation. 1989, 1991, 1993. *Crime in the United States—1988, 1990, 1992.* From *Uniform Crime Reports.* Washington, DC: Federal Bureau of Investigation.

Feshbach, Norma Deitch. 1982. "Sex Differences in Empathy." In *The Development of Prosocial Behavior,* ed. Nancy Eisenberg. New York: Academic Press.

Fine, Gary Alan. 1987. *With the Boys: Little League Baseball and Preadolescent Behavior.* Chicago: University of Chicago Press.

Fraiberg, Selma. 1961. Address to the Child Study Association of America.

———. 1977. *Every Child's Birthright: In Defense of Mothering.* New York: Basic Books.

Freud, Sigmund. 1930. *Civilization and Its Discontents*. London: Hogarth Press.

Garbarino, James, and Wendy Groninger. 1983. "Child Abuse, Delinquency, and Crime." Working paper number 807. Chicago: National Committee for the Prevention of Child Abuse.

Glueck, Sheldon, and Eleanor Glueck. 1964. *Ventures in Criminology: Selected Recent Papers*. London: Tavistock Publications.

Greven, Philip. 1990. *Spare the Child: The Religious Roots of Punishment and the Psychological Impact of Physical Abuse*. New York: Alfred A. Knopf.

Gross, Larry. 1974. "The 'Real' World of Television." *Today's Education* (January–February):86–87.

Hamburg, David A. 1992. *Today's Children: Creating a Future for a Generation in Crisis*. New York: Times Books.

Hayes, E. Kent. 1989. *Why Good Parents Have Bad Kids: How To Make Sure That Your Child Grows Up Right*. New York: Doubleday.

Hoffman, Martin L. 1978. "Empathy, Its Development and Prosocial Implications." *Nebraska Symposium on Motivation* 25:169–218.

Horney, Karen. 1950. *Neurosis and Human Growth*. New York: W. W. Norton.

Johnson, David W., and Roger T. Johnson. 1985. "Motivational Processes in Cooperative, Competitive, and Individualistic Learning Situations." In *Research on Motivation in Education*, vol. 2, ed. Carole Ames and Russell Ames. Orlando, FL: Academic Press.

Klatell, David. 1982. "TV as Entertainment and Information." In *TV & Teens: Experts Look at the Issues*, ed. Meg Schwartz. Reading, MA: Addison-Wesley.

Kohlberg, Lawrence. 1971. "From Is to Ought: How To Commit the Naturalistic Fallacy and Get Away with It in the Study of Moral Development." In *Cognitive Development and Epistemology*, ed. Theodore Mischel. New York: Academic Press.

Kohn, Alfie. 1986. *No Contest: The Case against Competition*. Boston: Houghton Mifflin.

Kohut, Heinz. 1989. "Thoughts on Narcissism and Narcissistic Rage." In *The Search for the Self: Selected Writings of Heinz Kohut*, vol. 2, ed. Paul Ornstein. Madison, CT: International Universities Press.

Kramer, Rita. 1988. *At a Tender Age: Violent Youth and Juvenile Justice*. New York: Henry Holt.

Kvaraceus, William C. 1966. *Anxious Youth: Dynamics of Delinquency*. Columbus, OH: Charles E. Merrill Books.

La Haye, Beverly. 1977. *How To Develop Your Child's Temperament.* Irvine, CA: Harvest House Publishers.

Lefkowitz, Monroe M., et al. 1977. *Growing Up To Be Violent: A Longitudinal Study of the Development of Aggression.* New York: Pergamon Press.

Lewis, Dorothy Otnow, et al. 1980. "Violent Juvenile Delinquents: Psychiatric, Neurological, Psychological, and Abuse Factors." *Annual Progress in Child Psychiatry and Child Development.*

————. 1988. "Neuropsychiatric, Psychoeducational, and Family Characteristics of 14 Juveniles Condemned to Death in the United States." *American Journal of Psychiatry* 145, no. 5 (May):584–589.

Linnoila, Markku, et al. 1983. "Low Cerebrospinal Fluid 5-Hydroxyindoacetic Acid Concentration Differentiates Impulsive from Non-Impulsive Violent Behavior." *Life Sciences* 33:2609–2614.

Maccoby, Eleanor. 1980. "Sex Differences in Aggression: A Rejoinder and Reprise." *Child Development* 51:964–980.

Maccoby, Eleanor, and Carol Nagy Jacklin. 1974. *The Psychology of Sex Differences,* vol. 1. Stanford, CA: Stanford University Press.

Magid, Ken, and Carole A. McKelvey. 1987. *High Risk: Children without a Conscience.* New York: Bantam Books.

Malmquist, Carl. 1971. "Premonitory Signs of Homicidal Juvenile Aggression." *American Journal of Psychiatry* 128:461–462.

Marans, Steven R., and Donald J. Cohen. 1993. "Children and Inner-City Violence: Strategies for Intervention." In *Psychological Effects of War and Violence on Children,* ed. Lewis A. Leavitt and Nathan A. Fox. Northvale, NJ: Lawrence Erlbaum Associates.

Maslow, Abraham H. 1970. *Motivation and Personality,* revised edition. New York: Harper and Row.

Maurer, A. 1976. "Physical Punishment of Children." Paper presented at the California State Psychological Convention, Anaheim, CA.

May, Rollo. 1972. *Power and Innocence: A Search for the Sources of Violence.* New York: W. W. Norton.

Mead, Margaret. 1961. *Cooperation and Competition among Primitive Peoples.* Boston: Beacon Press.

Miedzian, Myriam. 1991. *Boys Will Be Boys: Breaking the Link between Masculinity and Violence.* New York: Doubleday.

Miller, Alice. 1983. *For Your Own Good: Hidden Cruelty in Child-Rearing and the Roots of Violence.* Translated by Hildegarde and Hunter Hannum. New York: Farrar, Straus and Giroux.

Miller, Warren B. 1962. "Lower Class Culture as a Generating Milieu of Gang Delinquency." In *The Sociology of Crime and Delinquency*, ed. Marvin E. Wolfgang, Leonard Savitz, and Norman Johnson. New York: John Wiley and Sons.

Montagu, Ashley. 1976. *The Nature of Human Aggression*. New York: Oxford University Press.

Morgan, Ted. 1975. "'They Think I Can Kill Because I'm 14.'" *New York Times Magazine* 19 January 1975.

Nagler, Michael N. 1982. *America without Violence: Why Violence Persists and How You Can Stop It*. Covelo, CA: Island Press.

National Council of Juvenile and Family Court Judges. 1994. *Where We Stand: An Action Plan for Dealing with Violent Juvenile Crime*. Reno, NV: National Council of Juvenile and Family Court Judges.

National Institute of Mental Health. 1982. *Television and Behavior: Ten Years of Scientific Progress and Implications for the 80's, Volume 1: Summary Report*. Rockville, MD: National Institute of Mental Health.

Nelson, Linden L., and Spencer Kagan. 1972. "Competition: The Star-Spangled Scramble." *Psychology Today* (September):53–56.

Novak, Michael. 1976. *The Joy of Sports: End Zones, Bases, Baskets, Balls, and the Consecration of the American Spirit*. New York: Basic Books.

Olweus, Dan, Jack Block, and Marian Radke-Yarrow, eds. 1986. *The Development of Antisocial and Prosocial Behavior*. New York: Academic Press.

Palermo, Dave. 1986. "'Good Kids' Who Kill: Violent 80s To Blame?" *Los Angeles Times*, 2 March.

Petti, Theodore, and Leonard Davidman. 1981. "Homicidal School-Age Children: Cognitive Style and Demographic Features." *Child Psychiatry and Human Development* 12:82–85.

Phillips, David P. 1983. "The Impact of Mass Media Violence on U.S. Homicides," *American Sociological Review* 48 (August):560–568.

Pleck, Joseph H. 1983. *The Myth of Masculinity*. Cambridge, MA: MIT Press.

Prothrow-Stith, Deborah, with Michaele Weissman. *Deadly Consequences: How Violence Is Destroying Our Teenage Population and a Plan To Begin Solving the Problem*. New York: HarperCollins.

Richards, Pamela, Richard A. Berk, and Brenda Forster. 1979. *Crime as Play: Delinquency in a Middle-Class Suburb*. Cambridge, MA: Ballinger.

Rosner, Richard, et al. 1978. "Adolescents Accused of Murder and Manslaughter: A Five-Year Descriptive Study." *Bulletin of the American Academy of Psychiatry and Law* 4.

Roth, Jeffrey. 1994a. "Psychoactive Substances and Violence." National *Institute of Justice Research in Brief* (February).

———. 1994b. "Understanding and Preventing Violence." *National Institute of Justice Research in Brief* (February).

Rubenstein, Ruth P. 1977. "Changes in Self-Esteem and Anxiety in Competitive and Noncompetitive Camps." *Journal of Social Psychology* 102.

Sage, George H. 1978. "Psychosocial Implications of Youth Sports Programs." *Arena Review* 2 (Winter):18–22.

Samenow, Stanton E. 1989. *Before It's Too Late: Why Some Kids Get into Trouble—and What Parents Can Do about It.* New York: Times Books.

Schwartz, Meg, ed. 1982. *TV & Teens: Experts Look at the Issues.* Reading, MA: Addison-Wesley.

Sheley, Joseph F., and James D. Wright. 1993. "Gun Acquisition and Possession in Selected Juvenile Samples." *National Institute of Justice Research in Brief* (December).

Slaby, Ronald G., and Wendy Conklin Roedell. 1982. "The Development and Regulation of Aggression in Young Children." In *Psychological Development in the Elementary Years,* ed. Judith Worell. New York: Academic Press.

Smith, Melinda. 1991. "Mediation and the Juvenile Offender." *Update on Law-Related Education* 45 (Spring/Summer):7–10.

Snyder, Howard. 1993. *Arrest Rates of Youth 1991.* Pittsburgh: National Center for Juvenile Justice (July).

Socarides, Charles W. 1982. "Abdicating Fathers, Homosexual Sons: Psychoanalytic Observations on the Contribution of the Father to the Development of Male Homosexuality." In *Father and Child: Developmental and Clinical Perspectives,* ed. Stanley H. Cath, Alan R. Gurwitt, and John Munder Ross. Boston: Little, Brown and Company.

Somers, Anne. 1976. "Violence, Television, and the Health of American Youth." *New England Journal of Medicine* 294, no. 15 (8 April):811–817.

Sorrells, James. 1977. "Kids Who Kill." *Crime and Delinquency* 23:312–320.

Straus, Murray A., Richard J. Gelles, and Suzanne Steinmetz. 1980. *Behind Closed Doors: Violence in the American Family.* Garden City, NY: Anchor Books.

"Tale of a Young Mugger." 1976. *New York Times,* 11 April.

U.S. Department of Justice. 1976. *The Link between Learning Disabilities and Juvenile Delinquency.* Washington, DC: National Institute for Juvenile Justice and Delinquency Prevention.

Vissing, Y. M., et al. 1991. "Verbal Aggression by Parents and Psychosocial Problems of Children." *Child Abuse and Neglect* 15, no. 3:223–238.

Wallis, Claudia. 1985. "Children Having Children." *Time* (9 December):79–90.

Welsh, Ralph S. 1976. "Severe Parental Punishment and Delinquency: A Developmental Theory." *Journal of Child Clinical Psychology* 35, no. 1:17–21.

Widom, Cathy Spatz. 1992. "The Cycle of Violence." *National Institute of Justice Research in Brief* (October).

Willock, Brent. 1986. "Narcissistic Vulnerability in the Hyperaggressive Child: The Disregarded (Unloved, Uncared-for) Self." *Psychoanalytic Psychology* 3:59–80.

Wilson, Edward O. 1982. *On Human Nature.* New York: Bantam Books.

Wilson, James Q., and Richard J. Herrnstein. 1985. *Crime and Human Nature.* New York: Simon and Schuster.

Winn, Marie. 1981. *Children without Childhood.* New York: Pantheon Books.

———. 1985. *The Plug-in Drug: Television, Children, and the Family.* New York: Viking Press.

Wintemute, Garen, et al. 1992. "Policy Options of Firearm Violence: An Exploration of Regulation, Litigation and Research on Firearm Violence." In *Improving the Health of the Poor: Strategies for Prevention,* ed. Sarah E. Samuels and Mark D. Smith. Menlo Park, CA: The Henry J. Kaiser Family Foundation.

Wolfgang, Marvin E., Robert M. Figlio, and Thorsten Sellin. 1972. *Delinquency in a Birth Cohort.* Chicago: University of Chicago Press, 1972.

Chronology 2

Pre-Twentieth Century

The American Humane Association was founded in 1877 and is the only national organization working to protect both children and animals from abuse, neglect, cruelty, and exploitation. Their Children's Division works to break the cycle of abuse through training, risk assessment, research, and policy development programs initiated to provide effective child protective systems. They began their efforts by working to protect animals, and added children to their repertoire when they realized that no other organization existed to help and protect children.

Prior to 1899, courts in the United States followed an old common-law provision that divided childhood into two stages. Children under 7 years old could not be charged or prosecuted for any crime because they were not capable of thinking or acting with criminal intent. Children between 7 and 14 were also believed to be incapable of thinking or acting with criminal intent, but under certain circumstances, prosecutors could argue that the child knew the difference between good and evil, and therefore could be tried and sentenced for criminal behavior. At age 14, under the law at that time, children became adults.

In 1899, the Illinois legislature enacted the nation's first juvenile act establishing the first juvenile court. Before this, children accused of criminal acts were treated as adults. Hearings were conducted in any available court, because there were no juvenile courts and, if found guilty, children were sentenced as adults.

In England, as late as 1780, children could be tried, convicted, and hung for committing any of more than 200 crimes.

Twentieth Century

1915 The movement to remove children from adult prisons is just beginning. Historical records suggest that juveniles are beginning to be detained in converted private residences, county infirmaries, and hospitals instead of adult jails and prisons. Several major cities design and build facilities specifically for detaining juveniles. These facilities hold all children needing care outside of their own homes; no one sees the need to distinguish between juvenile delinquents and abused and neglected children and to separate these two groups.

1932 The first institution opens in Cleveland, Ohio, that is designed with living and sleeping units that separate juvenile delinquents from other children; areas are divided based on age and on activity. Professionals finally realize that delinquents should be separated from other children.

1954 This year sees the first hearings in the United States Senate on television and violence. Senator Estes Kefauver believes that watching violence on television contributes to the growing crime rate. As chairman of the Senate Subcommittee on Juvenile Delinquency, he convenes the first hearings on this subject.

1961 Senator Thomas Dodd of Connecticut, as chairman of the Senate Subcommittee on Juvenile Delinquency, holds hearings on what he believes to be the broadcast industry's overwhelming and opportunistic use of violence. Evidence is produced that shows how network executives push for higher ratings by strongly encouraging, and in some cases ordering, programmers and film studios to increase the level and amount of violence in programs they offer. Dr. Albert Bandura, professor of psychology at Stanford University, cites study after study that shows young children, imitating behavior that they have just seen on a violent television show, play more aggressively than when they have not seen a violent show. Nothing results from the hearings, because Senator Dodd appears to lose his enthusiasm for the investigation. His staff members claim that his change of attitude is a direct result of his friendships with members of the broadcast industry.

1962   C. Henry Kempe, a pediatrician from Denver, in an article in the *Journal of the American Medical Association,* describes the "battered child syndrome," characteristics of physically abused children that all physicians should be able to determine, helping them more easily identify abused children. This is the first formal recognition of child abuse in the medical community. This article results in a surge of research on abuse—physical, sexual, and psychological—and brings national attention to the seriousness and extent of child abuse.

Lord of the Flies by William Golding is published. This book elicits a shocked reaction from many adults who cannot believe that children can act so violently against each other as well as from parents who think the book is too violent for children to read.

1967   Dr. George Gerbner, dean of the Annenberg School of Communications at the University of Pennsylvania, and Dr. Larry Gross begin their annual study of the extent and nature of violence in network television programs. The study is funded by the National Institute of Mental Health and consists of trained observers tabulating the number and types of violent acts contained in each season's programming. This results in a Violence Index, comparing the number and types of violent actions by each network and by year.

The National Citizens Committee for Broadcasting uses the Gerbner Index to identify those advertisers whose commercials often appear on the most violent programs identified by this index and starts a campaign to persuade these advertisers to support less violent programming.

1967 On May 15 a new era in juvenile court history begins. The Gerald Gault decision, by the United States Supreme Court, changes the way that juveniles are treated in juvenile courts. The sheriff of Gila County, Arizona, had placed Gerald Gault, 15 years old, and a friend in custody after a woman complained about receiving a lewd telephone call from one of the boys. Gault was arrested, and even though he denied making the call, officials made no attempt to prove the woman's claim; in fact the juvenile court's only contact with the woman was one phone call from a juvenile officer. The woman never appeared at the hearing, Gerald and his parents were not allowed to read the probation officer's referral report, and Gerald was sentenced to a state juvenile institution until he turned 21. The Supreme Court hears the case and rules that notice of a court hearing must be given with sufficient time to allow a proper defense and must detail the charges to be made, that the child and his parents must be notified of the child's right to be represented by counsel, that the constitutional privilege against self-incrimination applies to juveniles, and that sworn testimony in juvenile courts should be the same as in adult hearings—specifically, that without a valid confession, testimony by witnesses available for cross-examination was essential for a delinquency finding. These findings suggest to many observers that a due process revolution has been mandated for juvenile courts.

1972 The U.S. Surgeon General's *Report on Violence,* formally titled *Television and Social Behavior,* is published. It establishes a tentative causal relationship between television violence and aggressive behavior among young viewers. Citing over 100 published papers, including 50 studies, it concludes that children exposed to violence on television have increased levels of aggressive behavior. The report quickly becomes the focal point in the movement to reform the television industry.

The C. Henry Kempe National Center for the Prevention and Treatment of Child Abuse and Neglect opens to provide a clinically based resource for training, consultation, program development and education, and research in all forms of child abuse and neglect. The center is committed to multidisciplinary approaches to improve the recognition, treatment, and prevention of all forms of abuse and neglect.

The Children's Creative Response to Conflict (CCRC) is established by the New York Quaker Project on Community Conflict. Realizing that the beginnings of violence are often planted in children at an early age, the CCRC is one of the first programs to help adults and children develop new ways of looking at conflicts and to help them develop solutions. Workshops are offered to help students, parents, teachers, and concerned individuals develop skills in one or more of the program's central themes: cooperation, communication, affirmation, creative conflict resolution, mediation, and bias awareness.

1973   George Gerbner's annual study of the extent and nature of violence in network television programs is expanded to include a study of the effects of television violence on both child and adult viewers.

1974   The Juvenile Justice and Delinquency Prevention Act of 1974 is passed by Congress. This act consolidates many previous laws enacted by Congress on the subject of youth crime and delinquency, and focuses on diversion, de-institutionalization, and the separation of juvenile from adult offenders. It sets up an Office of Juvenile Justice and Delinquency Prevention, a National Advisory Committee on Juvenile Justice and Delinquency Prevention, and a National Institute for Juvenile Justice and Delinquency Prevention to serve as a clearinghouse, and provides block grants to develop programs emphasizing the prevention of delinquency.

The National Center on Child Abuse and Neglect (NCCAN) is established by the Child Abuse Prevention and Treatment Act (PL 93-247) as the primary federal agency charged with helping states and communities address the problems of child maltreatment. NCCAN oversees all federal child abuse and neglect efforts and allocates child maltreatment funds appropriated by Congress. The organization is responsible for conducting

1974   research on the causes, prevention, and treatment of
(cont.) child abuse and neglect; collecting, analyzing, and dis-
         seminating information to professionals concerned with
         child abuse and neglect; increasing public awareness of
         the problems of child maltreatment; and assisting states
         and communities in developing programs related to the
         prevention, identification, and treatment of child abuse
         and neglect.

         Marian Wright Edelman organizes the Children's De-
         fense Fund (CDF) to protect America's youth. She wants
         to provide a strong and effective voice for all children,
         educating the nation about the needs of children and en-
         couraging the support of children before they get sick,
         drop out of school, or get into trouble.

1975   A study by Senator Birch Bayh, chairman of the U.S.
         Senate Subcommittee to Investigate Juvenile Delin-
         quency, concludes in a report on *Our Nation's Schools—A
         Report Card* that violent acts committed by and against
         children in the nation's schools are increasing. The study
         finds that between 1970 and 1973 confiscations of deadly
         weapons have increased 54.4 percent, assaults on stu-
         dents have increased by 85.3 percent, and murders have
         increased by 18.5 percent in the nation's schools.

1978   The New York State Legislature passes and the governor
         signs into law the Juvenile Offender Law, informally
         known as the Willie Bosket law. This legislation results
         from the public outrage at the crimes and punishments of
         Willie Bosket, who has committed over 2,000 crimes, in-
         cluding 25 stabbings, while he was between the ages of 9
         and 15. The crimes that finally push the legislature to
         enact the Juvenile Offender Law take place during an
         eight-day crime spree in which 15-year-old Willie robs
         several people and shoots and kills two of them. He is
         found guilty of both murders and is placed in the custody
         of the New York State Division for Youth for five years.
         This is the maximum penalty allowed under the law at
         the time; however, the Juvenile Offender Law now allows
         for juveniles to be tried and sentenced as adults if they
         commit certain crimes while they are still juveniles—i.e.,

if they are charged with murder when they are 13, 14, or 15, or charged with other violent felonies.

1980   The National Commission on Youth issues a report entitled *The Transition of Youth to Adulthood: A Bridge Too Long.* Through this report, the commission hopes to generate widespread discussion and debate on a variety of topics to help shorten the transition to adulthood for American youth. Their recommendations include encouraging television viewers to continue to pressure broadcasters to decrease levels of television violence, reforming the juvenile justice system, preventing youth crime and delinquency, and eliminating status offender classifications.

     Behind Closed Doors: Violence in American Families is published. The authors, sociologists Murray Straus, Richard Gelles, and Suzanne Steinmetz, conducted an in-depth study of family violence and this book summarizes their findings. One of the first books to explore the extent of family violence, it is often considered a definitive work about family violence; its authors estimate that, as of 1975, between 3.1 and 4 million children had been assaulted by their parents sometime during their childhood, and between 1 and 1.9 million children were assaulted by their parents in 1975.

     The Violent Juvenile Offender Program is funded by the U.S. Congress.

     The Office of Juvenile Justice and Delinquency Prevention (OJJDP), U.S. Department of Justice, initiates a study of violent youth crime in five cities—Boston, Denver, Memphis, Newark, and Phoenix. Each of these areas has high rates of violent youth crime and OJJDP wants to determine the most effective ways of treating chronic violent juvenile offenders.

1982   Richard Jahnke, 16, kills his father. This is the first case of a parricide—a child murdering a parent—to receive national attention since Lizzie Borden killed her parents. Living in Cheyenne, Wyoming, with his father, mother,

1982
(*cont.*)
and sister, Richard was a good student and member of the ROTC. However, his father was a strict disciplinarian, known to beat his wife and his children severely when they did anything to displease him. This particular night, Richard's father shoves him and tells him to be out of the house by the time he (the father) returns home. After his father leaves, Richard gathers all the guns in the house and waits in the garage for his father to return; he stations his sister in the living room with a gun in case his father gets past him. When his father returns, Richard kills him. He and his sister are charged with first degree murder, sentenced to between 5 and 15 years, and after serving 1 year, are pardoned by the governor of Wyoming after an intense public outcry.

The National Institute of Mental Health publishes a report called *Television and Behavior: Ten Years of Scientific Progress and Implications for the Eighties,* which looks at the relationship between violence on television and aggressive, violent behavior. One of the report's conclusions is that children who are exposed to violence on television may accept violence as normal behavior. They may not be able to distinguish between the fantasy of television and the reality of daily life, and even believe that television is reality.

1983
The National Conference of State Legislatures believes a relationship between child abuse and delinquency does exist, and this issue is important enough to hold two briefings for all state legislators. The briefings review current research being conducted as well as findings that suggest a relationship does exist between abuse and delinquency.

1984
A conference on "Child Abuse: Prelude to Delinquency?" draws together researchers, practitioners, and policy makers with extensive experience in child abuse and/or delinquency. The conference is organized by the Office of Juvenile Justice and Delinquency Prevention (OJJDP), the National Center on Child Abuse and Neglect (NCCAN), and the National Committee for the Prevention of Child Abuse. Recommendations include the need for additional research on the relationship between child abuse and

delinquency as well as intervention and prevention strategies.

The U.S. government creates the Attorney General's Task Force on Family Violence.

1985   The Parents' Music Resource Center is founded to pressure the music and video industry to become responsible for what they are selling, specifically the lewd and/or violent lyrics of music and actions in videos. The Center participates in hearings before the Senate Commerce Committee on the sexual and violent nature of rock music lyrics. By 1990, the industry proclaims that all albums, tapes, and discs will have standardized warning labels.

1988   George Comstock, a professor of public communication at Syracuse University, reviews the research concerning television violence and aggressive behavior. He finds that a majority of the studies report that watching violence on television does not help children relieve violent feelings, but rather increases levels and incidence of antisocial, aggressive behavior.

President Ronald Reagan vetoes the Children's Television Act of 1988.

The United States Supreme Court rules, in *Thompson v. Oklahoma*, that the State of Oklahoma cannot execute William Wayne Thompson, who was 15 years old when he and three older friends brutally beat and murdered his former brother-in-law. Thompson admitted he had kicked the murder victim in the head, "cut his throat and chest, and shot him in the head" (Ewing 1990, 124). Thompson's death sentence is vacated, with five justices agreeing that it is cruel and unusual punishment to execute someone under the age of 16 and therefore proscribed by the Eighth Amendment.

1989   The United States Supreme Court again takes up the issue of death sentences for juveniles. This time, two cases, *Stanford v. Kentucky* and *Wilkins v. Missouri*, are heard at the same time by the Court. The basic question

1989   is "whether the Eighth Amendment forbids the execu-
(*cont.*)   tion of individuals for crimes they committed while ei-
       ther 16 or 17 years old" (Ewing 1990, 124). This time the
       court agrees with the death sentences, letting them
       stand, because the justices believe that there is no general
       agreement by society that it is wrong to execute these or
       other juveniles under the age of 18 who commit heinous
       crimes.

1990   Dalton Prejean dies in the electric chair after killing a
       state trooper when he was 17. He is the first youth to die
       in the electric chair after the 1989 Supreme Court ruling
       allowing youths to be sentenced to death. Earlier, he had
       served only a little more than two years in a juvenile in-
       stitution for murdering a taxi driver when he was 14.

       The New York City police commissioner responds to the
       record-setting number of homicides committed in New
       York City in 1989 by suggesting a new approach to vio-
       lence. He suggests that churches start teaching children
       moral values, schools start teaching students how to re-
       solve conflicts peacefully, and that medical professionals
       study the causes of violence.

       Congress passes the Children's Television Act, which di-
       rects the Federal Communications Commission (FCC) to
       consider, when renewing a television station's broadcast
       license, the station's compliance with certain program-
       ming requirements. These requirements include broad-
       casting programs that meet the educational needs of
       children and activities that will enhance the educational
       value of programming for children.

1992   The Center for the Study and Prevention of Violence is
       initiated at the University of Colorado in Boulder. The
       center's purpose is to provide information and assis-
       tance to groups and individuals studying the causes of
       violence and to suggest ways of preventing violence,
       especially youth violence. The center's Information
       House gathers research literature relating to violence and
       offers bibliographic searches of its on-line data base on
       requested topics. Information is gathered on research,
       programs, curricula, videos, books and journal articles,

1992
(*cont.*) and other sources of information about the causes of violence and prevention strategies, and all this information is then included in an on-line data base. Abstracts are written and included in this data base. Reviews of literature include evaluating juvenile violence prevention, violence and the schools, the effects of the mass media on violence, the family and juvenile violence, gangs, guns and violence, and alcohol and drugs and their influence on juvenile violence. Technical assistance is provided to individuals and groups developing or evaluating programs on preventing violence. The center also has a research component, analyzing data and developing and conducting other projects to understand the causes of violence.

1993 In England, on February 12, two 10-year-old boys lure 2-year-old James Bulger away from his mother in a shopping mall in Liverpool. They drag and push the toddler for four kilometers until they reach a secluded spot where they beat him to death with bricks and a metal bar. They then partially strip him and leave his body on a railroad track where it is sliced in two by a passing train. The 10-year-olds are charged with James Bulger's abduction and murder and in December are found guilty on both counts. The boys are detained indefinitely at separate facilities for dangerous children. The world is shocked at the viciousness of this crime and the young age of the offenders.

Notes

Ewing, Charles Patrick. 1990. *When Children Kill: The Dynamics of Juvenile Homicide.* Lexington, MA: Lexington Books.

Biographical Sketches 3

T. Berry Brazelton (b. 1918)

Brazelton is believed by many to be the successor to Benjamin Spock. After completing his training in pediatric medicine (he was granted his M.D. degree from Columbia University in 1943 and completed a residency at Massachusetts General Hospital and a pediatric residency at Children's Hospital in 1947), he studied child psychiatry. He became increasingly concerned over the conditions under which children were being raised, and in 1988 helped launch Parent Action, a grassroots lobbying organization for parents. He saw more children being raised in poverty and more two-parent families trying to raise their children while both parents worked full-time, and he believed something should be done to help them out.

Over the years, Brazelton has lobbied Congress for guaranteed parental leave, flexible working arrangements, and improved day care. Not only has he supported these initiatives, but he has continued to conduct research in order to help parents understand their children and interact with them in a positive way. Through his research, he determined that children were not blank slates or lumps of clay to be molded by their parents, but rather complex, responsive individuals with their own moods and behavior characteristics. He believes that infants' behavior can be modified by parents who are properly trained. Brazelton's emphasis on providing support for caring but overworked parents has distanced him from many of his colleagues. He initially believed that mothers with young children should not work outside of the home, but later modified his thinking and suggested that they stay home at least for the first several months of the baby's life. In 1988 he participated with congressional representative Patricia Schroeder (D-Colorado) on a national tour to bring attention to family issues. He also worked with Schroeder as a member of the National Commission on Children to gain passage of a law providing parents with up to 4 months of leave to care for a newborn or a newly adopted child, or for family illness. President Bill Clinton later signed a bill allowing up to 12 weeks of unpaid leave to employees of large companies.

Brazelton is still concerned with the environment that children are growing up in today, worrying that parents must have a sense of control over their children's lives and be able to teach them values and morals, and not feel overwhelmed by too many pressures.

Marian Wright Edelman (b. 1939)

As a student at Spelman College, Marian Wright Edelman spent her junior year studying at the Sorbonne in France and traveled across the Soviet Union, with thoughts of a career in foreign service. However, when she returned to the United States, her interest in civil rights grew as she participated in sit-ins in Atlanta in 1960, and was arrested with 14 other students during one sit-in. Her interest in civil rights became a career focus and, after graduating from Spelman as valedictorian in 1960, she decided to become a lawyer. While at Yale Law School, she continued to participate in civil rights activities, traveling to Mississippi to help in a voter registration drive in 1963.

After graduating from Yale in 1963, Edelman became one of the first two interns at the NAACP Legal Defense and Education Fund in Mississippi. She became the first black woman to pass the Mississippi bar and opened her own law office, working to help get demonstrating students out of jail and participating in several school desegregation cases. She also served on the board of the Child Development Group of Mississippi, an organization representing one of the largest Head Start programs in the country.

In 1968, with a Ford Foundation grant, she moved to Washington, D.C., to start the Washington Research Project, founded to discover how current and new laws could help the poor. She met Peter Edelman while in Mississippi; he was a legislative assistant to Robert F. Kennedy. Soon after Kennedy was shot, they were married and moved to Boston. Marian became director of the Harvard University Center for Law and Education, but often flew back to Washington to continue her duties as head of the Washington Research Project, the forerunner of the Children's Defense Fund (CDF). The CDF was founded in 1973 to protect the children of America by providing a strong and effective voice for all children, educating the nation about the needs of children, and encouraging the support of children before they get physically sick, drop out of school, or get into trouble.

Edelman still leads the CDF, with headquarters in Washington and state offices in Ohio, Texas, and Minnesota, and local offices in Cleveland, Ohio, and Washington, D.C. Concerned about children and violence, Edelman started the Violence Prevention Project, CDF's most recent effort to provide a safe start for all children in America. The project focuses on federal legislation, public education, and community mobilization in order to begin to curb the cycle of violence plaguing our schools, families, and communities. CDF and the Black Community Crusade for Children, a CDF-coordinated effort to mobilize the black community, have organized the Anti-Violence Network. This network includes over 100 primarily community-based organizations dedicated to preventing violence. The network's purpose is to build a grassroots effort to influence and shape public policy in the field of violence prevention and to enhance the effectiveness of the member groups. CDF has also developed a violence component to its Child Watch Visitation Program, which provides a vivid demonstration to community leaders on the effects of violence on children.

Edelman returned to live in Washington, D.C., with her husband, became chairman of the board of trustees at Spelman College in 1980, and has served on the boards of many organizations concerned with child welfare, including the Carnegie Council on Children, the March of Dimes, and the United Nations International Children's Emergency Fund (UNICEF).

George Gerbner (b. 1919)

As the dean of the University of Pennsylvania's Annenberg School of Communications, George Gerbner has had the opportunity to study television violence and its effects on behavior of viewers, young and old. He has conducted research on a variety of communications topics over the past 40 years. While earning his M.S. and Ph.D. (1955) in communication from the University of Southern California (USC), Gerbner taught journalism, English, and social science at John Muir College in Pasadena, was responsible for publications and general educational curriculum planning for the city of Pasadena, was a research associate in the cinema department at USC, and taught a course on the social aspects of mass communication at El Camino College in Torrance, California. After earning his Ph.D., he became an assistant professor at the University of Illinois Institute of Communications Research, studying the relationship between the mass media and the images they create in the public's mind.

By 1964, Gerbner was named dean of the Annenberg School of Communications. The National Commission on the Causes and Prevention of Violence asked him to study the effects of violence in the mass media, especially television violence. Along with Dr. Larry Gross, Gerbner began an annual study of the extent and nature of violence in network television programs. The study was funded by the National Institute of Mental Health and consisted of trained observers tabulating the number and types of violent acts contained in each season's programming. This resulted in a Violence Index, comparing the number and types of violent actions broadcast by each network and by year. In 1973, the study was expanded to include the study of the effects of television violence on child and adult viewers.

In 1967, the National Citizens Committee for Broadcasting used the Gerbner Index to identify those advertisers whose commercials often appeared on the most violent programs, according to this index, and started a campaign to persuade these advertisers to support less violent programming.

By 1969, the National Institute of Mental Health awarded an annual grant to the Annenberg School of Communications for Gerbner to continue monitoring television violence. While network television executives have disputed his findings, based on what they perceive as flaws in his research, Gerbner stands by his research design and its findings. He has encouraged the teaching of critical viewing skills to students in schools, creating a wider market in television production to lessen its dependence on advertising dollars, and fostering public debate on the value and place of television in society.

Sheldon Glueck (1896–1980) and Eleanor Glueck (1898–1972)

Sheldon Glueck was born in Warsaw, Poland, and became a naturalized citizen of the United States in 1920. He attended Georgetown School of Law, George Washington University, and Harvard University, and was granted the following degrees: A.B., A.M., LL.B., LL.M., S.S.D., Ph.D., and Sc.D. He taught in the Department of Social Ethics at Harvard and at Harvard Law School and was particularly interested in the relationship between law and psychiatry, delinquency research, and delinquency prevention. He received many awards for his work in criminal justice.

Eleanor Touroff was born in Brooklyn, New York, and received an A.B. from Barnard College in English, an M.Ed. in 1923, and an Ed.D. in 1925 from Harvard Graduate School of Education. She also attended the New York School of Social Work. She was a research criminologist in the Department of Social Ethics. For 20 years, Eleanor was a research associate for the Harvard Law School Research Project into the Causes, Treatment, and Prevention of Juvenile Delinquency; she and Sheldon were co-directors of the program for seven years. They were married in 1922 and started a lifelong study of crime and delinquency.

The Gluecks studied the etiology of delinquency, ways of predicting who would become delinquent, prevention strategies, the correctional system, the role that working mothers played in juvenile delinquency, the family's role, other factors thought to cause delinquent behavior, and other areas of crime and delinquency using a multidisciplinary approach. They understood the influence that social forces, including poverty, alcoholism, poor health conditions, weak family structure and support, and inadequate education, could have on juveniles, and which could lead to delinquent behavior.

They believed that the fields of psychiatry, psychology, social work, and education should all play a role in the juvenile justice system. They worked with the system to help develop predictors of future delinquency to assist in treatment and prevention efforts. They developed the Social Prediction Tables, which were used to help identify children who had the potential to become delinquents by the age of six years; these tables were based on data collected from older delinquents. While many sociologists criticized these prediction tables because of the methods the Gluecks used to develop them, the validity of these tables has been verified through studies conducted in several countries.

Alice Miller

With a Ph.D. in psychology and sociology, Alice Miller has been a practicing psychoanalyst and instructor in psychoanalysis for over 20 years. When her book *Thou Shalt Not Be Aware* was first published in Germany in 1981, Dr. Miller was virtually the only person writing about the sexual abuse of children in Europe. She visited the United States in 1982 and was delighted to see that her topic was being written about openly in this country. She believes that children are "used and misused for adults' needs, including sexual needs, to a much greater extent than we realize." She thinks emotions blocked because of this abuse inevitably lead to emotional and physical problems. While she attempted to integrate her theories into the mainstream of psychoanalytic theory, she realized that this was an impossible task. She says,

> It took time for me to accept the fact that psycho-analysis, too, of necessity shares the taboos of the society to which it belongs; realizing this, I tried to understand from what source these taboos received their extraordinary power. I began my search within the framework of psychoanalysis because this was the field I knew best, but the answers I found fell outside its boundaries and cast new light on the foundations of society as a whole. In almost every area of life I found the tendency to ignore the prevalence of child abuse and to deny its lasting effects. This attitude is found not only in psychoanalysis, where it has been given additional reinforcement by the drive theory, but also in the new therapeutic schools, for it conforms to the unwritten laws of our society and remains unconscious as long as it is not directly confronted. (Miller 1986, 309–310)

Miller argues that therapists must start listening to the children and identifying with them in order to understand them. Therapists must become advocates for their clients instead of representing current societal theories and values. They must not spare the parents at any cost, understanding the ways in which sexuality can be used to control or have power over those weaker in society.

Ashley Montagu (b. 1905)

Ashley Montagu is probably one of the foremost anthropologists in the world. With a Ph.D. in anthropology from Columbia University, his numerous writings have focused on the relationship between cultural factors and the physical and behavioral evolution of humans. He believes that the environment and the culture one is brought up in, rather than genetics, determine many human characteristics. This environment-versus-heredity theory has been applied by him in a variety of areas, including human aggression, racism, sexism, and child-rearing techniques. In *The Nature of Human Aggression,* Montagu debunks the theories of Konrad Lorenz, Robert Ardrey, Desmond Morris, Anthony Storr, Sigmund Freud, Charles Darwin, Erich Fromm, Sheldon and Eleanor Glueck, and others prominent in this field who believe that mankind is innately aggressive and depraved.

Reviewing the research on instinct and adaptation, cannibalism and aggression, the use of tools and weapons, cooperation, the brain and aggression, territoriality, war and violence, and the social and political consequences of believing in innate aggression, Montagu argues that genes interacting with the social environment lead to aggressive, even violent behavior. He theorizes that no one is born with aggressive, violent impulses, and that explanations for aggression and violent behavior are more complicated than many experts believe. Montagu believes that no child who is adequately loved becomes aggressive or violent. He also believes that humans have no aggressive instincts, and that everything we know we learn from other human beings. In his books, *Culture and Human Development* and *The Meaning of Love,* he emphasizes the characteristics of social cooperation and love as important selection factors in evolution, doing so long before these factors were emphasized by the modern sociobiologists.

Deborah Prothrow-Stith (b. 1954)

As a physician, the former public health commissioner of Massachusetts, and a top administrator at the Harvard School of Public Health, Deborah Prothrow-Stith has become an authority in the study of violent children as a public health problem. She has focused on developing a violence prevention curriculum for schools. Her primary belief is that teenage violence is a public health problem as well as a problem for the criminal justice system. She has examined adolescent violence in disadvantaged neighborhoods, looking at the causes of violence, primarily among poor, young black males, the group at highest risk for violence. She examines social, psychological, racial, cultural, and economic factors that may contribute to youth violence. She conducted research at a Boston high school, describing the fears, insecurities, and other emotions the students experience growing up in a violent environment. Ultimately, she has proposed workable ways to reduce the incidence of violence among our nation's adolescents. She began by developing an anti-violence curriculum for students as a student at Harvard Medical School. Her senior project was to create a public health intervention curriculum to help curb adolescent violence, incorporating materials from three disciplines: criminal justice, mental health, and the biological sciences.

Janet Reno (b. 1938)

Janet Reno attended Dade County, Florida, public schools, received a B.S. in chemistry from Cornell University, and was granted her LL.B. degree from Harvard Law School in 1963. She was sworn in as the United States Attorney General, the first woman to hold that post, on 12 March 1993. She is known for her no-nonsense way of getting things done as well as for her compassion. As attorney general, she believes that any program focusing on preventing violent youth crime must incorporate primary prevention tactics, including prenatal care and intervention programs for children growing up in poverty.

Reno has spoken out repeatedly about the importance of helping children grow up to be responsible, honest, and caring adults. She advocates that they must also learn that they are responsible for their actions and will be punished for breaking the law. Before becoming attorney general, Reno spent 15 years as the chief prosecutor for Dade County, where she became known for her genuine concern for disadvantaged juveniles and her ability to develop creative ways to help reduce juvenile crime. She has argued for neighborhood resource teams—composed of a police officer, a social worker, a nurse, and a housing expert—to work with low-income communities to reduce crime. She formed one such team in West Perrine, Florida, and was heavily involved in their activities. After the program was initiated, West Perrine experienced a 60 percent reduction in crime.

Reno has been equally successful in her children's rights advocacy efforts. In Florida, she reformed the juvenile justice system, prosecuted child abuse cases aggressively, and pursued delinquent fathers for child support. In dealing with the drug problems among youth, she initiated an innovative drug court in which nonviolent, first-time offenders were sent for counseling instead of being sent to prison; results show that over half of those completing the program have remained drug free.

Stanton Samenow (b. 1941)

Stanton Samenow received his Ph.D. in clinical psychology from the University of Michigan in 1968, after completing his undergraduate work at Yale University in 1963. Currently in private practice, he was a clinical-research psychologist for the Program for the Investigation of Criminal Behavior from 1970 through 1978, and was a member of the President's Law Enforcement Task Force on Victims of Crime in 1982. Dr. Samenow has learned a great deal from years of evaluating and counseling juvenile and adult offenders. With Samuel Yochelson, he co-wrote the three-volume *The Criminal Personality: Inside the Criminal Mind* in 1984, and *Before It's Too Late: Why Some Kids Get into Trouble—and What Parents Can Do about It* in 1989. In *Before It's Too Late,* he provides instructive insights for approaches parents can take in dealing with their antisocial, problem child.

While the environment certainly can play a role in personality formation, Dr. Samenow believes that children make choices as they respond to their environment. Parents are responsible for teaching their children right from wrong, and instilling moral and ethical principles and positive values, but children choose to accept or reject these teachings. He has identified seven common indications of antisocial behavior, maintained that the tendency to blame the environment is wrong and that antisocial children know the difference between right and wrong but choose to believe that the rules don't apply to them. While the decision to act responsibly lies with the child, Dr. Samenow continues to show parents how they can help their children learn to make the right choices.

Patricia Schroeder (b. 1940)

In her more than 20 years as a Democrat representing the First Congressional District of Colorado, including most of the city and county of Denver, Patricia Schroeder has focused on family issues, women's rights issues, and women's health issues. She is considered the dean of the Colorado delegation to Congress and is the "most senior woman in Congress."

In 1988 Schroeder participated in a national tour to bring

attention to family issues. While she was a member of the National Commission on Children, she worked to enact passage of a law that would provide parents with up to 4 months of leave to care for a newborn, a newly adopted child, or a family member. Congress later passed, and President Bill Clinton signed into law, a bill allowing up to 12 weeks of unpaid leave to employees of large companies.

Schroeder received her J.D. in 1964 from Harvard Law School after completing her undergraduate work at the University of Minnesota.

Murray A. Straus (b. 1926)

Murray Straus is prominently known in the field of family violence and child abuse and neglect. He received his B.A. in 1948 from the University of Wisconsin, his M.S. in 1949, and his Ph.D. in sociology from the University of Wisconsin in 1956. He was a member of the board of directors of the National Council on Family Relations from 1963 through 1970, and has been the director of the Family Research Laboratory at the University of New Hampshire since 1980.

Along with his colleagues Richard Gelles and Suzanne Steinmetz, he pioneered one of the first comprehensive research studies on family violence in America. They studied the extent and breadth of family violence and what that violence meant to the participants. After examining a variety of forms of violence culled from over 2,000 interviews, their research shows, for the first time, the extent of violent acts toward children, including many actions that could injure, maim, or kill them. The evidence shows that violence in the home is the primary source of our violent society.

Notes

Miller, Alice. 1986. *Thou Shalt Not Be Aware: Society's Betrayal of the Child.* Translated by Hildegarde and Hunter Hannum. New York: Meridian.

Montagu, Ashley. 1976. *The Nature of Human Aggression.* New York: Oxford University Press.

Prothrow-Stith, Deborah, with Michaele Weissman. 1991. *Deadly Consequences: How Violence Is Destroying Our Teenage Population and a Plan To Begin Solving the Problem.* New York: HarperCollins.

Samenow, Stanton E. 1989. *Before It's Too Late: Why Some Kids Get into Trouble—and What Parents Can Do about It.* New York: Times Books.

Straus, Murray A., Richard J. Gelles, and Suzanne Steinmetz. 1980. *Behind Closed Doors: Violence in the American Family.* Garden City, NY: Anchor Books.

Facts and Statistics 4

This chapter presents general facts and statistics relating to violent children, excerpts from relevant documents from a variety of organizations, excerpts from three relevant U.S. Supreme Court decisions, and excerpts from the Juvenile Justice and Delinquency Prevention Act of 1974.

Statistics

According to the *Uniform Crime Reports*, published by the Federal Bureau of Investigation, the number of juveniles arrested for committing a serious violent crime, including murder, rape, robbery, and aggravated assault, increased by 50 percent between 1987 and 1991. Also between 1987 and 1991, there was an 85 percent increase in juvenile arrests for murder. In 1991, 122,900 juveniles were arrested for committing a serious violent crime, including 3,400 for murder, 6,300 for forcible rape, 44,500 for robbery, and 68,700 for aggravated assault. Between 1987 and 1991, the use of guns in homicides by juveniles increased from 64 percent to 78 percent (*Crime in the United States 1988, 1990, 1992*, 1989, 1991, 1993). Minority, disadvantaged, and vulnerable youth are most often affected by violence with guns. Gunshot wounds are the leading cause of death for black males between the ages of 15 and 34 and black females between the ages of 15 and 29. Black teenagers, between 1984 and 1988, were 2.8 times more likely to die from gunshot wounds than all natural causes combined. Between 1984 and 1988, the homicide rate for black males between the ages of 15 and 19 doubled; this entire increase was a result of firearm homicide. Almost one-half (48 percent) of all deaths among black male teenagers and almost 20 percent of all deaths of black female teenagers are a result of gun violence (Wintemute et al. 1992).

Blacks also are more likely to be arrested for violent crime than whites. For example, in 1991, black youth were arrested at a rate of 1,456 per 100,000 while the rate for white youths was 293 per 100,000 (Thornberry 1994).

> Youth are not only overrepresented as violent offenders, they also are overrepresented as victims of violent crimes. For Americans between the ages of 15 and 19, homicide by gunfire is the second leading cause of death. . . . Although youth violence affects all segments of American society, it has particularly devastating effects on people of color. Homicide has long been the leading cause of death among young African-American males. In 1987, for example, the death rate due to firearm homicides for African-American males ages 15 to 19 was 49.2 per 100,000; the rate for white males of the same age was only 5.1 per 100,000. (Thornberry 1994, 9)

Because many studies are case studies of individuals or descriptive studies of small groups of violent juveniles, it is often difficult to develop a clear picture of who these children are. This difficulty may also occur because there are many circumstances in which children kill.

The Office of Juvenile Justice and Delinquency Prevention in the U.S. Department of Justice put together a fact sheet on juveniles and violence that provides a wide-ranging view on how many juveniles are affected by violence and how many participate in violent activities. The Children's Defense Fund also has collected statistics on children and violence. Both of these documents are excerpted below.

Juveniles and Violence:
Juvenile Offending and Victimization

Office of Juvenile Justice and Delinquency Prevention
Fact Sheet no. 3, July 1993

Current national data do not exist on the actual level of violent crime committed by juveniles. Policy makers and researchers rely on the FBI's *Uniform Crime Reports* of arrests of youth under the age of 18 as an indicator of the level of juvenile crime in the United States. Although only 5 percent of all juvenile arrests are for violent offenses, these arrests increased dramatically over the 5-year period from 1987 to 1991.

- Between 1987 and 1991, the number of Violent Crime Index arrests of juveniles increased by 50 percent—twice the increase for persons 18 years of age or older. Most alarming, juvenile arrests for murder increased by 85 percent, compared with 21 percent for those age 18 and older.
- The estimated 122,900 Violent Crime Index arrests of juveniles in 1991 was the highest number in history, with 3,400 arrests for murder, 6,300 for forcible rape, 44,500 for robbery, and 68,700 for aggravated assault.
- Juveniles accounted for 17 percent of all violent crime arrests in 1991.
- Three of every 10 juvenile murder arrests involved a victim under age 18.
- Juveniles' use of guns in homicides increased from 64 percent to 78 percent between 1987 and 1991, during which time juvenile arrests for weapons violations increased 62 percent.
- In 1991 the nearly 50,000 juvenile weapons arrests accounted for more than 1 out of 5 weapons arrests. Black youth were arrested for weapons law violations at a rate triple that of white youth.
- The 1991 violent crime arrest rate for black youth was 5 times higher than that of white youth (1,456 per 100,000 compared with 283 per 100,000).
- In 1990, 1 in 5 high school students reported carrying a weapon somewhere, at least once, during the past month. One in 20 had carried a firearm.

- Among students who carried a weapon, knives and razors were more likely to be carried (55 percent) than were firearms (20 percent). More than half of the black males who carried a weapon carried a gun.

Contrary to popular perceptions of the risk of violent crime, teenagers are victimized at higher rates than adults. In the *National Crime Victimization Surveys (1985–1988)* youth under age 20 made up only 14 percent of the survey population, yet they accounted for 30 percent of violent crime victimizations.

- An estimated 960,000 youth between ages 12 and 19 were the victims of 1.9 million violent crimes—rape, robbery, and assault—each year between 1985 and 1988.
- Approximately 67 out of every 1,000 teenagers were victims of a violent crime each year, compared with 26 per 1,000 persons age 20 or older (1985–1988).
- Teen victimizations were most likely to occur in or around school—37 percent of the violent crime victimizations of youth between 12 and 15 years old occurred at school, compared with 17 percent of those 16 to 19 years of age.
- Schools with gangs had higher victimization rates. Twelve percent of the students reporting gangs at school were victimized compared with 8 percent of those who reported no gang presence.
- FBI data show that in 1991 more than 2,200 youth under age 18 were murdered in the U.S.—an average of more than 6 youth homicide victims each day.
- Although the prevalence of homicides of children age 13 and under has been relatively stable, teen homicides (age 14–17) have more than doubled—from 4 per 100,000 in 1984 to 11 per 100,000 in 1991.
- Adolescent homicide victims, those aged 10–17, were most often killed by a friend or other acquaintance (61 percent).
- More than 70 percent of teenage homicide victims were shot to death. The overwhelming majority of youth homicide victims in the 10–17 age range were male (73 percent).
- In 1991 more than 83 percent of murder victims between ages 15 and 19 were killed with firearms, compared with 66 percent of all murder victims.

The Children's Defense Fund Statistics on Children and Violence

- The National Education Association reports that, every day in the United States, 40 children are killed or injured by guns.
- In 1990, guns were used to kill 222 American children under the age of 10, and 6,795 American adolescents, teenagers, and young adults under the age of 25. These figures exclude the numbers of children and youths who use guns to commit suicide.
- Since 1988, teenage boys in the United States generally have been more likely to die from gunshot wounds than from all natural causes combined, according to the National Center for Health Statistics.
- In a mere three years—between 1987 and 1990—gunshot wounds among children ages 16 and under in urban areas nearly doubled, according to the National Pediatric Trauma Registry.
- The Harlem Hospital in New York reports that the majority of children admitted with gunshot wounds already have lost a family member to a fatal, gun-related injury.
- A study in *The New England Journal of Medicine* found that young men in Harlem are less likely to live to age 40 than their counterparts in Bangladesh.
- Homicide is the leading cause of death among black youths ages 18 to 24. According to the Centers for Disease Control, between 1984 and 1988, the murder rate of black youths between the ages of 15 and 19 rose by 100 percent.
- During a six-month period in 1988–1989, more than 400,000 students were victims of violent crime at school. A 1990 survey of students at 31 Illinois high schools revealed that 1 in 20 students had carried a gun to school. California schools reported a 200 percent increase in gun confiscations from students between 1986 and 1990. In a 1987 survey of high-school students, 48 percent of tenth-grade boys and 34 percent of eighth-grade boys said they could get a handgun if they wanted one.
- In New York City, arrests on gun charges increased by 75

percent between 1987 and 1990 for youngsters ages 7 to 15.

- A recent Northeastern University study found that arrests for murder of boys 12 years of age and under doubled between 1985 and 1991.
- Violent acts are the daily fare of millions of American children who watch television an average of 21 hours per week. *TV Guide* reports a violent incident is shown, on average, every six minutes.
- The United States spends at least one billion dollars annually on hospital costs associated with the treatment of individuals who have been shot and who, frequently, have no health insurance.
- According to the Center to Prevent Handgun Violence, in 1990, handguns were used to murder 13 people in Sweden, 91 people in Switzerland, 87 people in Japan, 68 people in Canada, 22 people in Great Britain, and 10 people in Australia. By comparison, handguns were used to murder 10,567 people in the United States.

Documents

This section provides excerpts from some of several organizations and associations relating to children and violence. The American Psychological Association (APA) examined violence and youth and developed recommendations for public policy. The National Council of Juvenile and Family Court Judges (NCJFCJ) developed an action plan to respond to violent juvenile crime. The American Humane Association (AHA) developed eight steps for people to take to reduce or eliminate violence in their lives. The Children's Defense Fund (CDF) advocates ten steps to stop the war against American children. Also included are a policy statement regarding violence from the National Cable Television Association and standards for depicting violence in television programs from the Network Television Association.

The APA convened a Committee on Violence and Youth to explore the findings of earlier and current research studies and to apply these findings to the current problem of violent youth. They developed several recommendations in the area of public policy to prevent violent acts by youth or to lessen the effects of these violent acts.

Report of the American Psychological Association Commission on Violence and Youth, Volume I

Recommendations for Public Policy

Although violence involving youth is increasingly prevalent and lethal, it is not inevitable. On the basis of psychology's understanding of how violent behavior is learned and transmitted, the Commission on Violence and Youth of the American Psychological Association encourages adoption of the following broad and coordinated set of remedies to prevent youth violence or mitigate its effects.

1. Early childhood interventions can help children learn to deal with social conflict effectively and nonviolently . . .

1.1 We recommend that Congress ask all relevant federal agencies to identify successful and promising interventions, programs, and resources for preventing and treating youth violence and develop and disseminate a report that is based on these programs . . .

1.2 We recommend that funding and technical assistance for implementing local violence prevention programs be distributed through such mechanisms as state block grant programs. Special attention should be directed to continuous comprehensive intervention and follow-up in health and educational programs for families at risk for violence. Such families would include very young mothers, single-parent families, those with parental mental health or substance abuse problems, those with parental histories of violent offenses or domestic violence, and those at high risk for child neglect and abuse. We also ask Congress to expand funding for Head Start and other school readiness programs both to improve the overall quality of such programs and to include all eligible children.

1.3 We encourage parent-teacher associations, community health centers, child care centers, and other organizations at which parents gather, to provide parent-child management training programs to foster the development of a repertoire of parental disciplining techniques to replace coercive ones. These programs should include behavior management and social skills training curricula, which have been shown to be effective in improving family communication and reducing child behavior problems.

2. Schools can become a leading force in providing the safety and the effective educational programs by which children can learn to reduce and prevent violence . . .

2.1 We ask Congress to encourage federally supported efforts to develop, implement, and evaluate violence prevention and aggression reduction curricula for use in the schools from early childhood through the teen years. Such efforts would involve teacher training, training for other school personnel, curricular activities, coordinated parental support activities, and technical assistance in implementing programs that apply techniques known to be effective in reducing aggression and preventing violence.

2.2 We recommend that school systems take a long view of children's education regarding violence and make every effort to develop and implement a coordinated, systematic, and developmentally and culturally appropriate program for violence prevention beginning in the early years and continuing throughout adolescence.

2.3 We ask state educational agencies to support the development, implementation, and evaluation of programmatic comprehensive school-based violence prevention programs designed to provide a safe learning environment and to teach students sound and effective principles of violence prevention. Furthermore, we underscore the need to provide a safe school environment for all children.

2.4 We recommend that professional organizations involved with school-based programs prepare and disseminate effective and promising program materials, assessment tools, and evaluation findings germane to violence prevention for broad and flexible use by schools even while ongoing research attempts to improve their effectiveness and adapt them for particular circumstances and local cultural groups. Such organizations would include the American Psychological Association, the National Association of School Psychologists, the National Education Association, and the National Association for the Education of Young Children, among others.

2.5 We encourage schools to engage in the early identification of children who show emotional and behavioral problems related to violence and to provide to them or refer them for appropriate educational experiences and psychological interventions.

2.6 We ask Congress, state governments, and local governments to support the funding and development of after-school programs and recreational activities in schools with high proportions of at-risk children and youth. Initiation into gangs and delinquency is commonly linked to unsupervised time after school.

2.7 We recommend that those state governments and school boards that have not already done so adopt policies and provide training to prohibit the use of corporal punishment in schools and to encourage positive behavior management techniques to maintain school discipline and safety. We also encourage early childhood educators and health practitioners to teach parents alternative methods of discipline in the home.

2.8 We recommend that violence reduction training be made a part of preservice and inservice training for teachers, administrators, school staff, and health professionals likely to serve children of school age.

3. All programmatic efforts to reduce and prevent violence will benefit from heightened awareness of cultural diversity . . .

3.1 We call for a variety of efforts aimed at increasing sensitivity to cultural differences and reducing discrimination and prejudice that create a climate conducive to violence. Such efforts should begin in the earliest school years with specialized curricula for children and be continued throughout the school years. To foster more widespread acceptance of cultural diversity, human relations education should be provided for adults in a variety of settings, including public and private employment, the armed services, churches, and schools.

3.2 We recommend that all public programs designed to reduce or prevent youth violence be developed, implemented, and evaluated with a sensitivity to cultural differences and with the continued involvement of the groups and the communities they are designed to serve. Current programs designed to prevent violence should also be reviewed for their appreciation and integration of diverse cultural perspectives.

4. Television and other media can contribute to the solutions rather than to the problems of youth violence . . .

4.1 We call upon the Federal Communications Commission (FCC) to review, as a condition for license renewal, the programming and outreach efforts and accomplishments of television stations in helping to solve the problem of youth violence. . . . We also call on the FCC to institute rules that would require broadcasters, cable operators, and other telecasters to avoid programs containing an excessive amount of dramatized violence during "child viewing hours" between 6 am and 10 pm.

4.2 We ask Congress to support a national educational violence prevention campaign involving television programming and related educational outreach activities to address the dire need for public education to help prevent youth violence in America. This campaign would be based on our best available scientific evidence about which changes will be most effective in helping to prevent violence, and our best educational and media strategies for fostering such change.

4.3 We recommend that the Film Rating System be revised to take into account the violence content that is harmful to children and youth. We also recommend that producers and distributors of television and video programming be required to provide clear and easy to use warning labels for violent material to permit viewers to make informed choices.

5. Major reductions in the most damaging forms of youth violence can be achieved by limiting youth access to firearms and by teaching children and youth how to prevent firearm violence . . .

5.1 We support the initiative of the U.S. Public Health Service to reduce weapon-carrying by adolescents.

5.2 We recommend that Congress provide funding for the development, implementation, and evaluation of school-based programs to educate children regarding the prevention of firearm violence and the reduction of both unintentional and intentional death and injury caused by firearms.

6. Reduction of youth involvement with alcohol and other drugs can reduce violent behavior . . .

6.1 We encourage community, school, family, and media involvement in prevention and treatment programs that focus on the links between substance abuse and the prevalence of violence.

6.2 We encourage federal, state, and local agencies to provide funding for such education, prevention, and treatment programs.

7. Psychological health services for young perpetrators, victims, and witnesses of violence can ameliorate the damaging effects of violence and reduce further violence . . .

7.1 We recommend that public mental health services be reallocated so that more services are available for prevention and for early treatment of children and families with problems of aggression and violence.

7.2 We recommend that more treatment programs be developed and increased counseling services for victims be made available to the large numbers of young children and youth who witness high levels of violence in their homes, streets, and schools.

8. Education programs can reduce the prejudice and hostility that lead to hate crimes and violence against social groups . . .

8.1 We encourage schools, colleges, and universities to adopt human relations education to dispel stereotypes, encourage broader intercultural understanding and appreciation, and reduce the incidence of hate violence. Training in mediation techniques should be provided to community leaders.

8.2 We recommend that effective interventions be developed to help victims of hate violence to recover from attacks.

8.3 We recommend that, in conjunction with these efforts, the U.S. Civil Rights Commission undertake a review of federal antidiscrimination laws, statutes, and regulations regarding race, ethnicity, religion, gender, sexual orientation, and physical disability.

8.4 We recommend that federal, state, and local governments pursue strict enforcement of antidiscrimination laws regarding race, ethnicity, religion, gender, sexual orientation, and physical disability.

9. When groups become mobs, violence feeds on itself . . .

9.1 We recommend that human relations training for community leaders and police be conducted jointly.

9.2 We recommend that police departments implement or expand their training and community policing efforts, that these efforts include social and cultural sensitivity training, and that increased participation by members of the community be included in these efforts.

10. Psychologists can act individually and in our professional organizations to reduce violence among youth . . .

10.1 We propose that the American Psychological Association resolution on television violence and children's aggression be modified to cover all the mass media, including film and video as well as television.

10.2 We recommend that the American Psychological Association develop video and other educational materials designed to enhance the critical viewing skills of teachers, parents, and children regarding media violence and how to prevent its negative effects.

10.3 We recommend that the American Psychological Association revise and expand its current policy on handgun control to incorporate the following as APA policy:

—Support for nationwide restrictive licensing of firearm ownership based on attainment of legal voting age; clearance following a criminal record background check; and demonstrated skill in firearm knowledge, use, and safety.
—Support for federal, state, and local governments to increase specific legal, regulatory, and enforcement efforts to reduce widespread, easy, and unsupervised access to firearms by children and youth.

10.4 We propose that the American Psychological Association hold a series of training programs for its members on youth violence with special sessions for clinicians and for researchers.

10.5 We recommend that the American Psychological Association take an active role in identifying model interventions that have been demonstrated to be effective in preventing or reducing youth violence. These should be disseminated to professional audiences and to the general public.

10.6 We recommend that psychologists review the research findings presented in this and other reports and provide consultation to community groups interested in implementing programs to prevent youth violence.

10.7 We suggest that psychologists make a coordinated presentation of models of successful violence prevention programs at such workshops as the Vermont Conference on Primary Prevention.

10.8 We recommend that the American Psychological Association sponsor further reviews of influencing factors in violence—for example, gender, ethnicity, psychophysiology, and substance abuse.

10.9 We recommend that the report and recommendations of this Commission on Violence and Youth be presented to Congress, to the U.S. Department of Health and Human

Services, to the U.S. Commission on Civil Rights, to the U.S. Department of Justice, and to other relevant agencies.

10.10 We recommend that education and training on youth violence be incorporated into the graduate preparation of psychologists. We also recommend that psychological training programs institute cultural sensitivity courses and training to increase cultural awareness and sensitivity to underrepresented groups that are affected by violence.

Excerpts from *Where We Stand: An Action Plan for Dealing with Violent Juvenile Crime*, National Council of Juvenile and Family Court Judges

In January 1994, the National Council of Juvenile and Family Court Judges called for vigorous new concerted action by policy makers and juvenile and criminal justice professionals to stem violent crime by juveniles. A task force of experienced judges is now working with federal and state legislators to adopt legislation to provide juvenile judges with the authority and resources to deal more effectively with violent juvenile crime at the state and local government levels.

Recent analysis by the National Council of Juvenile and Family Court Judges has confirmed the validity of the recommendations in its 1984 report on *The Juvenile Court and Serious Offenders*. The recommendations were developed by judges from the metropolitan areas of the United States, where over half the violent juvenile crimes occur. With funding provided by the United States Department of Justice, Office of Juvenile Justice and Delinquency Prevention, the National Council drew on the expertise of criminal and juvenile professionals to formulate a comprehensive plan for preventing and controlling juvenile violent crime.

This country must adopt a long-term effort to reduce violent juvenile crimes. The National Council believes that this effort first requires an expansion and redirection of existing resources to more effective crime prevention efforts involving families, schools and community organizations. As the *Serious Offenders* report observed, when social institutions are strong, communities well organized, and parents and schools competent and caring, there is a comparably small violent juvenile crime problem.

Beyond prevention there are numerous actions that the National Council believes should be implemented by state and local governments with financial, technical assistance and research efforts from the state and federal levels. These efforts are designed to assure that protection of public safety remains the paramount goal of the juvenile court in dealing with violent juvenile crime. They should focus on the comparably small number of repeat violent offenders. They include:

- Assuring that juvenile courts can hold violent juvenile offenders fully accountable for their crimes. Resources must be directed to imposition of swift and sure sanctions which are proportionate to the crime, to the culpability of the juvenile and to the juvenile's prior record.
- Providing adequate resources to the juvenile courts to conduct thorough diagnostic assessments of juveniles and to develop individualized dispositions for juveniles based on the circumstances of the crime and the problems and needs of the juvenile offender.
- Renewing the commitment to rehabilitation of violent juvenile offenders consistent with the paramount public safety goal.
- Providing legislation, with rational guidelines for the protection of public safety and individual rights, under which state and local juvenile judges can transfer violent juvenile offenders to adult criminal courts. These guidelines must recognize that there are violent juvenile offenders for whom the resources and processes of the juvenile court cannot (1) effectively rehabilitate the juvenile, (2) provide an appropriate long-term sanction, or (3) adequately protect the public.
- Opening the juvenile court to the public for fact-finding hearings involving violent juvenile crime and transfers to criminal court.
- Providing juvenile court records to police and criminal courts.
- Expanding local community-based secure and nonsecure programs for violent juvenile offenders with adequate public safety controls and with involvement of and assistance to the families of violent offenders.
- Assuring that existing programs for dealing with violent juvenile offenders derive maximum utility from current levels of financial support.
- Developing better supervised and controlled re-entry programs for violent juvenile offenders who are being released into the community from secure institutions.
- Improving and expanding training and technical

assistance programs for juvenile justice professionals to assure the most effective use of the limited resources which are available for dealing with violent juvenile offenders.

The American Humane Association's Eight Steps to a Non-Violent Future

1. Take animal and child abuse seriously, and report it to your local humane society or child welfare agency. Abuse must be stopped. People who repeatedly and intentionally hurt animals or children need incarceration, counseling, or other intervention.

2. Encourage professionals, such as judges, animal control officers, doctors, social workers, teachers, and ministers to familiarize themselves with the link between cruelty to animals and family violence.

3. If you have children, practice positive parenting styles that do not rely on corporal punishment. To learn about such methods consult with your local mental health center, social service agency, or the United Way.

4. Instill compassion and humane values in young people by showing that you value people, animals, and the environment.

5. Question the glorification of violence in sports, the media, and entertainment. Nonviolent problem-solving skills, compassion, and self-control must be valued by society to be valued by children.

6. If animal or child abuse was part of your personal history, you may need to seek professional counseling to fully understand the effect these acts have had on you and your family. Often the cycle of violence can be broken by a desire to stop the abuse.

7. Use your political voice, and vote on issues relevant to education, social service delivery, and allocation of funds toward improving the quality of life for people and animals in your community and country.

8. Support organizations that protect animals and children from abuse by volunteering or financially contributing.

The Children's Defense Fund's 10 Steps To Stop the War Against Children in America

Every American must work to transform our nation's priorities, give children first call on our personal and collective time, resources, and leadership and take the following steps:

1. Make sure as a parent, teacher, religious or civic leader that you do not engage in violence or teach children by word or deed that violence is the way to resolve conflicts and disputes. Remove guns from your home and encourage others to do so.
2. Immediately urge the President, Congress, and state and local officials to ensure children's physical security by working for a cease-fire in the violent gun war against children and for strong, federal, state, and local legislation and regulation to control the manufacture, sale, and possession of non-sporting firearms and ammunition in private hands. All guns should be treated and regulated as the dangerous products they are.
3. Implement immediately a range of effective safety plans to protect children in school, to and from school, and in their neighborhoods. Safe houses, safe corridors, peace zones, and after-school opportunities must be established in every violence-stricken neighborhood and be monitored by citizen, parent, and law enforcement vigils. Children and youths need to see adults caring enough to protect them so they do not have to resort to guns to protect themselves.
4. Every community must provide children and youths safe and positive alternatives to the streets through summer, weekend, and after-school programs to keep children safe and connected to caring adults and role models. Follow the Black Student Leadership Network (BSLN) example of running recreational, academic, and cultural enrichment programs for children utilizing the Summer Food Service Program. Write us for more information.
5. Create youth jobs and training opportunities to provide legitimate routes to success. Providing work opportunities for our youths will help to ensure that they become productive and contributing adults. Creating a job is a lot cheaper than building a new prison cell. Tell this to the President, Congress, and local officials and urge them to invest in jobs.
6. Start parent education and family support programs that will help parents better protect, nurture, and support their children, and seek to prevent teen pregnancy. New federal Family Preservation and Support

Services Program funds should be used to expand services in communities that will strengthen families, prevent family violence and alcohol and drug abuse, and get special help to young parents.

7. Involve your congregation in a massive Children's Sabbath celebration of and Moral Witness for children and against violence on October 14–16, 1994. Protestant, Catholic, Jewish, Moslem, and African American religious action materials are available from CDF to help conduct study groups, prayer circles, teach-ins, and worship services on violence and to examine what can be done. And join with and involve youths from your college campuses and high schools who are seeking to jump-start a community dialogue and actions against violence. Contact us for information.

8. Inform yourself and others firsthand about the violence plaguing children in your community and what you can do by participating in a Child Watch. Then help a child write a letter to local, state, and national officials explaining how violence affects him or her and voicing ideas about reducing violence. CDF has Child Watch anti-violence materials and training available to help local leaders understand the conditions in which our children live and what can be done.

9. Monitor the television shows, movies, and video games children watch and the music they buy and listen to. Turn off violent programs and explain that violence is deadly—not entertaining. Then voice your concerns to networks, producers, and sponsors. Children need to hear positive values from adults to counter negative cultural signals. And they need adults to vigorously fight racial discrimination and hate crimes that contribute to community violence and division.

10. Join the movement to Leave No Child Behind and work to make sure that every child gets a Healthy Start, a Head Start, a Fair Start, and a Safe Start. . . . Take the Pledge for Children if you are a parent, grandparent, or surrogate parent.

Industry Policy Statement Regarding Violence Issued by the National Cable Television Association, 27 January 1993

We believe that the depiction of violence is a legitimate dramatic and journalistic representation of an unavoidable part of human existence. We also believe that the gratuitous use of violence depicted as an easy and convenient solution to human problems is harmful to our industry and society. We therefore discourage and will strive to reduce the frequency of such exploitive uses of violence while preserving our right to show programs that convey the real meaning and consequences of violent behavior. To all these ends, we will seek to improve communications with our viewers regarding the nature of violence appearing in our programs.

Standards for Depiction of Violence in Television Programs Issued by the Network Television Association, 11 December 1992

1. Conflict and strife are the essence of drama and conflict often results in physical or psychological violence. However, all depictions of violence should be relevant and necessary to the development of character, or to the advancement of theme or plot.
2. Gratuitous or excessive depictions of violence (or redundant violence shown solely for its own sake) are not acceptable.
3. Programs should not depict violence as glamorous, nor as an acceptable solution to human conflict.
4. Depictions of violence may not be used to shock or stimulate the audience.
5. Scenes showing excessive gore, pain or physical suffering are not acceptable.
6. The intensity and frequency of the use of force, and other factors relating to the manner of its portrayal, should be measured under a standard of reasonableness so that the program, on the whole, is appropriate for a home viewing medium.
7. Scenes which may be instructive in nature, e.g., which depict in an imitable manner the use of harmful

devices or weapons, describe readily usable techniques for the commission of crimes, or show replicable methods for the evasion of detection or apprehension, should be avoided. Similarly, ingenious, unique or otherwise unfamiliar methods of inflicting pain or injury are unacceptable if easily capable of imitation.

8. Realistic depictions of violence should also portray, in human terms, the consequences of that violence to its victims and its perpetrators. Callousness or indifference to suffering experienced by victims of violence should be avoided.

9. Exceptional care must be taken in stories or scenes where children are victims of or are threatened by acts of violence (physical, psychological or verbal).

10. The portrayal of dangerous behavior which would invite imitation by children, including portrayals of the use of weapons or implements readily accessible to this impressionable group, should be avoided.

11. Realistic portrayals of violence as well as scenes, images or events which are unduly frightening or distressing to children should not be included in any program specifically designed for that audience.

12. The use of real animals shall conform to accepted standards of humane treatment. Fictionalized portrayals of abusive treatment should be strictly limited to the legitimate requirements of plot development.

13. Extreme caution must be exercised in any themes, plots or scenes which mix sex and violence. Rape and other sexual assaults are violent, not erotic, behavior.

14. The scheduling of any program, commercial or promotional material, including those containing violent depictions, should take into consideration the nature of the program, its content and the likely composition of the intended audience.

15. Certain exceptions to the foregoing may be acceptable, as in the presentation of material whose overall theme is clearly and unambiguously anti-violent.

Court Decisions and Legislation

In this section, excerpts from three relevant Supreme Court decisions are presented, as well as excerpts from the Juvenile

Justice and Delinquency Prevention Act of 1974. The first Supreme Court decision, *In Re Gault,* had a major impact on the way juveniles are treated in juvenile courts. The Supreme Court ruled that notice of a court hearing must be given with sufficient time to allow a proper defense and must detail the charges to be made, that the child and his or her parents must be notified of the child's right to be represented by counsel, that the constitutional privilege against self-incrimination applies to juveniles, and that sworn testimony in juvenile court should be the same as in adult hearings.

The next court decision, *Thompson v. Oklahoma,* reversed a lower court decision sentencing 15-year-old William Wayne Thompson to death for the beating and murder of his former brother-in-law. Five justices agreed that the death sentence for this juvenile was cruel and unusual punishment and was therefore proscribed by the Eighth Amendment to the Constitution.

The final Supreme Court decision includes two cases heard and decided together, *Stanford v. Kentucky* and *Wilkins v. Missouri.* This case also focused on the issue of executing individuals for crimes they committed while 16 or 17 years old. In these cases, the Supreme Court agreed with the death sentences, letting the lower court decisions stand.

The Juvenile Justice and Delinquency Prevention Act of 1974, as amended, is the final document excerpted in this section. The act consolidated many of the earlier laws enacted by Congress relating to youth crime and delinquency, focusing on diversion, de-institutionalization, and the separation of juveniles from adult offenders.

In Re Gault et al., 387 U.S. 1

This is an appeal under *28 U.S.C. § 1257 (2)* from a judgment of the Supreme Court of Arizona affirming the dismissal of a petition for a writ of habeas corpus. *99 Ariz. 181, 407 P. 2d 760 (1965).* The petition sought the release of Gerald Francis Gault, appellants' 15-year-old son, who had been committed as a juvenile delinquent to the State Industrial School by the Juvenile Court of Gila County, Arizona. The Supreme Court of Arizona affirmed dismissal of the writ against various arguments which included an attack upon the constitutionality of the Arizona Juvenile Code because of its alleged denial of procedural due process rights to juveniles charged with being "delinquents." The court agreed that the constitutional guarantee of due process of law is applicable in such proceedings. It held that Arizona's Juvenile Code is to be read as "impliedly" implementing the "due process concept." It then proceeded to identify and describe "the particular elements which constitute due process in a juvenile hearing." It concluded that the proceedings ending in commitment of Gerald Gault did not offend those requirements. We do not agree, and we reverse. We begin with a statement of the facts.

I.

On Monday, June 8, 1964, at about 10 a.m., Gerald Francis Gault and a friend, Ronald Lewis, were taken into custody by the Sheriff of Gila County. Gerald was then still subject to a six months' probation order which had been entered on February 25, 1964, as a result of his having been in the company of another boy who had stolen a wallet from a lady's purse. The police action on June 8 was taken as the result of a verbal complaint by a neighbor of the boys, Mrs. Cook, about a telephone call made to her in which the caller or callers made lewd or indecent remarks. It will suffice for purposes of this opinion to say that the remarks or questions put to her were of the irritatingly offensive, adolescent, sex variety.

At the time Gerald was picked up, his mother and father were both at work. No notice that Gerald was being taken into custody was left at the home. No other steps were taken to advise them that their son had, in effect, been arrested. Gerald was taken to the Children's Detention Home. When his mother arrived home at about 6 o'clock, Gerald was not there. Gerald's older brother was sent to look for him at the trailer home of the Lewis family. He apparently learned then that Gerald was in custody. He so informed his mother. The two of them went to the Detention Home. The deputy probation officer, Flagg, who was also superintendent of the Detention Home, told Mrs. Gault "why Jerry was there" and said that a hearing would be held in Juvenile Court at 3 o'clock the following day, June 9.

Officer Flagg filed a petition with the court on the hearing day, June 9, 1964. It was not served on the Gaults. Indeed, none of them saw this petition until the habeas corpus hearing on August 17, 1964. The petition was entirely formal. It made no reference to any factual basis for the judicial action which it initiated. It recited only that "said minor is under the age of eighteen years, and is in need of the protection of this Honorable

Court; [and that] said minor is a delinquent minor." It prayed for a hearing and an order regarding "the care and custody of said minor." Officer Flagg executed a formal affidavit in support of the petition.

On June 9, Gerald, his mother, his older brother, and Probation Officers Flagg and Henderson appeared before the Juvenile Judge in chambers. Gerald's father was not there. He was at work out of the city. Mrs. Cook, the complainant, was not there. No one was sworn at this hearing. No transcript or recording was made. No memorandum or record of the substance of the proceedings was prepared. Our information about the proceedings and the subsequent hearing on June 15, derives entirely from the testimony of the Juvenile Court Judge, Mr. and Mrs. Gault and Officer Flagg at the habeas corpus proceeding conducted two months later. From this, it appears that at the June 9 hearing Gerald was questioned by the judge about the telephone call. There was conflict as to what he said. His mother recalled that Gerald said he only dialed Mrs. Cook's number and handed the telephone to his friend, Ronald. Officer Flagg recalled that Gerald had admitted making the lewd remarks. Judge McGhee testified that Gerald "admitted making one of these [lewd] statements." At the conclusion of the hearing, the judge said he would "think about it." Gerald was taken back to the Detention Home. He was not sent to his own home with his parents.

On June 11 or 12, after having been detained since June 8, Gerald was released and driven home. There is no explanation in the record as to why he was kept in the Detention Home or why he was released. At 5 p.m. on the day of Gerald's release, Mrs. Gault received a noted signed by Officer Flagg. it was on plain paper, not letterhead. Its entire text was as follows:

"Mrs. Gault:
"Judge McGHEE has set Monday June 15, 1964 at 11:00 A.M. as the date and time for further Hearings on Gerald's delinquency.
"/s/ Flagg"

At the appointed time on Monday, June 15, Gerald, his father and mother, Ronald Lewis and his father, and Officers Flagg and Henderson were present before Judge McGhee. Witnesses at the habeas corpus proceeding differed in their recollections of Gerald's testimony at the June 15 hearing. Mr. and Mrs. Gault recalled that Gerald again testified that he had only dialed the number and that the other boy had made the remarks. Officer Flagg agreed that at this hearing Gerald did not admit making the lewd remarks. But Judge McGhee recalled that "there was some admission again of some of the lewd statements. He . . . he didn't admit any of the more serious lewd statements." Again, the complainant, Mrs. Cook, was not present. Mrs. Gault asked that Mrs. Cook be present "so she could see which boy that done the talking, the dirty talking over the phone." The Juvenile Judge said "she didn't have to be present at that hearing." The judge did not speak to Mrs. Cook or communicate with her at any time. Probation Officer Flagg had talked to her once—over the telephone on June 9.

At this June 15 hearing a "referral report" made by the probation officers was filed with the court, although not disclosed to Gerald or his parents. This listed the charge as "Lewd Phone Calls." At the conclusion of the hearing, the judge committed Gerald as a juvenile delinquent to the State Industrial School "for the period of his minority [that is, until 21], unless sooner discharged by due process of law." An order to that effect was entered. It recites that "after a full hearing and due deliberation, the Court finds that said minor is a delinquent child, and that said minor is of the age of 15 years."

No appeal is permitted by Arizona law in juvenile cases. On August 3, 1964, a petition for a writ of habeas corpus was filed with the Supreme Court of Arizona and referred by it to the Superior Court for hearing.

The Superior Court dismissed the writ, and appellants sought review in the Arizona Supreme Court. That court stated that it considered appellants' assignments of error as urging (1) that the Juvenile Code *ARS § 8-201 to § 8-239,* is unconstitutional because it does not require that parents and children be apprised of the specific charges, does not require proper notice of a hearing, and does not provide for an appeal; and (2) that the proceedings and order relating to Gerald constituted a denial of due process of law because of the absence of adequate notice of the charge and the hearing; failure to notify appellants of certain constitutional rights including the rights to counsel and to confrontation, and the privilege against self-incrimination; the use of unsworn hearsay testimony; and the failure to make a record of the proceedings. Appellants further asserted that it was error for the Juvenile Court to remove Gerald from the custody of his parents without a showing and finding of their unsuitability, and alleged a miscellany of other errors under state law.

The Supreme Court handed down an elaborate and wide-ranging opinion affirming dismissal of the writ and stating the court's conclusions as to the issues raised by appellants and other aspects of the juvenile process. In their jurisdictional statement and brief in this Court, appellants do not urge upon us all of the points passed upon by the Supreme Court of Arizona. They urge that we hold the Juvenile Code of Arizona invalid on its face or as applied in this case because, contrary to the Due Process Clause of the Fourteenth Amendment, the juvenile is taken from the custody of his parents and committed to a state institution pursuant to proceedings in which the Juvenile Court has virtually unlimited discretion, and in which the following basic rights are denied:

1. Notice of the charges;
2. Right to counsel;
3. Right to confrontation and cross-examination;
4. Privilege against self-incrimination;
5. Right to a transcript of the proceedings; and
6. Right to appellate review.

We shall not consider other issues which were passed upon by the Supreme Court of Arizona. We emphasize that we indicate no opinion as to whether the decision of that court with respect to such other issues does or does not conflict with requirements of the Federal Constitution.

II.

[T]here is no reason why, consistently with due process, a State cannot continue, if it deems it appropriate, to provide and to improve provision for the confidentiality of records of police contacts and court action relating to juveniles. It is interesting to note, however, that the Arizona Supreme Court used the confidentiality argument as a justification for the type of notice which is here attacked as inadequate for due process purposes. The parents were given merely general notice that their child was charged with "delinquency." No facts were specified. The Arizona court held, however, as we shall discuss, that in addition to this general "notice," the child and his parents must be advised "of the facts involved in the case" no later than the initial hearing by the judge. Obviously, this does not "bury" the word about the child's transgressions. It merely defers the time of disclosure to a point when it is of limited use to the child or his parents in preparing his defense or explanation.

Further, it is urged that the juvenile benefits from informal proceedings in the court. The early conception of the Juvenile Court proceeding was one in which a fatherly judge touched the heart and conscience of the erring youth by talking over his problems, by paternal advice and admonition, and in which, in extreme situations, benevolent and wise institutions of the State provided guidance and help "to save him from a downward career." Then, as now, goodwill and compassion were admirably prevalent. But recent studies have, with surprising unanimity, entered sharp dissent as to the validity of this gentle conception. They suggest that the appearance as well as the actuality of fairness, impartiality and orderliness—in short, the essentials of due process—may be a more impressive and more therapeutic attitude so far as the juvenile is concerned. For example, in a recent study, the sociologists Wheeler and Cottrell observe that when the procedural laxness of the "parens patriae" attitude is followed by stern disciplining, the contrast may have an adverse effect upon the child, who feels that he has been deceived or enticed. They conclude as follows: "Unless appropriate due process of law is followed, even the juvenile who has violated the law may not feel that he is being fairly treated and may therefore resist the rehabilitative efforts of court personnel." Of course, it is not suggested that juvenile court judges should fail appropriately to take account, in their demeanor and conduct, of the emotional and psychological attitude of the juveniles with whom they are confronted. While due process requirements will, in some instances, introduce a degree of order and regularity to Juvenile Court proceedings to determine delinquency, and in contested cases will introduce some elements of the adversary system, nothing will require that the conception of the kindly juvenile judge be replaced by its opposite, nor do we here rule upon the question whether ordinary due process requirements must be observed with respect to hearings to determine the disposition of the delinquent child.

Ultimately, however, we confront the reality of that portion of the Juvenile Court process with which we deal in this case. A boy is charged with misconduct. The boy is committed to an institution where he may be restrained of liberty for years. It is of no constitutional consequence—and of limited practical meaning— that the institution to which he is committed is called an

Industrial School. The fact of the matter is that, however euphemistic the title, a "receiving home" or an "industrial school" for juveniles is an institution of confinement in which the child is incarcerated for a greater or lesser time. His world becomes "a building with whitewashed walls, regimented routine and institutional hours. . . . " Instead of mother and father and sisters and brothers and friends and classmates, his world is peopled by guards, custodians, state employees, and "delinquents" confined with him for anything from waywardness to rape and homicide.

In view of this, it would be extraordinary if our Constitution did not require the procedural regularity and the exercise of care implied in the phrase "due process." Under our Constitution, the condition of being a boy does not justify a kangaroo court. The traditional ideas of Juvenile Court procedure, indeed, contemplated that time would be available and care would be used to establish precisely what the juvenile did and why he did it—was it a prank of adolescence or a brutal act threatening serious consequences to himself or society unless corrected? Under traditional notions, one would assume that in a case like that of Gerald Gault, where the juvenile appears to have a home, a working mother and father, and an older brother, the Juvenile Judge would have made a careful inquiry and judgment as to the possibility that the boy could be disciplined and dealt with at home, despite his previous transgressions. Indeed, so far as appears in the record before us, except for some conversation with Gerald about his school work and his "wanting to go to . . . Grand Canyon with his father," the points to which the judge directed his attention were little different from those that would be involved in determining any charge of violation of a penal statute. The essential difference between Gerald's case and a normal criminal case is that safeguards available to adults were discarded in Gerald's case. The summary procedure as well as the long commitment was possible because Gerald was 15 years of age instead of over 18.

If Gerald had been over 18, he would not have been subject to Juvenile Court proceedings. For the particular offense immediately involved, the maximum punishment would have been a fine of $5 to $50, or imprisonment in jail for not more than two months. Instead, he was committed to custody for a maximum of six years. If he had been over 18 and had committed an offense to which such a sentence might apply, he would have been entitled to substantial rights under the Constitution of the United States as well as under Arizona's laws and constitution.

The United States Constitution would guarantee him rights and protections with respect to arrest, search and seizure, and pretrial interrogation. It would assure him of specific notice of the charges and adequate time to decide his course of action and to prepare his defense. He would be entitled to clear advice that he could be represented by counsel, and, at least if a felony were involved, the State would be required to provide counsel if his parents were unable to afford it. If the court acted on the basis of his confession, careful procedures would be required to assure its voluntariness. If the case went to trial, confrontation and opportunity for cross-examination would be guaranteed. So wide a gulf between the State's treatment of the adult and of the child requires a bridge sturdier than mere verbiage, and reasons more persuasive than cliché can provide. As Wheeler and Cottrell have put it, "The rhetoric of the juvenile court movement has developed without any necessarily close correspondence to the realities of court and institutional routines."

In *Kent v. United States [383 U.S. 541 (1966)]*, we stated that the Juvenile Court Judge's exercise of the power of the state as parens patriae was not unlimited. We said that "the admonition to function in a 'parental' relationship is not an invitation to procedural arbitrariness." With respect to the waiver by the Juvenile Court to the adult court of jurisdiction over an offense committed by a youth, we said that "there is no place in our system of law for reaching a result of such tremendous consequences without ceremony—without hearing, without effective assistance of counsel, without a statement of reasons." We announced with respect to such waiver proceedings that while "We do not mean . . . to indicate that the hearing to be held must conform with all of the requirements of a criminal trial or even of the usual administrative hearing; but we do hold that the hearing must measure up to the essentials of due process and fair treatment." We reiterate this view, here in connection with a juvenile court adjudication of "delinquency," as a requirement which is part of the Due Process Clause of the Fourteenth Amendment of our Constitution.

We now turn to the specific issues which are presented to us in the present case.

III.
Notice of Charges

We cannot agree with the court's conclusion that adequate notice was given in this case. Notice, to comply with due process requirements, must be given sufficiently in advance of scheduled court proceedings so that reasonable opportunity to prepare will be afforded, and it must "set forth the alleged misconduct with particularity." It is obvious, as we have discussed above, that no purpose of shielding the child from the public stigma of knowledge of his having been taken into custody and scheduled for hearing is served by the procedure approved by the court below. . . . Due process of law requires notice of the sort we have described—that is, notice which would be deemed constitutionally adequate in a civil or criminal proceeding. It does not allow a hearing to be held in which a youth's freedom and his parents' right to his custody are at stake without giving them timely notice, in advance of the hearing, of the specific issues that they must meet. Nor, in the circumstances of this case, can it reasonably be said that the requirement of notice was waived.

IV.
Right to Counsel

We conclude that the Due Process Clause of the Fourteenth Amendment requires that in respect of proceedings to determine delinquency which may result in commitment to an institution in which the juvenile's freedom is curtailed, the child and his parents must be notified of the child's right to be represented by counsel retained by them, or if they are unable to afford counsel, that counsel will be appointed to represent the child.

At the habeas corpus proceeding, Mrs. Gault testified that she knew that she could have appeared with counsel at the juvenile hearing. This knowledge is not a waiver of the right to counsel which she and her juvenile son had, as we have defined it. They had a right expressly to be advised that they might retain counsel and to be confronted with the need for specific consideration of whether they did or did not choose to waive the right. If they were unable to afford to employ counsel, they were entitled in view of the seriousness of the charge and the potential commitment, to appointed counsel, unless they chose waiver. Mrs. Gault's knowledge that she could employ counsel was not an "intentional relinquishment or abandonment" of a fully known right.

V.
Confrontation, Self-Incrimination, Cross-Examination

We conclude that the constitutional privilege against self-incrimination is applicable in the case of juveniles as it is with respect to adults. We appreciate that special problems may arise with respect to waiver of the privilege by or on behalf of children, and that there may well be some differences in technique—but not in principle—depending upon the age of the child and the presence and competence of parents. The participation of counsel will, of course, assist the police, Juvenile Courts and appellate tribunals in administering the privilege. If counsel was not present for some permissible reason when an admission was obtained, the greatest care must be taken to assure that the admission was voluntary, in the sense not only that it was not coerced or suggested, but also that it was not the product of ignorance of rights or of adolescent fantasy, fright or despair.

The "confession" of Gerald Gault was first obtained by Officer Flagg, out of the presence of Gerald's parents, without counsel and without advising him of his right to silence, as far as appears. The judgment of the Juvenile Court was stated by the judge to be based on Gerald's admissions in court. Neither "admission" was reduced to writing, and, to say the least, the process by which the "admissions" were obtained and received must be characterized as lacking the certainty and order which are required of proceedings of such formidable consequences. Apart from the "admissions," there was nothing upon which a judgment or finding might be based. There was no sworn testimony. Mrs. Cook, the complainant, was not present. The Arizona Supreme Court held that "sworn testimony must be required of all witnesses including police officers, probation officers and others who are part of or officially related to the juvenile court structure." We hold that this is not enough. No reason is suggested or appears for a different rule in respect of sworn testimony in juvenile courts than in adult tribunals. Absent a valid confession adequate to support the determination of the Juvenile Court, confrontation and sworn testimony by witnesses available for cross-examination were essential for a finding of "delinquency" and an order committing Gerald to a state institution for a maximum of six years.

The recommendations in the Children's Bureau's "Standards

for Juvenile and Family Courts" are in general accord with our conclusions. They state that testimony should be under oath and that only competent, material and relevant evidence under rules applicable to civil cases should be admitted in evidence. The New York Family Court Act contains a similar provision.

As we said in *Kent v. United States, 383 U.S. 541, 554 (1966),* with respect to waiver proceedings, "there is no place in our system of law for reaching a result of such tremendous consequences without ceremony. . . ." We now hold that, absent a valid confession, a determination of delinquency and an order or commitment to a state institution cannot be sustained in the absence of sworn testimony subjected to the opportunity for cross-examination in accordance with our law and constitutional requirements.

VI.
Appellate Review and Transcript of Proceedings

Appellants urge that the Arizona statute is unconstitutional under the Due Process Clause because, as construed by its Supreme Court, "there is no right of appeal from a juvenile court order. . . ." The court held that there is no right to a transcript because there is no right to appeal and because the proceedings are confidential and any record must be destroyed after a prescribed period of time. Whether a transcript or other recording is made, it held, is a matter for the discretion of the juvenile court.

This Court has not held that a State is required by the Federal Constitution "to provide appellate courts or a right to appellate review at all." In view of the fact that we must reverse the Supreme Court of Arizona's affirmance of the dismissal of the writ of habeas corpus for other reasons, we need not rule on this question in the present case or upon the failure to provide a transcript or recording of the hearings—or, indeed, the failure of the Juvenile Judge to state the grounds for his conclusion. Cf. *Kent v. United States, supra, at 561,* where we said, in the context of a decision of the juvenile court waiving jurisdiction to the adult court, which by local law, was permissible: ". . . it is incumbent upon the Juvenile Court to accompany its waiver order with a statement of the reasons or considerations therefor." As the present case illustrates, the consequences of failure to provide an appeal, to record the proceedings, or to make findings or state the grounds for the juvenile court's conclusion may be to throw a burden upon the machinery for habeas corpus, to saddle the reviewing process with the burden of attempting to reconstruct a record, and to impose upon the Juvenile Judge the unseemly duty of testifying under cross-examination as to the events that transpired in the hearings before him.

For the reasons stated, the judgment of the Supreme Court of Arizona is reversed and the cause remanded for further proceedings not inconsistent with this opinion.

Thompson v. Oklahoma, 455 S. Ct. 2687

Justice Stevens announced the judgment of the Court and delivered an opinion in which Justice Brennan, Justice Marshall, and Justice Blackmun join.

Petitioner was convicted of first-degree murder and sentenced to death. The principal question presented is whether the execution of that sentence would violate the constitutional prohibition against the infliction of "cruel and unusual punishments" because petitioner was only 15 years old at the time of his offense.

I.

Because there is no claim that the punishment would be excessive if the crime had been committed by an adult, only a brief statement of facts is necessary. In concert with three older persons, petitioner actively participated in the brutal murder of his former brother-in-law in the early morning hours of January 23, 1983. The evidence disclosed that the victim had been shot twice, and that his throat, chest, and abdomen had been cut. He also had multiple bruises and a broken leg. His body had been chained to a concrete block and thrown into a river where it remained for almost four weeks. Each of the four participants was tried separately and each was sentenced to death.

Because petitioner was a "child" as a matter of Oklahoma law, the District Attorney filed a statutory petition, see *Okla. Stat., Tit. 10, § 1112(b) (1981),* seeking an order finding "that said child is competent and had the mental capacity to know and appreciate the wrongfulness of his [conduct]." App. 4. After a hearing, the trial court concluded "that there are virtually no reasonable prospects for rehabilitation of William Wayne Thompson within the juvenile system and that William Wayne Thompson should be held accountable for his acts as if he were an adult and should be certified to stand trial as an adult."

At the guilt phase of petitioner's trial, the prosecutor introduced three color photographs showing the condition of the victim's body when it was removed from the river. Although the Court of Criminal Appeals held that the use of two of those photographs was error, it concluded that the error was harmless because the evidence of petitioner's guilt was so convincing. However, the prosecutor had also used the photographs in his closing argument during the penalty phase. The Court of Criminal Appeals did not consider whether this display was proper.

At the penalty phase of the trial, the prosecutor asked the jury to find two aggravating circumstances: that the murder was especially heinous, atrocious, or cruel; and that there was a probability that the defendant would commit criminal acts of violence that would constitute a continuing threat to society. The jury found the first, but not the second, and fixed petitioner's punishment as death.

The Court of Criminal Appeals affirmed the conviction and sentence, *724 P. 2d 780 (1986),* citing its earlier opinion in *Eddings v. State, 616 P. 2d 1159 (1980),* rev'd on other grounds, *455 U.S. 104 (1982),* for the proposition that "once a minor is certified to stand trial as an adult, he may also, without violating the Constitution, be punished as an adult." *24 P. 2d, at 784.* We granted certiorari to consider whether a sentence of death is cruel and unusual punishment for a crime committed by a 15-year-old child, as well as whether photographic evidence that a state court deems erroneously admitted but harmless at the guilt phase nevertheless violates a capital defendant's constitutional rights by virtue of its being considered at the penalty phase.

II.

The authors of the Eighth Amendment drafted a categorical prohibition against the infliction of cruel and unusual punishments, but they made no attempt to define the contours of that category. They delegated that task to future generations of judges who have been guided by the "evolving standards of decency that mark the progress of a maturing society." *Trop v. Dulles, 356 U.S. 86, 101 (1958)* (plurality opinion) (Warren, C.J.). In performing that task the Court has reviewed the work product of state legislatures and sentencing juries, and has carefully considered the reasons why a civilized society may accept or reject the death penalty in certain types of cases. Thus, in confronting the question whether the youth of the defendant—more specifically, the fact that he was less than 16 years old at the time of his offense—is a sufficient reason for denying the State the power to sentence him to death, we first review relevant legislative enactments, then refer to jury determinations, and finally explain why these indicators of contemporary standards of decency confirm our judgment that such a young person is not capable of acting with the degree of culpability that can justify the ultimate penalty.

III.

Justice Powell has repeatedly reminded us of the importance of "the experience of mankind, as well as the long history of our law, recognizing that there are differences which must be accommodated in determining the rights and duties of children as compared with those of adults. Examples of this distinction abound in our law: in contracts, in torts, in criminal law and procedure, in criminal sanctions and rehabilitation, and in the right to vote and to hold office."*Goss v. Lopez, 419 U.S. 565, 590–591 (1975)* (dissenting opinion). Oklahoma recognizes this basic distinction in a number of its statutes. Thus, a minor is not eligible to vote, to sit on a jury, to marry without parental consent, or to purchase alcohol or cigarettes. Like all other States, Oklahoma has developed a juvenile justice system in which most offenders under the age of 18 are not held criminally responsible. Its statutes do provide, however, that a 16- or 17-year-old charged with murder and other serious felonies shall be considered an adult. Other than the special certification procedure that was used to authorize petitioner's trial in this case "as an adult," apparently there are no Oklahoma statutes, either civil or criminal, that treat a person under 16 years of age as anything but a "child."

The line between childhood and adulthood is drawn in different ways by various States. There is, however, complete or near unanimity among all 50 States and the District of Columbia in treating a person under 16 as a minor for several important purposes. In no State may a 15-year-old vote or serve on a jury. Further, in all but one State a 15-year-old may not drive without parental consent, and in all but four States a 15-year-old may not marry without parental consent. Additionally, in those States that have legislated on the subject, no one under age 16 may purchase pornographic materials (50 States), and in most States that have some form of legalized gambling, minors are not permitted to participate without parental consent (42 States). Most relevant, however, is the fact that all States have enacted legislation designating the maximum age for juvenile court jurisdiction at no less than 16. All of this legislation is consistent with the experience of mankind, as well as the long history of our law, that the normal 15-year-old is not prepared to assume the full responsibilities of an adult.

Most state legislatures have not expressly confronted the question of establishing a minimum age for imposition of the death penalty. In 14 States, capital punishment is not authorized at all, and in 19 others capital punishment is authorized but no minimum age is expressly stated in the death penalty statute. One might argue on the basis of this body of legislation that there is no chronological age at which the imposition of the death penalty is unconstitutional and that our current standards of decency would still tolerate the execution of 10-year-old children. We think it self-evident that such an argument is unacceptable; indeed, no such argument has been advanced in this case. If, therefore, we accept the premise that some offenders are simply too young to be put to death, it is reasonable to put this group of statutes to one side because they do not focus on the question of where the chronological age line should be drawn. When we confine our attention to the 18 States that have expressly established a minimum age in their death penalty statutes, we find that all of them require that the defendant have attained at least the age of 16 at the time of the capital offense.

The conclusion that it would offend civilized standards of decency to execute a person who was less than 16 years old at the time of his or her offense is consistent with the views that have been expressed by respected professional organizations, by other nations that share our Anglo-American heritage, and by the leading members of the Western European community. Thus, the American Bar Association and the American Law Institute have formally expressed their opposition to the death penalty for juveniles. Although the death penalty has not been entirely abolished in the United Kingdom or New Zealand (it has been abolished in Australia, except in the State of New South Wales, where it is available for treason and piracy), in neither of those countries may a juvenile be executed. The death penalty has been abolished in West Germany, France, Portugal, The Netherlands, and all of the Scandinavian countries, and is available only for exceptional crimes such as treason in Canada, Italy, Spain, and Switzerland. Juvenile executions are also prohibited in the Soviet Union.

IV.

The second societal factor the Court has examined in determining the acceptability of capital punishment to the American sensibility is the behavior of juries. In fact, the infrequent and haphazard handing out of death sentences by capital juries was a prime factor underlying our judgment in *Furman v. Georgia, 408 U.S. 238 (1972)*, that the death penalty, as then administered in unguided fashion, was unconstitutional.

While it is not known precisely how many persons have been executed during the 20th century for crimes committed under the age of 16, a scholar has recently compiled a table revealing this number to be between 18 and 20. All of these occurred during the first half of the century, with the last such execution taking place apparently in 1948. In the following year this Court observed that this "whole country has traveled far from the period in which the death sentence was an automatic and commonplace result of convictions. . . ." *Williams v. New York, 337 U.S. 241, 247 (1949)*. The road we have traveled during the past four decades—in which thousands of juries have tried murder cases—leads to the unambiguous conclusion that the imposition of the death penalty on a 15-year-old offender is now generally abhorrent to the conscience of the community.

Department of Justice statistics indicate that during the years 1982 through 1986 an average of over 16,000 persons were arrested for willful criminal homicide (murder and non-negligent manslaughter) each year. Of that group of 82,094 persons, 1,393 were sentenced to death. Only 5 of them, including the petitioner in this case, were less than 16 years old at the time of the offense. Statistics of this kind can, of course, be interpreted in different ways, but they do suggest that these five young offenders have received sentences that are "cruel and unusual in the same way that being struck by lightning is cruel and unusual." *Furman v. Georgia, 408 U.S., at 309* (Stewart, J., concurring).

V.

"Although the judgments of legislatures, juries, and prosecutors weigh heavily in the balance, it is for us ultimately to judge whether the Eighth Amendment permits imposition of the death penalty" on one such as petitioner who committed a heinous murder when he was only 15 years old. *Enmund v. Florida, 458 U.S. 782, 797 (1982).* In making that judgment, we first ask whether the juvenile's culpability should be measured by the same standard as that of an adult, and then consider whether the application of the death penalty to this class of offenders "measurably contributes" to the social purposes that are served by the death penalty.

It is generally agreed "that punishment should be directly related to the personal culpability of the criminal defendant." *California v. Brown, 479 U.S. 538, 545 (1987)* (O'Connor, J., concurring). There is also broad agreement on the proposition that adolescents as a class are less mature and responsible than adults. We stressed this difference in explaining the importance of treating the defendant's youth as a mitigating factor in capital cases:

> But youth is more than a chronological fact. It is a time and condition of life when a person may be most susceptible to influence and to psychological damage. Our history is replete with laws and judicial recognition that minors, especially in their earlier years, generally are less mature and responsible than adults. Particularly "during the formative years of childhood and adolescence, minors often lack the experience, perspective, and judgment" expected of adults. *Bellotti v. Baird, 443 U.S. 622, 625 (1979).* (*Eddings v. Oklahoma, 455 U.S. 104, 115–116 [1982]* [footnotes omitted]).

To add further emphasis to the special mitigating force of youth, Justice Powell quoted the following passage from the *1978 Report of the Twentieth Century Fund Task Force on Sentencing Policy Toward Young Offenders:*

> [A]dolescents, particularly in the early and middle teen years, are more vulnerable, more impulsive, and less self-disciplined than adults. Crimes committed by youths may be just as harmful to victims as those committed by older persons, but they deserve less punishment because adolescents may have less

> capacity to control their conduct and to think in
> long-range terms than adults. Moreover, youth crime
> as such is not exclusively the offender's fault; of-
> fenses by the young also represent a failure of family,
> school, and the social system, which share responsi-
> bility for the development of America's youth. *455
> U.S., at 115, n. 11.*

Thus, the Court has already endorsed the proposition that less
culpability should attach to a crime committed by a juvenile
than to a comparable crime committed by an adult. The basis
for this conclusion is too obvious to require extended explanation. Inexperience, less education, and less intelligence make the
teenager less able to evaluate the consequences of his or her
conduct while at the same time he or she is much more apt to
be motivated by mere emotion or peer pressure than is an adult.
The reasons why juveniles are not trusted with the privileges
and responsibilities of an adult also explain why their irrespon-
sible conduct is not as morally reprehensible as that of an adult.

"The death penalty is said to serve two principal social
purposes: retribution and deterrence of capital crimes by
prospective offenders." *Gregg v. Georgia, 428 U.S. 153, 183 (1976)*
(joint opinion of Stewart, Powell and Stevens, JJ.). In Gregg we
concluded that as "an expression of society's moral outrage at
particularly offensive conduct," retribution was not "inconsistent with our respect for the dignity of men." Ibid. Given the
lesser culpability of the juvenile offender, the teenager's capacity for growth, and society's fiduciary obligations to its children,
this conclusion is simply inapplicable to the execution of a 15-
year-old offender.

For such a young offender, the deterrence rationale is
equally unacceptable. The Department of Justice statistics indicate that about 98 percent of the arrests for willful homicide involved persons who were over 16 at the time of the offense.
Thus, excluding younger persons from the class that is eligible
for the death penalty will not diminish the deterrent value of
capital punishment for the vast majority of potential offenders.
And even with respect to those under 16 years of age, it is obvious that the potential deterrent value of the death sentence is
insignificant for two reasons. The likelihood that the teenage offender has made the kind of cost-benefit analysis that attaches
any weight to the possibility of execution is so remote as to be
virtually nonexistent.

And, even if one posits such a cold-blooded calculation by a 15-year-old, it is fanciful to believe that he would be deterred by the knowledge that a small number of persons his age have been executed during the 20th century. In short, we are not persuaded that the imposition of the death penalty for offenses committed by persons under 16 years of age has made, or can be expected to make, any measurable contribution to the goals that capital punishment is intended to achieve. It is, therefore, "nothing more than the purposeless and needless imposition of pain and suffering," *Coker v. Georgia, 433 U.S., at 592,* and thus an unconstitutional punishment.

VI.

Petitioner's counsel and various amici curiae have asked us to "draw a line" that would prohibit the execution of any person who was under the age of 18 at the time of the offense. Our task today, however, is to decide the case before us; we do so by concluding that the Eighth and Fourteenth Amendments prohibit the execution of a person who was under 16 years of age at the time of his or her offense.

The judgment of the Court of Criminal Appeals is vacated, and the case is remanded with instructions to enter an appropriate order vacating petitioner's death sentence.

Justice Scalia, with whom the Chief Justice and Justice White join, dissenting.

Thompson v. Oklahoma

The Dissenting Opinion

If the issue before us today were whether an automatic death penalty for conviction of certain crimes could be extended to individuals younger than 16 when they commit the crimes, thereby preventing individualized consideration of their maturity and moral responsibility, I would accept the plurality's conclusion that such a practice is opposed by a national consensus, sufficiently uniform and of sufficiently long standing, to render it cruel and unusual punishment within the meaning of the Eighth Amendment. We have already decided as much, and more, in *Lockett v. Ohio, 438 U.S. 586 (1978).* I might even agree with the plurality's conclusion if the question were whether a person under 16 when he commits a crime can be deprived of the benefit of a rebuttable presumption that he is not mature and responsible enough to be punished as an adult. The question posed here, however, is radically different from both of these. It is whether there is a national consensus that no criminal so much as one day under 16, after individuated consideration of his circumstances, including the overcoming of a presumption that he should not be tried as an adult, can possibly be deemed mature and responsible enough to be punished with death for any crime. Because there seems to me no plausible basis for answering this last question in the affirmative, I respectfully dissent.

I.

I begin by restating the facts since I think that a fuller account of William Wayne Thompson's participation in the murder, and of his certification to stand trial as an adult, is helpful in understanding the case. The evidence at trial left no doubt that on the night of January 22–23, 1983, Thompson brutally and with premeditation murdered his former brother-in-law, Charles Keene, the motive evidently being, at least in part, Keene's physical abuse of Thompson's sister. As Thompson left his mother's house that evening, in the company of three older friends, he explained to his girlfriend that "we're going to kill Charles." Several hours later, early in the morning of January 23, a neighbor, Malcolm "Possum" Brown, was awakened by the sound of a gunshot on his front porch. Someone pounded on his front door shouting: "Possum, open the door, let me in. They're going to kill me." Brown telephoned the police, and then opened the front door to see a man on his knees attempting to repel blows with his arms and hands. There were four other men on the porch. One was holding a gun and stood apart, while the other three were hitting and kicking the kneeling man, who never attempted to hit back. One of them was beating the victim with an object 12 to 18 inches in length. The police called back to see if the disturbance was still going on, and while Brown spoke with them on the telephone the men took the victim away in a car.

Several hours after they had left Thompson's mother's house, Thompson and his three companions returned. Thompson's girlfriend helped him take off his boots, and heard him say: "[W]e killed him. I shot him in the head and cut his throat and threw him in the river." Subsequently, the former wife of one of Thompson's accomplices heard Thompson tell his mother that "he killed him. Charles was dead and Vicki didn't have to worry about him anymore." During the days following the murder Thompson made other admissions. One witness testified that she asked Thompson the source of some hair adhering to a pair of boots he was carrying. He replied that was where he had kicked Charles Keene in the head. Thompson also told her that he had cut Charles' throat and chest and had shot him in the head. Another witness testified that when she told Thompson that a friend had seen Keene dancing in a local bar, Thompson remarked that that would be hard to do with a bullet in his head. Ultimately, one of Thompson's codefendants admitted that after Keene had been shot twice in the head Thompson had cut Keene "so the fish could eat his body." Thompson and a codefendant had then thrown the body into the Washita River, with a chain and blocks attached so that it would not be found. On February 18, 1983, the body was recovered. The Chief Medical Examiner of Oklahoma concluded that the victim had been beaten, shot twice, and that his throat, chest, and abdomen had been cut.

On February 18, 1983, the State of Oklahoma filed an information and arrest warrant for Thompson, and on February 22 the State began proceedings to allow Thompson to be tried as an adult. Under Oklahoma law, anyone who commits a crime when he is under the age of 18 is defined to be a child, unless he is 16 or 17 and has committed murder or certain other specified crimes, in which case he is automatically certified to stand trial as an adult. *Okla. Stat., Tit. 10, § 1101, § 1104.2 (Supp. 1987).* In addition, under the statute the State invoked in the present case, juveniles may be certified to stand trial as adults if: (1) the State can establish the "prosecutive merit" of the case, and (2) the court certifies, after considering six factors, that there are no reasonable prospects for rehabilitation of the child within the juvenile system. *Okla. Stat., Tit. 10, § 1112(b) (1981).*

At a hearing on March 29, 1983, the District Court found probable cause to believe that the defendant had committed first-degree murder and thus concluded that the case had prosecutive merit. A second hearing was therefore held on April 21, 1983, to determine whether Thompson was amenable to the juvenile system, or whether he should be certified to stand trial as an adult. A clinical psychologist who had examined Thompson testified at the second hearing that in her opinion Thompson understood the difference between right and wrong but had an antisocial personality that could not be modified by the juvenile justice system. The psychologist testified that Thompson believed that because of his age he was beyond any severe penalty of the law, and accordingly did not believe there would be any severe repercussions from his behavior. Numerous other witnesses testified about Thompson's prior abusive behavior. Mary Robinson, an employee of the Oklahoma juvenile justice system, testified about her contacts with Thompson during several of his previous arrests, which included arrests for assault and battery in August 1980; assault and battery in October 1981; attempted burglary in May 1982; assault and battery with a knife in July 1982; and assault with a deadly weapon in February 1983. She testified that Thompson had been provided with all the counseling the State's Department of Human Services had available, and that none of the counseling or placements seemed to improve his behavior. She recommended that he be certified to stand trial as an adult. On the basis of the foregoing testimony, the District Court filed a written order certifying Thompson to stand trial as an adult. That was appealed and ultimately affirmed by the Oklahoma Court of Criminal Appeals.

Thompson was tried in the District Court of Grady County between December 4 and December 9, 1983. During the guilt phase of the trial, the prosecutor introduced three color photographs showing the condition of the victim's body when it was removed from the river. The jury found Thompson guilty of first-degree murder. At the sentencing phase of the trial, the jury agreed with the prosecution on the existence of one aggravating circumstance, that the murder was "especially heinous, atrocious, or cruel." As required by our decision in *Eddings v. Oklahoma, 455 U.S. 104, 115–117 (1982),* the defense was permitted to argue to the jury the youthfulness of the defendant as a mitigating factor. The jury recommended that the death penalty be imposed, and the trial judge, accordingly, sentenced Thompson to death. Thompson appealed, and his conviction and capital sentence were affirmed. Standing by its earlier decision in *Eddings v. State, 616 P. 2d, 1159, 1166–1167 (1980),* rev'd on other grounds, *455 U.S. 104 (1982),* the Oklahoma Court of Criminal Appeals held that "once a minor is certified to stand trial as an adult, he may also, without violating the Constitution, be punished as an adult." *724 P. 2d 780, 784 (1986).* It also held that admission of two of the three photographs was error in the guilt phase of the proceedings, because their prejudicial effect outweighed their probative value; but found that error harmless in light of the overwhelming evidence of Thompson's guilt. It held that their prejudicial effect did not outweigh their probative value in the sentencing phase, and that they were therefore properly admitted, since they demonstrated the brutality of the crime. Thompson petitioned for certiorari with respect to both sentencing issues, and we granted review. *479 U.S. 1084 (1987).*

II.

A.

As the foregoing history of this case demonstrates, William Wayne Thompson is not a juvenile caught up in a legislative scheme that unthinkingly lumped him together with adults for purposes of determining that death was an appropriate penalty for him and for his crime. To the contrary, Oklahoma first gave careful consideration to whether, in light of his young age, he should be subjected to the normal criminal system at all. That question having been answered affirmatively, a jury then considered whether, despite his young age, his maturity and moral responsibility were sufficiently developed to justify the sentence of death. In upsetting this particularized judgment on the basis of a constitutional absolute, the plurality pronounces it to be a fundamental principle of our society that no one who is as little as one day short of his 16th birthday can have sufficient maturity and moral responsibility to be subjected to capital punishment for any crime. As a sociological and moral conclusion that is implausible; and it is doubly implausible as an interpretation of the United States Constitution.

Stanford v. Kentucky and Wilkins v. Missouri, 109 S. Ct. 2969, 110 S. Ct. 23

These two consolidated cases require us to decide whether the imposition of capital punishment on an individual for a crime committed at 16 or 17 years of age constitutes cruel and unusual punishment under the Eighth Amendment.

The first case . . . involves the shooting death of 20-year-old Barbel Poore in Jefferson County, Kentucky. Petitioner Kevin Stanford committed the murder on January 7, 1981, when he was approximately 17 years and 4 months of age. Stanford and his accomplice repeatedly raped and sodomized Poore during and after their commission of a robbery at a gas station where she worked as an attendant. They then drove her to a secluded area near the station, where Stanford shot her point-blank in the face and then in the back of her head. The proceeds from the robbery were roughly 300 cartons of cigarettes, two gallons of fuel, and a small amount of cash. A corrections officer testified that petitioner explained the murder as follows: "'[H]e said, I had to shoot her, [she] lived next door to me and she would recognize me. . . . I guess we could have tied her up or something or beat [her up] . . . and tell her if she tells, we would kill her. . . . Then, after he said that he started laughing.'"

After Stanford's arrest, a Kentucky juvenile court conducted hearings to determine whether he should be transferred for trial as an adult under *Ky Rev Stat Ann § 208.170.* That statute provided that juvenile court jurisdiction could be waived and an offender tried as an adult if he was either charged with a Class A felony or capital crime, or was over 16 years of age and charged with a felony. Stressing the seriousness of petitioner's offenses and the unsuccessful attempts of the juvenile system to treat him for numerous instances of past delinquency, the juvenile court found certification for trial as an adult to be in the best interest of petitioner and the community.

Stanford was convicted of murder, first-degree sodomy, first-degree robbery, and receiving stolen property, and was sentenced to death and 45 years in prison. The Kentucky Supreme Court affirmed the death sentence, rejecting Stanford's "deman[d] that he has a constitutional right to treatment." Finding that the record clearly demonstrated that "there was no program or treatment appropriate for the appellant in the juvenile justice system," the court held that the juvenile court did not err in certifying petitioner for trial as an adult. The court also stated that petitioner's "age and the possibility that he might be rehabilitated were mitigating factors appropriately left to the consideration of the jury that tried him."

The second case before us today . . . involves the stabbing death of Nancy Allen, a 26-year-old mother of two who was working behind the sales counter of the convenience store she and David Allen owned and operated in Avondale, Missouri. Petitioner Heath Wilkins committed the murder on July 27, 1985, when he was approximately 16 years and 6 months of age. The record reflects that Wilkins' plan was to rob the store and murder "whoever was behind the counter" because "a dead person can't talk." While Wilkins' accomplice, Patrick Stevens, held Allen, Wilkins stabbed her, causing her to fall to the floor. When Stevens had trouble operating the cash register, Allen spoke up to assist him, leading Wilkins to stab her three more times in her chest. Two of these wounds penetrated the victim's heart. When Allen began to beg for her life, Wilkins stabbed her four more times in the neck, opening her carotid artery. After helping themselves to liquor, cigarettes, rolling papers, and approximately $450 in cash and checks, Wilkins and Stevens left Allen to die on the floor.

Because he was roughly six months short of the age of majority for purposes of criminal prosecution, *Mo Rev Stat § 211.021(1) (1986)*, Wilkins could not automatically be tried as an adult under Missouri law. Before that could happen, the juvenile court was required to terminate juvenile court jurisdiction and certify Wilkins for trial as an adult under *§ 211.071*, which permits individuals between 14 and 17 years of age who have committed felonies to be tried as adults. Relying on the "viciousness, force and violence" of the alleged crime, petitioner's maturity, and the failure of the juvenile justice system to rehabilitate him after previous delinquent acts, the juvenile court made the necessary certification.

Wilkins was charged with first-degree murder, armed criminal action, and carrying a concealed weapon. After the court found him competent, petitioner entered guilty pleas to all charges. A punishment hearing was held, at which both the State and petitioner himself urged imposition of the death sentence. Evidence at the hearing revealed that petitioner had been in and out of juvenile facilities since the age of eight for various acts of burglary, theft, and arson, had attempted to kill his mother by putting insecticide into Tylenol capsules, and had killed several animals in his neighborhood. Although psychiatric testimony indicated that Wilkins had "personality disorders," the witnesses agreed that Wilkins was aware of his actions and could distinguish right from wrong.

Determining that the death penalty was appropriate, the trial court entered the following order:

> [T]he court finds beyond reasonable doubt that the following aggravating circumstances exist:
>
> 1. The murder in the first degree was committed while the defendant was engaged in the perpetration of the felony of robbery, and

2. The murder in the first degree involved depravity
of mind and that as a result thereof, it was outra-
geously or wantonly vile, horrible or inhuman.

On mandatory review of Wilkins' death sentence, the
Supreme Court of Missouri affirmed, rejecting the argument
that the punishment violated the Eighth Amendment. *736 SW2d
409 (1987).*

We granted certiorari in these cases, *488 U.S. 887, 102 L. Ed.
2d 208, 109 S. Ct. 217 (1988)* and *487 U.S. 1233, 101 L. Ed. 2d 930,
108 S. Ct. 2896 (1988),* to decide whether the Eighth Amendment precludes the death penalty for individuals who commit
crimes at 16 or 17 years of age.

II.

The thrust of both Wilkins' and Stanford's arguments is
that imposition of the death penalty on those who were juveniles when they committed their crimes falls within the Eighth
Amendment's prohibition against "cruel and unusual punishments." Wilkins would have us define juveniles as individuals
16 years of age and under; Stanford would draw the line at 17.

Neither petitioner asserts that his sentence constitutes one of
"those modes or acts of punishment that had been considered
cruel and unusual at the time that the Bill of Rights was
adopted." Nor could they support such a contention. At that
time, the common law set the rebuttable presumption of incapac-
ity to commit any felony at the age of 14, and theoretically permitted capital punishment to be imposed on anyone over the age
of 7. . . . In accordance with the standards of this common-law
tradition, at least 281 offenders under the age of 18 have been executed in this country, and at least 126 under the age of 17.

Thus petitioners are left to argue that their punishment is
contrary to the "evolving standards of decency that mark the
progress of a maturing society." They are correct in asserting
that this Court has "not confined the prohibition embodied in
the Eighth Amendment to 'barbarous' methods that were generally outlawed in the 18th century," but instead has interpreted
the Amendment "in a flexible and dynamic manner." In determining what standards have "evolved," however, we have
looked not to our own conceptions of decency, but to those of
modern American society as a whole. As we have said, "Eighth
Amendment judgments should not be, or appear to be, merely

the subjective views of individual Justices; judgment should be informed by objective factors to the maximum possible extent." This approach is dictated both by the language of the Amendment—which proscribes only those punishments that are both "cruel and unusual"—and by the "deference we owe to the decisions of the state legislatures under our federal system," *Gregg v. Georgia, 96 S. Ct. 2909.*

III.

"[F]irst" among the "'objective indicia that reflect the public attitude toward a given sanction'" are statutes passed by society's elected representatives. Of the 37 States whose laws permit capital punishment, 15 decline to impose it upon 16-year-old offenders and 12 decline to impose it on 17-year-old offenders. This does not establish the degree of national consensus this Court has previously thought sufficient to label a particular punishment cruel and unusual. In invalidating the death penalty for rape of an adult woman, we stressed that Georgia was the sole jurisdiction that authorized such a punishment, *Coker v. Georgia, 97 S. Ct. 1861.* In striking down capital punishment for participation in a robbery in which an accomplice takes a life, we emphasized that only eight jurisdictions authorized similar punishment, *Enmunds v. Florida, 102 S. Ct. 3368.* In finding that the Eighth Amendment precludes execution of the insane and thus requires an adequate hearing on the issue of sanity, we relied upon (in addition to this common-law rule) the fact that "no State in the Union" permitted such punishment. And in striking down a life sentence without parole under a recidivist statute, we stressed that "[i]t appears that [petitioner] was treated more severely than he would have been in any other State."

Since a majority of the States that permit capital punishment authorize it for crimes committed at age 16 or above, petitioners' cases are more analogous to *Tison v. Arizona, 107 S. Ct. 1676 (1987)* than Coker, Enmund, Ford, and Solem. In Tison, which upheld Arizona's imposition of the death penalty for major participation in a felony with reckless indifference to human life, we noted that only 11 of those jurisdictions imposing capital punishment rejected its use in such circumstances. As we noted earlier, here the number is 15 for offenders under 17 and 12 for offenders under 18. We think the same conclusion as in Tison is required in this case.

Petitioners make much of the recently enacted federal statute providing capital punishment for certain drug-related offenses, but limiting that punishment to offenders 18 and over. The Anti-Drug Abuse Act of 1988, *Public Law 100-690, 102 Stat. 4390, § 7001(1), 21 USC § 848(1) (1988 ed.).* That reliance is entirely misplaced. To begin with, the statute in question does not embody a judgment by the Federal Legislature that no murder is heinous enough to warrant the execution of such a youthful offender, but merely that the narrow class of offense it defines is not. The congressional judgment on the broader question, if apparent at all, is to be found in the law that permits 16- and 17-year-olds (after appropriate findings) to be tried and punished as adults for all federal offenses, including those bearing a capital penalty that is not limited to 18-year-olds. Moreover, even if it were true that no federal statute permitted the execution of persons under 18, that would not remotely establish—in the face of a substantial number of state statutes to the contrary—a national consensus that such punishment is inhumane, any more than the absence of a federal lottery establishes a national consensus that lotteries are socially harmful. To be sure, the absence of a federal death penalty for 16- or 17-year-olds (if it existed) might be evidence that there is no national consensus in favor of such punishment. It is not the burden of Kentucky and Missouri, however, to establish a national consensus approving what their citizens have voted to do; rather, it is the "heavy burden" of petitioners, *Gregg v. Georgia, 428 U.S. at 175, 96 S. Ct. 2909,* to establish a national consensus against it. As far as the primary and most reliable indication of consensus is concerned—the pattern of enacted laws—petitioners have failed to carry that burden.

IV.

A.

Wilkins and Stanford argue, however, that even if the laws themselves do not establish a settled consensus, the application of the laws does. That contemporary society views capital punishment of 16- and 17-year-old offenders as inappropriate is demonstrated, they say, by the reluctance of juries to impose, and prosecutors to seek, such sentences. Petitioners are quite correct that a far smaller number of offenders under 18 than over 18 have been sentenced to death in this country. From 1982 through 1988, for example, out of 2,106 total death sentences, only 15 were imposed on individuals who were 16 or under when they committed their crimes, and only 30 on individuals who were 17 at the time of the crime. And it appears that actual executions for crimes committed under age 18 accounted for only about two percent of the total number of executions that occurred between 1642 and 1986. As Wilkins points out, the last execution of a person who committed a crime under 17 years of age occurred in 1959. These statistics, however, carry little significance. Given the undisputed fact that a far smaller percentage of capital crimes are committed by persons under 18 than over 18, the discrepancy in treatment is much less than might seem. Granted, however, that a substantial discrepancy exists, that does not establish the requisite proposition that the death sentence for offenders under 18 is categorically unacceptable to prosecutors and juries. To the contrary, it is not only possible, but overwhelmingly probable, that the very considerations which induce petitioners and their supporters to believe that death should never be imposed on offenders under 18 cause prosecutors and juries to believe that it should rarely be imposed.

B.

This last point suggests why there is also no relevance to the laws cited by petitioners and their amici which set 18 or more as the legal age for engaging in various activities, ranging from driving to drinking alcoholic beverages to voting. It is, to begin with, absurd to think that one must be mature enough to drive carefully, to drink responsibly, or to vote intelligently, in order to be mature enough to understand that murdering another human being is profoundly wrong, and to conform one's conduct to that most minimal of all civilized standards. But even if the requisite degrees of maturity were comparable, the age statutes in question would still not be relevant. They do not represent a social judgment that all persons under the designated ages are not responsible enough to drive, to drink, or to vote, but at most a judgment that the vast majority are not. These laws set the appropriate ages for the operation of a system that makes its determinations in gross, and that does not conduct individualized maturity tests for each driver, drinker, or voter. The criminal justice system, however, does provide individualized testing. In the realm of capital punishment in particular, "individualized consideration [is] a constitutional requirement," *Lockett v. Ohio, 98 S. Ct. 2954 (1978)*, and one of the individualized mitigating factors that sentencers must be permitted to consider is the defendant's age, see *Eddings v. Oklahoma, 102 S. Ct. 869 (1982)*. Twenty-nine States, including both Kentucky and Missouri, have codified this constitutional requirement in laws specifically designating the defendant's age as a mitigating factor in capital cases. Moreover, the determinations required by juvenile transfer statutes to certify a juvenile for trial as an adult ensure individualized consideration of the maturity and moral responsibility of 16- and 17-year-old offenders before they are even held to stand trial as adults. The application of this particularized system to the petitioners can be declared constitutionally inadequate only if there is a consensus, not that 17 or 18 is the age at which most persons, or even almost all persons, achieve sufficient maturity to be held fully responsible for murder; but that 17 or 18 is the age before which no one can reasonably be held fully responsible. What displays society's views on this latter point are not the ages set forth in the generalized system of driving, drinking, and voting laws cited by petitioners and their amici, but the ages at which the States permit their particularized capital punishment systems to be applied.

V.

Having failed to establish a consensus against capital punishment for 16- and 17-year-old offenders through state and federal statutes and the behavior of prosecutors and juries, petitioners seek to demonstrate it through other indicia, including public opinion polls, the views of interest groups, and the positions adopted by various professional associations. We decline the invitation to rest constitutional law upon such uncertain foundations. A revised national consensus so broad, so clear, and so enduring as to justify a permanent prohibition upon all units of democratic government must appear in the operative acts (laws and the application of laws) that the people have approved.

We also reject petitioners' argument that we should invalidate capital punishment of 16- and 17-year-old offenders on the ground that it fails to serve the legitimate goals of penology. According to petitioners, it fails to deter because juveniles, possessing less developed cognitive skills than adults, are less likely to fear death; and it fails to exact just retribution because juveniles, being less mature and responsible, are also less morally blameworthy. In support of these claims, petitioners and their supporting amici marshall an array of socioscientific evidence concerning the psychological and emotional development of 16- and 17-year-olds.

If such evidence could conclusively establish the entire lack of deterrent effect and moral responsibility, resort to the Cruel and Unusual Punishments Clause would be unnecessary; the Equal Protection Clause of the Fourteenth Amendment would invalidate these laws for lack of rational basis. But as the adjective "socioscientific" suggests (and insofar as evaluation of moral responsibility is concerned perhaps the adjective "ethicoscientific" would be more apt), it is not demonstrable that no 16-year-old is "adequately responsible" or significantly deterred. It is rational, even if mistaken, to think the contrary. The battle must be fought, then, on the field of the Eighth Amendment; and in that struggle socioscientific, ethicoscientific, or even purely scientific evidence is not an available weapon. The punishment is either "cruel and unusual" (i.e., society has set its face against it) or it is not. The audience for these arguments, in other words, is not this Court but the citizenry of the United States. It is they, not we, who must be persuaded. For as we stated earlier, our job is to identify the "evolving standards of decency"; to determine, not what they should be, but what they are. We have no power under the Eighth Amendment to substitute our belief in the scientific evidence for the society's apparent skepticism. In short, we emphatically reject petitioner's suggestion that the issues in this case permit us to apply our "own informed judgment," *Brief for Petitioner in No. 87-6026 [Wilkins],* regarding the desirability of permitting the death penalty for crimes by 16- and 17-year-olds.

We reject the dissent's contention that our approach, by "largely return[ing] the task of defining the contours of Eighth Amendment protection to political majorities," leaves " '[c]onstitutional doctrine [to] be formulated by the acts of those institutions which the Constitution is supposed to limit.' " When this Court cast loose from the historical moorings consisting of the original application of the Eighth Amendment, it did not embark rudderless upon a wide-open sea. Rather, it limited the Amendment's extension to those practices contrary to the "evolving standards of decency that mark the progress of a maturing society." *Trop v. Dulles, 78 S. Ct. 590.* It has never been thought that this was a shorthand reference to the preferences of a majority of this Court. By reaching a decision supported neither by constitutional text nor by the demonstrable current standards of our citizens, the dissent displays a failure to appreciate that "those institutions which the Constitution is supposed to limit" include the Court itself. To say, as the dissent says, that "it is for us ultimately to judge whether the Eighth Amendment permits imposition of the death penalty,"—and to mean that as the dissent means it, i.e., that it is for us to judge, not on the basis of what we perceive the Eighth Amendment originally prohibited, or on the basis of what we perceive the society through its democratic processes now overwhelmingly disapproves, but on the basis of what we think "proportionate" and "measurably contributory to acceptable goals of punishment"—to say and mean that, is to replace judges of the law with a committee of philosopher-kings.

While the dissent is correct that several of our cases have engaged in so-called "proportionality" analysis, examining whether "there is a disproportion 'between the punishment imposed and the defendant's blameworthiness,'" and whether a punishment makes any "measurable contribution to acceptable goals of punishment," we have never invalidated a punishment on this basis alone. All of our cases condemning a punishment under this mode of analysis also found that the objective indicators of state laws or jury determinations evidenced a societal consensus against that penalty. In fact, the two methodologies blend into one another, since "proportionality" analysis itself can only be conducted on the basis of the standards set by our own society; the only alternative, once again, would be our personal preferences.

We discern neither a historical nor a modern societal consensus forbidding the imposition of capital punishment on any person who murders at 16 or 17 years of age. Accordingly, we conclude that such punishment does not offend the Eighth Amendment's prohibition against cruel and unusual punishment.

The judgments of the Supreme Court of Kentucky and the Supreme Court of Missouri are therefore affirmed.

Justice Brennan, with whom Justice Marshall, Justice Blackmun, and Justice Stevens join, dissenting.

Stanford v. Kentucky and *Wilkins v. Missouri*

The Dissenting Opinion

I believe that to take the life of a person as punishment for a crime committed when below the age of 18 is cruel and unusual punishment and hence is prohibited by the Eighth Amendment.

The method by which this Court assesses a claim that a punishment is unconstitutional because it is cruel and unusual is established by our precedents, and it bears little resemblance to the method four Members of the Court apply in this case. To be sure, we begin the task of deciding whether a punishment is unconstitutional by reviewing legislative enactments and the work of sentencing juries relating to the punishment in question to determine whether our Nation has set its face against a punishment to an extent that it can be concluded that the punishment offends our "evolving standards of decency." The Court undertakes such an analysis in this case.

I.

Our judgment about the constitutionality of a punishment under the Eighth Amendment is informed, though not determined by an examination of contemporary attitudes toward the punishment, as evidenced in the actions of legislatures and of juries. The views of organizations with expertise in relevant fields and the choices of governments elsewhere in the world also merit our attention as indicators whether a punishment is acceptable in a civilized society.

A.

The Court's discussion of state laws concerning capital sentencing gives a distorted view of the evidence of contemporary standards that these legislative determinations provide. Currently, 12 of the States whose statutes permit capital punishment specifically mandate that offenders under age 18 not be sentenced to death. When one adds to these 12 States the 15 (including the District of Columbia) in which capital punishment is not authorized at all, it appears that the governments in fully 27 of the States have concluded that no one under 18 should face the death penalty. A further three States explicitly refuse to authorize sentences of death for those who committed their offense when under 17, making a total of 30 States that would not tolerate the execution of petitioner Wilkins. Congress' most recent enactment of a death penalty statute also excludes those under 18.

. . . I do not suggest, of course, that laws of these States cut against the constitutionality of the juvenile death penalty—only that accuracy demands that the baseline for our deliberations should be that 27 States refuse to authorize a sentence of death in the circumstances of petitioner Stanford's case, and 30 would not permit Wilkins' execution; that 19 States have not squarely faced the question; and that only the few remaining jurisdictions have explicitly set an age below 18 at which a person may be sentenced to death.

B.

The application of these laws is another indicator the Court agrees to be relevant. The fact that juries have on occasion sentenced a minor to death shows, the Court says, that the death penalty for adolescents is not categorically unacceptable to juries. This, of course, is true; but it is not a conclusion that takes Eighth Amendment analysis very far. Just as we have never insisted that a punishment have been rejected unanimously by the States before we may judge it cruel and unusual, so we have never adopted the extraordinary view that a punishment is beyond Eighth Amendment challenge if it is sometimes handed down by a jury.

The Court speculates that this very small number of capital sentences imposed on adolescents [41 minors were sentenced to die between 1982 and 1988] indicates that juries have considered the youth of the offender when determining sentence, and have reserved the punishment for rare cases in which it is nevertheless appropriate. . . . It is certainly true that in the vast majority of cases, juries have not sentenced juveniles to death, and it seems to me perfectly proper to conclude that a sentence so rarely imposed is "unusual."

C.

Further indicators of contemporary standards of decency that should inform our consideration of the Eighth Amendment question are the opinions of respected organizations. Where organizations with expertise in a relevant area have given careful consideration to the question of a punishment's appropriateness, there is no reason why that judgment should not be entitled to attention as an indicator of contemporary standards. There is no dearth of opinion from such groups that the state-sanctioned killing of minors is unjustified. A number, indeed, have filed briefs amicus curiae in these cases, in support of petitioners. The American Bar Association has adopted a resolution opposing the imposition of capital punishment upon any person for an offense committed while under age 18, as has the National Council of Juvenile and Family Court Judges. The American Law Institute's Model Penal Code similarly includes a lower age limit of 18 for the death sentence. And the National Commission on Reform of the Federal Criminal Laws also recommended that 18 be the minimum age.

D.

Together, the rejection of the death penalty for juveniles by a majority of the States, the rarity of the sentence for juveniles, both as an absolute and a comparative matter, the decisions of respected organizations in relevant fields that this punishment is unacceptable, and its rejection generally throughout the world, provide to my mind a strong grounding for the view that it is not constitutionally tolerable that certain States persist in authorizing the execution of adolescent offenders. It is unnecessary, however, to rest a view that the Eighth Amendment prohibits the execution of minors solely upon a judgment as to the meaning to be attached to the evidence of contemporary values outlined above, for the execution of juveniles fails to satisfy two well-established and independent Eighth Amendment requirements—that a punishment not be disproportionate, and that it make a contribution to acceptable goals of punishment.

II.

Thus, in addition to asking whether legislative or jury rejection of a penalty shows that "society has set its face against it," the Court asks whether "a punishment is 'excessive' and unconstitutional" because there is disproportion "between the punishment imposed and the defendant's blameworthiness," or because it "makes no measurable contribution to acceptable goals of punishment and hence is nothing more than the purposeless and needless imposition of pain and suffering.

III.

Juveniles very generally lack that degree of blameworthiness that is, in my view, a constitutional prerequisite for the imposition of capital punishment under our precedents concerning the Eighth Amendment proportionality principle. The individualized consideration of an offender's youth and culpability at the transfer stage and at sentencing has not operated to ensure that the only offenders under 18 singled out for the ultimate penalty are exceptional individuals whose level of responsibility is more developed than that of their peers. In that circumstance, I believe that the same categorical assumption that juveniles as a class are insufficiently mature to be regarded as fully responsible that we make in so many other areas is appropriately made in determining whether minors may be subjected to the death penalty. As we noted in *Thompson v. Oklahoma, 108 S. Ct. 2687,* it would be ironic if the assumptions we so readily make about minors as a class were suddenly unavailable in conducting proportionality analysis. I would hold that the Eighth Amendment prohibits the execution of any person for a crime committed below the age of 18.

IV.

Under a second strand of Eighth Amendment inquiry into whether a particular sentence is excessive and hence unconstitutional, we ask whether the sentence makes a measurable contribution to acceptable goals of punishment. The two "principal social purposes" of capital punishment are said to be "retribution and the deterrence of capital crimes by prospective offenders." Unless the death penalty applied to persons for offenses committed under 18 measurably contributes to one of these goals, the Eighth Amendment prohibits it.

V.

There are strong indications that the execution of juvenile offenders violates contemporary standards of decency: a majority of States decline to permit juveniles to be sentenced to death; imposition of the sentence upon minors is very unusual even in those States that permit it; and respected organizations with expertise in relevant areas regard the execution of juveniles as unacceptable, as does international opinion. These indicators serve to confirm in my view my conclusion that the Eighth Amendment prohibits the execution of persons for offenses they committed while below the age of 18, because the death penalty is disproportionate when applied to such young offenders and fails measurably to serve the goals of capital punishment. I dissent.

The Juvenile Justice and Delinquency Prevention Act of 1974

Public Law 93-415, 42 U.S.C. 5601 et seq., as amended by:

The Fiscal Year Adjustment Act of 1976

The Crime Control Act of 1976

The Juvenile Justice Amendments of 1977

The Juvenile Justice Amendments of 1980

The Juvenile Justice, Runaway Youth, and Missing Children's Act Amendments of 1984

The Anti-Drug Abuse Act of 1988

Title VII, Subtitle F—Juvenile Justice and Delinquency Prevention Amendments of 1988

The Juvenile Justice and Delinquency Prevention Amendments of 1992

An Act to provide a comprehensive, coordinated approach to the problems of juvenile delinquency, and for other purposes.

Be it enacted by the Senate and House of Representatives of the United States of America in Congress assembled,
That this Act may be cited as the "Juvenile Justice and Delinquency Prevention Act of 1974."

Title I—Findings and Declaration of Purpose

Findings

Sec. 101. (a) The Congress hereby finds that—
  (1) juveniles accounted for almost half the arrests for serious crimes in the United States in 1974 and for less than one-third of such arrests in 1983;

(2) recent trends show an upsurge in arrests of adolescents for murder, assault, and weapon use;

(3) the small number of youth who commit the most serious and violent offenses are becoming more violent;

(4) understaffed, overcrowded juvenile courts, prosecutorial and public defender offices, probation services, and correctional facilities and inadequately trained staff in such courts, services, and facilities are not able to provide individualized justice or effective help;

(5) present juvenile courts, foster and protective care programs, and shelter facilities are inadequate to meet the needs of children, who, because of this failure to provide effective services, may become delinquents;

(6) existing programs have not adequately responded to the particular problems of the increasing numbers of young people who are addicted to or who abuse alcohol and other drugs, particularly nonopiate or polydrug abusers;

(7) juvenile delinquency can be reduced through programs designed to keep students in elementary and secondary schools through the prevention of unwarranted and arbitrary suspensions and expulsions;

(8) State and local communities which experience directly the devastating failures of the juvenile justice system do not presently have sufficient technical expertise or adequate resources to deal comprehensively with the problems of juvenile delinquency;

(9) existing Federal programs have not provided the direction, coordination, resources, and leadership required to meet the crisis of delinquency;

(10) the juvenile justice system should give additional attention to the problem of juveniles who commit serious crimes, with particular attention given to the areas of sentencing, providing resources necessary for informed dispositions, and rehabilitation;

(11) emphasis should be placed on preventing youth from entering the juvenile justice system to begin with; and

(12) the incidence of juvenile delinquency can be reduced through public recreation programs and activities designed to provide youth with social skills, enhance self-esteem, and encourage the constructive use of discretionary time.

(b) Congress finds further that the high incidence of delinquency in the United States today results in enormous annual cost and immeasurable loss of human life, personal security, and wasted human resources and that juvenile delinquency constitutes a growing threat to the national welfare requiring immediate and comprehensive action by the Federal Government to reduce and prevent delinquency.

Purpose

Sec. 102. (a) It is the purpose of this Act—

(1) to provide for the thorough and ongoing evaluation of all federally assisted juvenile justice and delinquency prevention programs;

(2) to provide technical assistance to public and private nonprofit juvenile justice and delinquency prevention programs;

(3) to establish training programs for persons, including professionals, paraprofessionals, and volunteers, who work with delinquents or potential delinquents or whose work or activities relate to juvenile delinquency programs;

(4) to establish a centralized research effort on the problems of juvenile delinquency, including the dissemination of the findings of such research and all data related to juvenile delinquency;

(5) to develop and encourage the implementation of national standards for the administration of juvenile justice, including recommendations for administrative, budgetary, and legislative action at the Federal, State, and local level to facilitate the adoption of such standards;

(6) to assist State and local communities with resources to develop and implement programs to keep students in elementary and secondary schools and to prevent unwarranted and arbitrary suspensions and expulsions;

(7) to establish a Federal assistance program to deal with the problems of runaway and homeless youth;

(8) to strengthen families in which juvenile delinquency has been a problem;

(9) to assist State and local governments in removing juveniles from jails and lockups for adults;

(10) to assist State and local governments in improving the administration of justice and services for juveniles who enter the system; and

(11) to assist States and local communities to prevent youth from entering the justice system to begin with.

(b) It is therefore the further declared policy of Congress to provide the necessary resources, leadership, and coordination–

(1) to develop and implement effective methods of preventing and reducing juvenile delinquency, including methods with a special focus on preserving and strengthening families so that juveniles may be retained in their homes;

(2) to develop and conduct effective programs to prevent delinquency, to divert juveniles from the traditional juvenile justice system and to provide critically needed alternatives to institutionalization;

(3) to improve the quality of juvenile justice in the United States;

(4) to increase the capacity of State and local governments and public and private agencies to conduct effective juvenile justice and delinquency prevention and rehabilitation programs and to provide research, evaluation, and training services in the field of juvenile delinquency prevention;

(5) to encourage parental involvement in treatment and alternative disposition programs; and

(6) to provide for coordination of services between State, local, and community-based agencies and to promote interagency cooperation in providing such services.

Part C—National Programs

Subpart I—National Institute for Juvenile Justice
and Delinquency Prevention

Establishment of National Institute for Juvenile Justice and Delinquency Prevention

Sec. 241. (a) There is hereby established within the Juvenile Justice and Delinquency Prevention Office a National Institute for Juvenile Justice and Delinquency Prevention.

(b) The National Institute for Juvenile Justice and Delinquency Prevention shall be under the supervision and direction of the Administrator.

(c) The activities of the National Institute for Juvenile Justice and Delinquency Prevention shall be coordinated with the activities of the National Institute of Justice in accordance with the requirements of section 201(b).

(d) It shall be the purpose of the Institute to provide—

(1) a coordinating center for the collection, preparation, and dissemination of useful data regarding the prevention, treatment, and control of juvenile delinquency; and

(2) appropriate training (including training designed to strengthen and maintain the family unit) for representatives of Federal, State, local law enforcement officers, teachers and special education personnel, recreation and park personnel, family counselors, child welfare workers, juvenile judges and judicial personnel, probation personnel, prosecutors and defense attorneys, correctional personnel (including volunteer lay personnel), persons associated with law-related education, youth workers, and representatives of private agencies and organizations with specific experience in the prevention, treatment, and control of juvenile delinquency.

(e) In addition to the other powers, express and implied, the Institute may—

(1) request any Federal agency to supply such statistics, data, program reports, and other material as the Institute deems necessary to carry out its functions;

(2) arrange with and reimburse the heads of Federal agencies for the use of personnel or facilities or equipment of such agencies;

(3) confer with and avail itself of the cooperation, services, records, and facilities of State, municipal, or other public or private local agencies;

(4) make grants and enter into contracts with public or private agencies, organizations, or individuals for the partial performance of any functions of the Institute;

(5) compensate consultants and members of technical

advisory councils who are not in the regular full-time employ of the United States, at a rate now or hereafter payable under section 5376 of title 5 of the United States Code and while away from home, or regular place of business, they may be allowed travel expenses, including per diem in lieu of subsistence, as authorized by section 5703 of title 5, United States Code for persons in the Government service employed intermittently; and

(6) assist through training, the advisory groups established pursuant to section 223(a)(3) or comparable public or private citizen groups in nonparticipating States in the accomplishment of their objectives consistent with this title.

(f)

(1) The Administrator, acting through the Institute, shall provide technical and financial assistance to an eligible organization composed of member representatives of the State advisory groups appointed under section 223(a)(3) to assist such organization to carry out the functions specified in paragraph (2).

(2) To be eligible to receive such assistance, such organization shall agree to carry out activities that include—

(A) conducting an annual conference of such member representatives for purposes relating to the activities of such State advisory groups;

(B) disseminating information, data, standards, advanced techniques, and program models developed through the Institute and through programs funded under section 261;

(C) reviewing Federal policies regarding juvenile justice and delinquency prevention;

(D) advising the Administrator with respect to particular functions or aspects of the work of the Office; and

(E) advising the President and Congress with regard to State perspectives on the operation of the Office and Federal legislation pertaining to juvenile justice and delinquency prevention.

(g) Any Federal agency which receives a request from the Institute, under subsection (e)(1) may cooperate with the Institute and shall, to the maximum extent practicable, consult with and furnish information and advice to the Institute.

Information Function

Sec. 242. The Administrator, acting through the National Institute for Juvenile Justice and Delinquency Prevention, shall—

(1) on a continuing basis, review reports, data, and standards relating to the juvenile justice system in the United States;

(2) serve as an information bank by collecting systematically and synthesizing the data and knowledge obtained from studies and research by public and private agencies, institutions, or individuals concerning all aspects of juvenile delinquency, including the prevention and treatment of juvenile delinquency; and

(3) serve as a clearing house and information center for the preparation, publication, and dissemination of all information regarding juvenile delinquency, including State and local juvenile delinquency prevention and treatment programs (including drug and alcohol programs and gender-specific programs) and plans, availability of resources, training and educational programs, statistics, and other pertinent data and information.

Research, Demonstration, and Evaluation Functions

Sec. 243. (a) The Administrator, acting through the National Institute for Juvenile Justice and Delinquency prevention, is authorized to—

(1) conduct, encourage, and coordinate research and evaluation into any aspect of juvenile delinquency, particularly with regard to new programs and methods which seek to strengthen and preserve families or which show promise of making a contribution toward the prevention and treatment of juvenile delinquency;

(2) encourage the development of demonstration projects in new, innovative techniques and methods to prevent and treat juvenile delinquency;

(3) establish or expand programs that, in recognition of varying degrees of the seriousness of delinquency behavior and the corresponding gradations in the responses of the juvenile justice system in response to that behavior, are designed to—

(i) encourage courts to develop and implement a continuum of post-adjudication restraints that bridge the gap between traditional probation and confinement in a correctional setting (including expanded use of probation, mediation, restitution, community service treatment, home detention, intensive supervision, electronic monitoring, boot camps and similar programs, and secure community-based treatment facilities linked to other support services such as health, mental health, education (remedial and special), job training, and recreation; and

(ii) assist in the provision by the Administrator of information and technical assistance, including technology transfer, to States in the design and utilization of risk assessment mechanisms to aid juvenile justice personnel in determining appropriate sanctions for delinquency behavior;

(4) encourage the development of programs which, in addition to helping youth take responsibility for their behavior, take into consideration life experiences which may have contributed to their delinquency when developing intervention and treatment programs;

(5) encourage the development and establishment of programs to enhance the States' ability to identify chronic serious and violent juvenile offenders who commit crimes such as rape, murder, firearms offenses, gang-related crimes, violent felonies, and serious drug offenses;

(5a) provide for the evaluation of all juvenile delinquency programs assisted under this title in order to determine the results and the effectiveness of such programs;

(6) provide for the evaluation of any other Federal, State, or local juvenile delinquency program;

(7) prepare, in cooperation with educational institutions, with Federal, State, and local agencies, and with appropriate individuals and private agencies, such studies as

it considers to be necessary with respect to the prevention and treatment of juvenile delinquency and the im-
provement of the juvenile justice system, including—

   (A) recommendations designed to promote effective
prevention and treatment, particularly by
strengthening and maintaining the family unit;

   (B) assessments regarding the role of family violence,
sexual abuse or exploitation, media violence, the
improper handling of youth placed in one State by
another State, the effectiveness of family-centered
treatment programs, special education, remedial
education, and recreation, and the extent to which
youth in the juvenile justice system are treated dif-
ferently on the basis of sex, race, or family income
and the ramifications of such treatment;

   (C) examinations of the treatment of juveniles
processed in the criminal justice system; and

   (D) recommendations as to effective means for deter-
ring involvement in illegal activities or promoting
involvement in lawful activities (including the
productive use of discretionary time through organized recreational activities on the part of gangs
whose membership is substantially composed of
juveniles);

 (8) disseminate the results of such evaluations and research and demonstration activities particularly to
persons actively working in the field of juvenile
delinquency;

 (9) disseminate pertinent data and studies to individuals,
agencies, and organizations concerned with the prevention and treatment of juvenile delinquency;

(10) develop and support model State legislation consistent with the mandates of this title and the standards
developed by the National Advisory Committee for
Juvenile Justice and Delinquency Prevention before
the date of the enactment of the Juvenile Justice,
Runaway Youth, and Missing Children's Act
Amendments of 1984;

(11) support research relating to reducing the excessive
proportion of juveniles detained or confined in secure
detention facilities, secure correctional facilities, jails,
and lockups who are members of minority groups;

(12) support independent and collaborative research,

research training, and consultation on social, psychological, educational, economic, and legal issues affecting children and families;

(13) support research related to achieving a better understanding of the commission of hate crimes by juveniles and designed to identify educational programs best suited to prevent and reduce the incidence of hate crimes committed by juveniles; and

(14) routinely collect, analyze, compile, publish, and disseminate uniform national statistics concerning—

(A) all aspects of juveniles as victims and offenders;

(B) the processing and treatment, in the juvenile justice system, of juveniles who are status offenders, delinquent, neglected, or abused; and

(C) the processing and treatment of such juveniles who are treated as adults for purposes of the criminal justice system.

(b) The Administrator shall make available to the public—

(1) the results of evaluations and research and demonstration activities referred to in subsection (a)(8); and

(2) the data and studies referred to in subsection (a)(9); that the Administrator is authorized to disseminate under subsection (a).

Technical Assistance and Training Functions

Sec. 244. The Administrator, acting through the National Institute for Juvenile Justice and Delinquency Prevention is authorized to—

(1) provide technical assistance and training assistance to Federal, State, and local governments and to courts, public and private agencies, institutions, and individuals in the planning, establishment, funding, operation, and evaluation of juvenile delinquency programs;

(2) develop, conduct, and provide for training programs for the training of professional, paraprofessional, and volunteer personnel, and other persons who are working with or preparing to work with juveniles, juvenile offenders (including juveniles who commit hate crimes), and their families;

(3) develop, conduct, and provide for seminars, workshops, and training programs in the latest proven effective techniques and methods of preventing and treating juvenile delinquency for law enforcement officers, juvenile judges, prosecutors and defense attorneys, and other court personnel, probation officers, correctional personnel, and other Federal, State, and local government personnel who are engaged in work relating to juvenile delinquency;

(4) develop technical training teams to aid in the development of training programs in the States and to assist State and local agencies which work directly with juveniles and juvenile offenders; and

(5) provide technical assistance and training to assist States and units of general local government to adopt the model standards issued under section 204(b)(7).

Establishment of Training Program

Sec. 245. (a) The Administrator shall establish within the Institute a training program designed to train enrollees with respect to methods and techniques for the prevention and treatment of juvenile delinquency, including methods and techniques specifically designed to prevent and reduce the incidence of hate crimes committed by juveniles. In carrying out this program the Administrator is authorized to make use of available State and local services, equipment, personnel, facilities, and the like.

(b) Enrollees in the training program established under this section shall be drawn from law enforcement and correctional personnel (including volunteer lay personnel), teachers and special education personnel, family counselors, child welfare workers, juvenile judges and judicial personnel, persons associated with law-related education, youth workers, and representatives of private agencies and organizations with specific experience in the prevention and treatment of juvenile delinquency.

Curriculum for Training Program

Sec. 246. The Administrator shall design and supervise a curriculum for the training program established by section 245 which shall utilize an interdisciplinary approach with respect to the prevention of juvenile delinquency, the treatment of juvenile delinquency, and the diversion of youths from the juvenile justice system. Such curriculum shall be appropriate to the needs of the enrollees of the training program and shall include training designed to prevent juveniles from committing hate crimes.

Participation in Training Program and State Advisory Group Conferences

Sec. 247. (a) Any person seeking to enroll in the training program established under section 245 shall transmit an application to the Administrator, in such form and according to such procedures as the Administrator may prescribe.

(b) The Administrator shall make the final determination with respect to the admittance of any person to the training program. The Administrator, in making such determination, shall seek to assure that persons admitted to the training program are broadly representative of the categories described in section 245(b).

(c) While participating as a trainee in the program established under section 245 or while participating in any conference held under section 241(f), and while traveling in connection with such participation, each person so participating shall be allowed travel expenses, including a per diem allowance in lieu of subsistence, in the same manner as persons employed intermittently in Government service are allowed travel expenses under section 5703 of title 5, United States Code. No consultation fee may be paid to such person for such participation.

Special Studies and Reports

Sec. 248. (a) Pursuant to 1988 amendments—

(1) Not later than 1 year after the date of the enactment of the Juvenile Justice and Delinquency Prevention Amendments of 1988, the Administrator shall begin to conduct a study with respect to the juvenile justice system—
(A) to review—
(i) conditions in detention and correctional facilities for juveniles; and
(ii) the extent to which such facilities meet recognized national professional standards; and

(B) to make recommendations to improve conditions in such facilities.

(2) (A) Not later than 1 year after the date of the enactment of the Juvenile Justice and Delinquency Prevention Amendments of 1988, the Administrator shall begin to conduct a study to determine—

    (i) how juveniles who are American Indians and Alaskan Natives and who are accused of committing offenses on and near Indian reservations and Alaskan Native villages, respectively, are treated under the systems of justice administered by Indian tribes and Alaskan Native organizations, respectively, that perform law enforcement functions;

    (ii) the amount of financial resources (including financial assistance provided by governmental entities) available to Indian tribes and Alaskan Native organizations that perform law enforcement functions, to support community-based alternatives to incarcerating juveniles; and

    (iii) the extent to which such tribes and organizations comply with the requirements specified in paragraphs (12)(A), (13), and (14) of section 223(a), applicable to the detention and confinement of juveniles.

(B) (i) for purposes of section 7(b) of the Indian Self-Determination and Education Assistance Act (25 U.S.C. 450e(b)), any contract, subcontract, grant, or subgrant made under paragraph (1) shall be deemed to be a contract, subcontract, grant, or subgrant made for the benefit of Indians.

    (ii) for purposes of section 7(b) of such Act and subparagraph (A) of this paragraph, references to Indians and Indian organizations shall be deemed to include Alaskan Natives and Alaskan Native organizations, respectively.

(3) Not later than 3 years after the date of the enactment of the Juvenile Justice and Delinquency Prevention Amendments of 1988, the Administrator shall submit a report to the chairman of the Committee of Education and Labor of the House of Representatives and the chairman of the Committee on the Judiciary of the Senate containing a description, and a summary of the

results, of the study conducted under paragraph (1) or (2), as the case may be.

Sec. 248. (b) Pursuant to 1992 Amendments—

(1) Not later than 1 year after the date of enactment of this subsection, the Comptroller General shall—
  (A) conduct a study with respect to juveniles waived to adult court that reviews—
    (i) the frequency and extent to which juveniles have been transferred, certified, or waived to criminal court for prosecution during the 5-year period ending December 1992;
    (ii) conditions of confinement in adult detention and correction facilities for juveniles waived to adult court; and
    (iii) sentencing patterns, comparing juveniles waived to adult court with juveniles who have committed similar offenses but have not been waived; and
  (B) submit to the Committee on Education and Labor of the House of Representatives and the Committee on the Judiciary of the Senate a report (including a compilation of State waiver statutes) on the findings made in the study and recommendations to improve conditions for juveniles waived to adult court.
(2) Not later than 1 year after the date of enactment of this subsection, the Comptroller General shall—
  (A) conduct a study with respect to admissions of juveniles for behavior disorders to private psychiatric hospitals, and to other residential and nonresidential programs that serve juveniles admitted for behavior disorders, that reviews—
    (i) the frequency with which juveniles have been admitted to such hospitals and programs during the 5-year period ending December 1992; and
    (ii) conditions of confinement, the average length of stay, and methods of payment for the residential care of such juveniles; and
  (B) submit to the Committee on Education and Labor of the House of Representatives and the Committee on the Judiciary of the Senate a report on the findings

made in the study and recommendations to improve procedural protections and conditions for juveniles with behavior disorders admitted to such hospitals and programs.

(3) Not later than 1 year after the date of enactment of this subsection, the Comptroller General shall—

(A) conduct a study of gender bias within State juvenile justice systems that reviews—

(i) the frequency with which females have been detained for status offenses (such as frequently running away, truancy, and sexual activity), as compared with the frequency with which males have been detained for such offenses during the 5-year period ending December 1992; and

(ii) the appropriateness of the placement and conditions of confinement for females; and

(B) submit to the Committee on Education and Labor of the House of Representatives and the Committee on the Judiciary of the Senate a report on the findings made in the study and recommendations to combat gender bias in juvenile justice and provide appropriate services for females who enter the juvenile justice system.

(4) Not later than 1 year after the date of enactment of this subsection, the Comptroller General shall—

(A) conduct a study of the Native American pass-through grant program authorized under section 223 (a)(5)(C) that reviews the cost-effectiveness of the funding formula utilized; and

(B) submit to the Committee on Education and Labor of the House of Representatives and the Committee on the Judiciary of the Senate a report on the findings made in the study and recommendations to improve the Native American pass-through grant program.

(5) Not later than 1 year after the date of enactment of this subsection, the Comptroller General shall—

(A) conduct a study of access to counsel in juvenile court proceedings that reviews—

(i) the frequency with which and the extent to which juveniles in juvenile court proceedings either have waived counsel or have obtained access to counsel during the 5-year period ending December 1992; and

(ii) a comparison of access to and the quality of counsel afforded juveniles charged in adult court proceedings with those of juveniles charged in juvenile court proceedings; and

(B) submit to the Committee on Education and Labor of the House of Representatives and the Committee on the Judiciary of the Senate a report on the findings made in the study and recommendations to improve access to counsel for juveniles in juvenile court proceedings.

(6) (A) Not later than 180 days after the date of enactment of this subsection, the Administrator shall begin to conduct a study and continue any pending study of the incidence of violence committed by or against juveniles in urban and rural areas in the United States.

(B) The urban areas shall include—
   (i) the District of Columbia;
   (ii) Los Angeles, California;
   (iii) Milwaukee, Wisconsin;
   (iv) Denver, Colorado;
   (v) Pittsburgh, Pennsylvania;
   (vi) Rochester, New York; and
   (vii) such other cities as the Administrator determines to be appropriate.

(C) At least one rural area shall be included.

(D) With respect to each urban and rural area included in the study, the objectives of the study shall be—
   (i) to identify characteristics and patterns of behavior of juveniles who are at risk of becoming violent or victims of homicide;
   (ii) to identify factors particularly indigenous to such areas that contribute to violence committed by or against juveniles;
   (iii) to determine the accessibility of firearms, and the use of firearms by or against juveniles;
   (iv) to determine the conditions that cause any increase in violence committed by or against juveniles;
   (v) to identify existing and new diversion, prevention, and control programs to ameliorate such conditions;
   (vi) to improve current systems to prevent and control violence by or against juveniles; and

(vii) to develop a plan to assist State and local governments to establish viable ways to reduce homicide committed by or against juveniles.

(E) Not later than 3 years after the date of enactment of this subsection, the Administrator shall submit a report to the Committee on Education and Labor of the House of Representatives and the Committee on the Judiciary of the Senate detailing the results of the study addressing each objective specified in subparagraph (D).

(7) (A) Not later than 1 year after the date of the enactment of this subsection, the Administrator shall—

(i) conduct a study described in subparagraph (B); and

(ii) submit to the chairman of the Committee on Education and Labor of the House of Representatives and the chairman of the Committee on the Judiciary of the Senate the results of the study.

(B) The study required by subparagraph (A) shall assess—

(i) the characteristics of juveniles who commit hate crimes, including a profile of such juveniles based on—

(I) the motives for committing hate crimes;

(II) the age, sex, race, ethnicity, education level, locality, and family income of such juveniles; and

(III) whether such juveniles are familiar with publications or organized groups that encourage the commission of hate crimes;

(ii) the characteristics of hate crimes committed by juveniles, including—

(I) the types of hate crimes committed;

(II) the frequency with which institutions and natural persons, separately determined, were the targets of such crimes;

(III) the number of persons who participated with juveniles in committing such crimes;

(IV) the types of law enforcement investigations conducted with respect to such crimes;

(V) the law enforcement proceedings commenced against juveniles for committing hate crimes; and

(VI) the penalties imposed on such juveniles as a result of such proceedings; and

(iii) the characteristics of the victims of hate crimes
committed by juveniles, including—
   (I) the age, sex, race, ethnicity, locality of the vic
       tims and their familiarity with the offender;
       and
   (II) the motivation behind the attack.

Notes

Federal Bureau of Investigation. 1989, 1991, 1993. *Uniform Crime Reports.* Washington, DC: Federal Bureau of Investigation.

Thornberry, Terence P. 1994. "Risk Factors for Youth Violence." In *Kids and Violence,* ed. Linda McCart. Washington, DC: National Governors' Association.

Wintemute, Garen, et al. 1992. "Policy Options of Firearm Violence: An Exploration of Regulation, Litigation and Research on Firearm Violence." In *Improving the Health of the Poor: Strategies for Prevention,* ed. Sarah E. Samuels and Mark D. Smith. Menlo Park, CA: The Henry J. Kaiser Family Foundation.

Organizations 5

This chapter describes organizations, listed alphabetically, that work in a variety of ways with violent children. They may be research oriented, prevention oriented, or service oriented. These organizations represent the types of services offered by programs throughout the country, but are only a sampling of the many organizations now dealing with violent children.

Academy of Criminal Justice Specialists (ACJS)
Northern Kentucky University
402 Nunn Hall
Nunn Drive
Highland Heights, KY 41099-5998
(606) 572-5634
Fax: (606) 572-6665

ACJS is a membership organization in the field of criminal justice education, research, and policy analysis. Its main purpose is to promote scholarly and professional activities in the criminal justice field. It provides a forum where the critical issues in criminal justice education, research, and operations are analyzed and debated. Membership is international and multidisciplinary.

Publications: Justice Quarterly and Journal of Criminal Justice Education.

African-American Males Initiatives
W. K. Kellogg Foundation
1 Michigan Avenue East
Battle Creek, MI 49017-4058
(616) 968-1611

This program provides grants to organizations serving African-American men and boys and has established a national advisory task force to provide direction for the effort. Activities focus on the delivery of multilayered services to individuals and leadership development. The program helps grassroots organizations develop well-conceived projects that give African-American men and boys opportunities to make positive changes in their lives; create community systems that break barriers that cause young people to feel isolated and poised for failure; improve the leadership skills of community leaders who develop and operate the projects; and establish successful models that can be replicated locally and nationally. Approximately 15,000 youth and 400 adults are expected to be directly affected by the original 15 projects; most are aimed at young people between the ages of 16 and 18 years.

Alternatives to Gang Membership
City of Paramount
16400 Colorado Avenue
Paramount, CA 90723
(310) 220-2140
Fax: (310) 630-2713

This joint venture between the city of Paramount and the Paramount Unified School District attempts to eliminate the source of future gang membership by teaching children the harmful consequences of this lifestyle, to not participate in it, and how to choose positive alternatives. Their approach is based on their belief that interest in gangs begins at an early age and a successful anti-gang program must emphasize early identification of children at risk. Their goal is to reduce gang membership and its destructive actions within the community. The program has three components: an elementary school anti-gang curriculum, an intermediate school follow-up program, and neighborhood meetings. Lessons in the elementary school curriculum focus on peer pressure, graffiti, the impact of gang activity on family members, drug abuse, and alternative activities. The intermediate school follow-up program reviews the information presented in the elementary school curriculum and also emphasizes self-esteem, the consequences of gang activities and a criminal lifestyle, higher education, and career opportunities. Neighborhood meetings, conducted by city staff members, educate parents about gangs and the consequences of gang involvement and provide parents with information, encouragement, and assistance in preventing their children from joining gangs.

American Correctional Association (ACA)
8025 Laurel Lakes Court
Laurel, MD 20707-5100
(800) 825-2665
Fax: (301) 206-5061

ACA is a membership organization composed of correctional administrators, wardens, prison and parole board members, probation officers, psychologists, educators, sociologists, and other individuals and groups involved and interested in the field of corrections. It promotes improved standards, develops adequate facilities, offers correspondence courses, and studies causes of juvenile delinquency, crime control methods, and prevention options.

Publications: When Children Kill—The Dynamics of Juvenile Homicide, by Charles Patrick Ewing, uses case studies to examine juvenile killers, their crimes, and the reasons why they kill. *Girls, Delinquency, and Juvenile Justice,* by Meda Chesney-Lind and Randall G. Shelden, discusses the nature and extent of female delinquency and includes theories of female delinquency and crime.

American Humane Association (AHA)
Children's Division
63 Inverness Drive E
Englewood, CO 80112-5117
(303) 792-9900
Fax: (303) 792-5333

AHA was founded in 1877 and is the only national organization working to protect both children and animals from abuse, neglect, cruelty, and exploitation. Their Children's Division works to break the cycle of abuse through training, risk assessment, research, and policy development programs initiated to provide effective child protective systems. Through their child advocacy efforts, better laws and public policy have been created. They offer continuing education programs that set program standards and program evaluation methods that have improved the quality of care and services; they have sponsored national conferences and regional workshops, and offer a variety of publications.

Publications: Publications include *Report on the Summit on Violence Towards Children and Animals,* November 1–3, 1991, and *Protecting Children and Animals: Agenda for a Non-Violent Future.*

American Youth Work Center (AYWC)
1751 N Street, NW, Suite 302
Washington, DC 20036
(202) 785-0764
Fax: (202) 728-0657

This organization represents and supports community-based youth-service programs through training, seminars, conferences, and research. A calendar of events includes many national and local conferences on topics such as juvenile justice, safe schools, child advocacy, child welfare, drugs and youth, gangs, and violent children. This organization serves all youth workers, including social workers, child welfare workers, law enforcement personnel, educators, program personnel, and all other professionals working with youth today.

Publications: Youth Today, a bimonthly newspaper that provides the latest news in the field of child welfare, juvenile delinquency treatment, and other important issues facing youth today.

Americans for Responsible Media
600 W. Rand Road
Arlington Heights, IL 60004
(708) 632-0516
Fax: (708) 632-0616

This organization is a media watchdog group, challenging broadcasters to practice responsible television. It began when two Chicago businessmen were unhappy with the media coverage of the riots that occurred after the Chicago Bulls won the 1992 National Basketball Association championship. They filed petitions with the Federal Communications Commission asking that broadcast licenses for two local stations not be renewed because their coverage of these riots included negligent information that encouraged rioters.

Anacostia/Congress Heights Partnership
2301 Martin Luther King, Jr. Avenue, SE
Washington, DC 20020
(202) 889-2102
Fax: (202) 678-3866

This program is a community organization that focuses on community building in a Washington, D.C., neighborhood. It initially focused on Children's Centers in public housing developments and churches, encouraging youth recreation and tutoring programs, parenting classes, and support groups. Its purpose is to help the most vulnerable families become independent and self-sufficient while strengthening the environment where these families live. It sponsors community discussions on relevant topics including violence. The Come See About Me program was created as a result of a community dialogue on violence; senior citizens and young people meet to provide the young people with positive role models and to build their self-esteem. The group also leads workshops on violence prevention in schools.

Boston Conflict Resolution Program
Boston Educators for Social Responsibility
11 Garden Street
Cambridge, MA 02138
(617) 492-8820
Fax: (617) 864-5164

This program focuses on violence prevention for students in elementary and middle schools. Teachers are provided with three days of training in conflict resolution, violence prevention, multicultural education and diversity, cooperation, anger management, and communication skills. This training assists teachers in increasing their mediation and conflict resolution skills in working with their students.

The Bureau for At-Risk Youth (BARY)
645 New York Avenue
Huntington, NY 11743
(800) 999-6884
(516) 673-4584
Fax: (516) 673-4544

This program offers parenting resource booklets on a variety of topics, including *About Juvenile Violence and Its Prevention*, offering parents ways to raise strong but nonaggressive children, and presents ways to help children deal with anger, conflicts, and aggression. Posters, pins, coloring books, and activity books are also available. It also offers several violence prevention videos.

California Wellness Foundation
Violence Prevention Initiative
6320 Canoga Avenue, Suite 1700
Woodland Hills, CA 91367-7111
(818) 593-6600

This foundation was created as an independent, private organization to improve the health of California residents. They participate in the design, development, and evaluation of health-promotion and disease-prevention programs and help develop strategies to encourage individuals and communities to adopt healthy lifestyles. Through the Violence Prevention Initiative, the foundation hopes to develop and evaluate a comprehensive multidisciplinary approach to combating youth violence throughout California. This initiative has four components: a leadership program, a community action program, a policy program, and a research program. The leadership program's goal is to strengthen communities by recognizing and promoting the importance of leadership in preventing acts of violence. The community action program provides resources and technical assistance to various communities to reduce youth violence through community health promotion programs. The policy program is working toward reducing violent deaths and injuries through changes in public policy. The research program focuses on expanding current knowledge about causes and prevention of youth violence; it will examine the relationship between violence and alcohol and other drugs, firearms and gang involvement, socioeconomic factors, and public health conditions. A community action grants program provides resources and technical assistance to communities that want to reduce youth violence through pilot collaborative health promotion programs.

Carnegie Council on Adolescent Development (CAD)
2400 N Street, NW, 6th Floor
Washington, DC 20037-1153
(202) 429-7979
Fax: (202) 775-0134

The Carnegie Corporation of New York established CAD in June 1986 to place the challenges of the adolescent years higher on the nation's agenda. The council works to stimulate continuing public attention to the risks and opportunities of the adolescent years and generates public and private support for measures that facilitate the critical transition to adulthood.

Publications: A Matter of Time: Risk and Opportunity in the Nonschool Hours is the result of a study to examine community programs for youth. The study included an extensive literature review, focus-group discussions, interviews with youth development leaders, commissioned papers, and site visits. It focuses on the changing structure of American society and the failure of families, schools, and community organizations to adapt to new social realities.

Center for Early Adolescence (CEA)
D-2 Carr Mill Town Center
University of North Carolina at Chapel Hill
Carrboro, NC 27510
(919) 966-1148
Fax: (919) 966-7657

As part of the School of Medicine at the University of North Carolina at Chapel Hill, CEA was founded in 1978 to promote the healthy growth and development of young adolescents by advocating for young adolescents and providing information services, research, training, and leadership development for those who can have a positive impact on adolescents. The center provides presentations and publications on relevant topics. Programs run by the center include major initiatives in urban middle-grades reform, promotion of adolescent literacy, community collaborations for youth, and the preparation of middle-grade teachers.

Center for the Study and Prevention of Violence
Institute of Behavioral Science
University of Colorado
910 28th Street
Campus Box 442
Boulder, CO 80309-0442
(303) 492-1032
Fax: (303) 443-3297

Founded in 1992, the center's purpose is to provide information and assistance to groups and individuals studying the causes of violence and ways of preventing violence, especially youth violence.

The center's Information House gathers research literature relating to violence and offers bibliographic searches of its on-line data base on requested topics. Information is gathered on research, programs, curricula, videos, books and journal articles, and other sources about causes of violence and prevention strategies, and then included in the on-line data base. Abstracts are written and included in this data base. Reviews of literature include evaluating juvenile violence prevention, violence and the schools, the effects of the mass media on violence, the family and juvenile violence, gangs, guns and violence, and alcohol and drugs and their influence on juvenile violence. Technical assistance is provided to individuals and groups developing or evaluating programs on preventing violence. The center also has a research component, analyzing data and developing and conducting other projects in an effort to understand the causes of violence.

Child Welfare League of America (CWLA)
440 First Street, NW, Suite 310
Washington, DC 20001
(202) 638-2952
Fax: (202) 638-4004

CWLA focuses on improving care and services for abused, neglected, or dependent children and youth, and their families. The league provides consultation services, conducts research, maintains a library and information services, develops standards for child welfare practice, and administers special projects.

Publications: Child Welfare: Journal of Policy, Practice, and Program presents articles for child welfare professionals.

Children's Creative Response to Conflict (CCRC)
Box 271
523 North Broadway
Nyack, NY 10960
(914) 358-4601
Fax: (914) 358-4924

CCRC was established in 1972 by the New York Quaker Project on Community Conflict. Realizing that the beginnings of violence are often planted in children at an early age, CCRC helps adults and children develop new ways of looking at conflicts and helps them develop solutions. Workshops are offered to help students, parents, teachers, and concerned individuals develop skills in one or more of the program's central themes: cooperation, communication, affirmation, creative conflict resolution, mediation, and bias awareness. Programs can be tailored to individual needs.

Publications: The Friendly Classroom for a Small Planet describes the program and provides exercises and activities that teach children the skills vital to nonviolent conflict resolution. CCRC also publishes a newsletter, *Sharing Space*, which provides a support network for those who seek to develop an affirming, cooperative classroom atmosphere. Other publications and cassettes are also available.

Children's Defense Fund (CDF)

25 E Street NW
Washington, DC 20001
(202) 628-8787
(800) CDF-1200
Fax: (202) 662-3510

CDF was founded to provide a strong and effective voice for all children, educating the nation about the needs of children and encouraging the support of children before they become physically sick, drop out of school, or get into trouble. The Violence Prevention Project is CDF's most recent effort to provide a safe start for all children in America. The project focuses on federal legislation, public education, and community mobilization in order to begin to curb the cycle of violence plaguing our schools, families, and communities. CDF and the Black Community Crusade for Children, a CDF-coordinated effort to mobilize the black community, have organized the Anti-Violence Network. This network includes over 100 primarily community-based organizations dedicated to preventing violence. The network's purpose is to build a grassroots effort to influence and shape public policy in the field of violence prevention and to enhance the effectiveness of the member groups. CDF has also developed a violence component to its Child Watch Visitation Program, which provides a vivid demonstration to community leaders on the effects of violence on children.

Publications: Publications include a violence prevention resource list and bibliography; *Violence Prevention,* a brochure that provides basic information on gun violence; and the March 1994 edition of *CDF Reports,* which focuses on gun violence.

CityKids Foundation (CKF)
57 Leonard Street
New York, NY 10013
(212) 925-3320

CKF is a nonprofit youth organization that trains young people to be leaders through the belief that if young people are given an opportunity, responsibility, and challenge to work, they will respond with creativity and understanding. The young people they bring together are from diverse ethnic, socioeconomic, and racial backgrounds. Using discussion groups, workshops, and peer-to-peer counseling, they are encouraged to talk to each other about issues important to them. Through CityKids Repertory performances, visual arts, books, videos, and music videos, they create the tools needed to ensure their voices are heard wherever possible.

Publications: Whatcha Gonna Do about Hate? is an educational music video that encourages children to discuss hatred and develop action plans to eradicate it. A book describing CityKids' multicultural expertise will be available to schools through the educational distribution system of Simon & Schuster, 1230 Avenue of the Americas, New York, NY 10020.

Committee for Children (CFC)
172 20th Avenue
Seattle, WA 98122
(800) 634-4449; Fax: (206) 322-7133
Seattle area: (206) 322-5050

CFC is a nonprofit organization providing educational materials, original research, training, and community education for the prevention of child abuse and youth violence. They offer a client support line for people who are in the process of implementing their programs, a preview library, and research assistance, and publish a *Prevention Update* newsletter.
Publications: Second Step™, a curriculum that teaches students about interpersonal violence, problem solving, empathy, and managing anger.

Community Board Program
1540 Market Street, Suite 490
San Francisco, CA 94102
(415) 552-1250
Fax: (415) 626-0595

The Community Board Program, a nonprofit organization, offers mediation services to the San Francisco community and provides conflict resolution program development and training assistance to schools, juvenile correctional facilities, and other agencies throughout the country. They have developed conflict resolution curricula for elementary and secondary schools, have helped develop a peer mediation model for juvenile correctional facilities, and are currently using youth organizing strategies in combination with problem-solving processes to reduce youth violence. Their Conflict Resolution Resources for Schools and Youth trains students as conflict managers to help other students resolve disputes by identifying and expressing their concerns and helping them resolve conflicts themselves.

Community Youth Gang Services (CYGS)
144 S. Fetterly Avenue
Los Angeles, CA 90022
(213) 266-4264

The CYGS program is one of the largest non-law-enforcement anti-gang programs in the country. It integrates prevention, intervention, and community mobilization combined with support from various justice agencies, using an interactive, multifaceted program called Target Area Strategy (TAS). TAS is a dual recovery plan aimed at reclaiming physical locations controlled by gangs as well as the youth affected by gangs, and has six major components: crisis intervention, community mobilization, prevention, parent-teacher education, job development, and graffiti removal. One component of its prevention activities is the Career Paths Program, a 15-week course presented in elementary schools that teaches kids about the negative aspects of gangs and promotes positive alternatives. Its Star Parenting Program provides parents with the tools necessary to address the complexities of parenthood and gang prevention.

Contra Costa County Health Services Department
Prevention Program
75 Santa Barbara Road
Pleasant Hill, CA 94523
(510) 646-6511
Fax: (510) 646-6520

This prevention program was started in 1982 to address two beliefs of the Health Services Department: that most major causes of death can be prevented and that prevention requires a multidisciplinary approach that must include many segments of a community. It focuses on violence as a public health problem and advocates a multidisciplinary approach to solving the problem. The prevention program, along with many community agencies, joined together to form the Alternatives to Violence and Abuse Coalition, which raises awareness of the many problems associated with violence and works to help prevent violence. Ten agencies also joined together to form the PACT Violence Prevention Coalition that focuses on identifying causes of violence, exploring options for reducing violence, and advocating for solutions in local communities. The program encourages youth to participate in activities and to be violence prevention leaders, and offers direct services to youth and families, leadership training, presentations to local community groups, networking, mutual policy development, and a variety of youth activities.

Direction Sports
600 Wilshire Boulevard, Suite 320
Los Angeles, CA 90017
(213) 627-9861

Direction Sports is a nonprofit organization that serves the emotional, educational, and recreational needs of disadvantaged youth. It attacks the problems associated with poor education at their roots by changing attitudes and motivation and by using team sports as the enticement for involvement. Its primary interest has been the development and refinement of peer-run programs, believing that the more involved youth are in solving their problems, the more success they will have. The program mixes athletics with academics to arm city youth with self-esteem. Employing inner-city teenagers to work as coaches and teachers for area youths, the program gives them viable alternatives to the gang, drug, and cruising culture of the streets. It focuses on two areas: to design programs that support the educational system and to enhance youths' self-esteem.

Drug Strategies
2445 M Street, NW, Suite 480
Washington, DC 20037
(202) 663-6090
Fax: (202) 663-6110

Drug Strategies, a nonprofit organization, promotes more effective approaches to solving the nation's drug problems, including both public and private initiatives that reduce the demand for drugs through prevention, education, treatment, and law enforcement efforts. A primary mission of this organization is to seek out workable prevention and treatment program models, and to compile the data collected into a form useful to those who need information about such programs.

Education Development Center, Inc. (EDC)
Child Safety Network
Adolescent Violence Prevention Resource Center
55 Chapel Street
Newton, MA 02158-1060
(617) 969-7100
Fax: (617) 244-3436

Founded in 1992, EDC established this resource center with funding from the U.S. Department of Health and Human Services, Maternal and Child Health Bureau. Its primary goal is to improve the delivery of youth violence prevention services. It provides state offices of maternal and child health with information, resources, materials, and technical assistance to help them develop new youth violence prevention programs and improve current programs.

Publications: Options, a bimonthly newsletter, offers articles on current topics concerning youth violence prevention, news from state maternal and child health agencies, conferences, and other resources, and announcements related to youth violence.

Educators for Social Responsibility (ESR)
23 Garden Street
Cambridge, MA 02138
(617) 492-1764
(800) 370-2515 (for ordering materials)
Fax: (617) 864-5164

ESR is a national nonprofit organization dedicated to children's ethical and social development. They develop and disseminate new ways of teaching and learning that help young people participate in shaping a better world. They offer programs and products that present divergent viewpoints, stimulate critical thinking, teach creative and productive ways of dealing with differences, promote cooperative problem solving, and foster informed decision making. Summer institutes for educators include Conflict Resolution; Diversity and Violence Prevention;

Teaching for Social Responsibility; Appreciating Diversity, Countering Bias and Multicultural Education; and Classroom as Community.

Publications: Publications include *Helping Teens Stop Violence: A Practical Guide for Counselors, Educators, and Parents*, which empowers young people to resist abuse and prevent violence in their relationships, and educational guides for conflict resolution.

Family Resource Coalition (FRC)
200 S. Michigan Avenue, Suite 1520
Chicago, IL 60604
(312) 341-0900
Fax: (312) 341-9361

FRC is a nonprofit national membership organization dedicated to family support. Membership ranges from those working with families in local communities, to state officials concerned with how best to deliver services, to Capitol Hill public policy analysts, to academicians. They maintain a data base on family support programs. They provide technical assistance, parent education materials, training, and consulting services.

Focus on the Family (FOF)
420 N. Cascade Avenue
Colorado Springs, CO 80903
(719) 531-5181
(800) 232-6459
Fax: (719) 531-3424

The objective of FOF is to reconnect families with the ageless wisdom of Judeo-Christian values. They believe that only a return to time-honored, traditional principles of morality, fidelity, and commitment will save the family. They provide a variety of referral services, a daily radio program that offers practical advice and inspiration on topics such as parenting and spiritual and emotional growth, and work to encourage government, business, and the entertainment industry to adopt policies that help strengthen the family.

Publications: monthly periodicals such as *Clubhouse*, for children between the ages of 8 and 12, which provides puzzles, activities, and faith-building stories all based on biblical values. *Brio* (for girls) and *Breakaway* (for boys) are filled with features for teens 12 years and up; and *Youthwalk*, published jointly with *Walk Thru the Bible*, helps teens develop a strong faith.

Fortune Society (FS)
39 W. 19th Street, 7th Floor
New York, NY 10011
(212) 206-7070
Fax: (212) 366-6323

The primary purpose of FS is to reach out to the ex-offender (16 years of age and older) who is recently released from prison and on parole or work-release status. Their Alternatives to Incarceration (ATI) program does court advocacy work for youth in trouble with the law. Over half of the staff members are ex-offenders who have considerable insight into the issues of child abuse and child violence, through their own experiences as well as the experience of others they have known.

Heartsprings, Inc.
P.O. Box 12158
Tucson, AZ 85732
(602) 298-5579
Fax: (602) 298-7430

A nonprofit organization, Heartsprings combines materials for children, local publicity, and corporate participation in helping children develop a variety of nonviolent interpersonal skills to help resolve conflicts. Heartsprings believes that children should be supported through each stage of development in learning how to deal with hostility and aggression. They have developed a "Pathways to Resiliency Series on Violence Alternatives" that provides intervention at each critical stage of development. Their PeaceBuilders curriculum works with teachers, students, families, counselors, principals, businesses, other staff, community, media and culture, police, government, and health care organizations to help prevent violence among children; the skills taught encourage cooperation, achievement, and success as a way of life.

Injury Prevention and Control Program (IPCP)
Massachusetts Department of Public Health
150 Tremont Street, 3rd Floor
Boston, MA 02111
(617) 727-1246
(800) CAR-SAFE (outside Boston metropolitan area)
Fax: (617) 727-0880

Started as the Statewide Comprehensive Injury Prevention Program (SCIPP), this state health department program recently added violence prevention and emergency medical services for children. The program is based on the theory that injuries can be predicted and prevented. Using advocates from throughout the community, including medical professionals, community agency staff, educators, and others, IPCP works to reduce injuries through education, technology, and legislation. Its Adolescent Violence Prevention Project helps develop community-based coalitions in Boston and Lawrence, Massachusetts. The Office of Violence Prevention involves many state agency programs to help develop opportunities to reduce interpersonal violence and intentional injury. Its primary objectives include coordinating and strengthening existing violence prevention activities; promoting and supporting the development of comprehensive community-based violence prevention initiatives within cities and towns in Massachusetts; increasing the dissemination of information on violence prevention to the public, schools, public health professionals, health care providers and others; and increasing the capacity of the department and other state agencies to address violence and intentional injury through integration into existing programs and grant-writing activities. The Injury Prevention Resource Center operates a data base of over 5,000 relevant violence materials; services are available to both professionals and the general public.

Its "Words, Not Weapons" campaign is cosponsored by the Massachusetts Department of Public Health, the Massachusetts Department of Education, the Governor's Alliance Against Drugs, the Massachusetts Committee of Criminal Justice, and several community-based organizations. The campaign's primary goals are to encourage open and straightforward discussion among teenagers about violence and coping with fear; develop violence prevention programs for schools that require students completing the violence prevention program to pledge not to carry weapons and to encourage others not to carry weapons; assist teachers and staff in addressing issues of violence that may arise in school; and involve parents, community-based organizations, and the media in supporting violence prevention initiatives.

**C. Henry Kempe National Center for the Prevention
and Treatment of Child Abuse and Neglect**
University of Colorado Health Sciences Center
Department of Pediatrics
1205 Oneida Street
Denver, CO 80220-2944
(303) 321-3963
Fax: (303) 329-3523

The Kempe Center was begun in 1972 to provide a clinically based
resource for training, consultation, program development and education, and research in all forms of child abuse and neglect. The
center is committed to multidisciplinary approaches to improve
recognition, treatment, and prevention. Programs to help children
and their families include Therapeutic Preschool, the Family Evaluation Team, the Child Advocacy and Protection Team, the Community Caring Project, the Perpetration Prevention Project, the
National Child Abuse and Neglect Clinical Resource Center, and
the Prevention Research Center for Family and Child Health.

Publications: Child Abuse and Neglect: The International Journal en-
compasses all areas of child abuse and neglect.

MAD DADS
2221 N. 24th Street
Omaha, NE 68110
(402) 451-3500

MAD (Men Against Destruction) DADS (Defending Against
Drugs and Social Disorder) was founded in 1989 at the Omaha
Pilgrim Baptist Church by a group of men who were fed up with
the gang violence and the flow of illegal drugs in their community. They encourage all strong, drug-free fathers—regardless of
race, social, economic, education, or professional background—to
provide positive parental role models and, by example, to address
city-wide issues concerning youth and their families. They provide weekend street patrols in troubled areas, reporting crime,
drug sales, and other destructive activities to the proper authorities. They provide positive community activities for youth, chap-
erone community events, and provide street counseling for those
in need at any time, day or night.

A division of MOMS AND KIDS works with the MAD
DADS, with chapters in Houston; Denver; New York City; Balti-
more; Columbus, Ohio; Greenville, Mississippi; several cities in
Florida; Council Bluffs, Iowa; and Omaha and Lincoln, Nebraska.

Mediascope
12711 Ventura Boulevard, Suite 250
Studio City, CA 91604
(818) 508-2080
Fax: (818) 508-2088

Founded in 1992, Mediascope is a nonprofit organization promoting positive presentations of social issues in the media, including television, film, music, and video games. Through its Media and Violence Project, and in conjunction with the entertainment, scientific, educational, and public health communities, Mediascope explores ways to solve the complex issue of depicting violence in a responsible and balanced manner on the screen. Activities include informational forums such as workshops and seminars where the creative community has an opportunity to meet and confer with media researchers, social scientists, psychologists, child development specialists, and violence prevention practitioners.

Additionally, Mediascope produces and disseminates publications relevant to media violence; initiates original research; convenes and facilitates entertainment industry round-table discussions; provides story and script consultations; offers a clearinghouse for research information; and provides referral services to community and school-based programs where writers can observe and interact with young people, including high-risk youth.

Publications: Film and Television Ratings: An International Assessment. An ethics curriculum for film and television schools is in development.

**National Association for the Education
of Young Children (NAEYC)**
1509 16th Street, NW
Washington, DC 20036-1426
(800) 424-2460
In Washington: (202) 232-8777
Fax: (202) 328-1846

NAEYC is the nation's largest professional organization of early-childhood educators. Its members are committed to advocating actions that address two major goals: first, to lower the incidence of violence in all forms in children's lives by advocating for appropriate public policies and actions at the national level; and second, to improve the abilities of teachers to help children deal with violence, promote children's resilience, and help families by improving services offered by professionals in early-childhood programs.

Publications: Media Violence and Children: A Guide for Parents is a brochure that provides information about the effects of children's repeated viewing of television violence and offers guidelines for parents. The NAEYC has also issued a position statement on violence in the lives of children. Brochures, videos, and books are available concerning discipline; social, emotional, and moral development; peace and anti-violence; and advocacy.

National Association for Mediation in Education (NAME)
205 Hampshire House
University of Massachusetts
Amherst, MA 01002
(413) 545-2462
Fax: (413) 545-4802

NAME encourages the development and implementation of conflict resolution programs and curricula in schools and universities. It teaches students and teachers about diversity and how to appreciate and build skills to work together despite their differences. NAME operates a clearinghouse for information and distributes appropriate materials; provides a support network through a newsletter, annual conferences, and regional networking activities; provides technical assistance for school programs; promotes a multicultural perspective; supports theory and research activities; and provides leadership in developing guidelines for conflict resolution training.

Publications: Annotated Bibliography for Teaching Conflict Resolution in Schools, containing materials on school mediation programs and activities, and the *Violence Prevention Packet* (second edition), which provides information and resources on school violence.

National Association of Counsel for Children (NACC)
1205 Oneida Street
Denver, CO 80220
(303) 322-2260
Fax: (303) 329-3523

NACC is a nonprofit organization founded in 1977 to enhance the well-being of children by promoting excellence in the field of children's law. With a multidisciplinary approach, it works to improve the legal protection and representation of children. The association promotes education, support services, and training for attorneys, guardians, and other children's advocates; works to enhance the efficiency and knowledge of attorneys representing children by providing a forum for exchanging information regarding legal cases; advocates for improvements in juvenile law; and organizes and conducts seminars.

National Association of Police Athletic Leagues (PALs)
200 Castlewood Drive, Suite 400
North Palm Beach, FL 33408-5696
(407) 844-1823
Fax: (407) 863-6120

One of the largest juvenile crime prevention programs, with over 3 million members PALs provides a forum for sharing information, promotes national training seminars, develops fund-raising programs, initiates public awareness projects, develops regional and national tournaments, and publishes a national newspaper. It promotes competition in the advancement of sportsmanship and citizenship. Local chapters throughout the nation offer a variety of activities, including sports programs, arts and crafts, dance, music, drama, social services, vocational guidance, remedial reading, gardening, field trips, and other popular youth activities. The organization works with neighborhood youth who are bored, apathetic, lonely, and are dealing with the countless problems of living in the city. The long-term goal is to reach these youths before they become delinquent.

National Center on Child Abuse and Neglect
National Clearinghouse on Child Abuse
and Neglect Information (NCCAN)
U.S. Dept. of Health and Human Services
P.O. Box 1182
Washington, DC 20013
(703) 385-7565
(800) 394-3366
Fax: (703) 385-3206

NCCAN was established in 1974 by the Child Abuse Prevention and Treatment Act (P.L. 93-247) as the primary federal agency charged with helping states and communities address the problems of child maltreatment. NCCAN oversees all federal child abuse and neglect efforts and allocates child maltreatment funds appropriated by Congress. They are responsible for conducting research on the causes, prevention, and treatment of child abuse and neglect; collecting, analyzing, and disseminating information to professionals concerned with child abuse and neglect; increasing public awareness of the problems of child maltreatment; and assisting states and communities in developing programs related to the prevention, identification, and treatment of child abuse and neglect.

NCCAN operates a clearinghouse for information on all aspects of child maltreatment. They provide services and products in a variety of areas. Manuals, reports, directories, catalogs, literature reviews, annotated bibliographies, and fact sheets are available through the clearinghouse. For a fee, the clearinghouse information specialists provide custom searches of the child abuse and neglect data base.

Publications: Publications include an annotated bibliography, *Anti-Social Behavior Resulting from Abuse.*

National Clearinghouse on Satanic Crime in America
USCCCN International, Inc.
P.O. Box 1185–Nixon Station
Edison, NJ 08818-1185
(908) 549-2599
Fax: (908) 549-2599

This organization's primary purpose is to serve as an awareness, training, and investigative research organization for crimes and criminal activities that appear to be satanic, occult, ritualistic, or gang-related. It maintains a data base of persons, registered and unregistered groups, and destructive activities related to cult and occult involvement, as well as demographics of criminal acts and timely educational materials. It offers publications, videos, training seminars, and related efforts.

Publications: Don't Touch That Gun, VHS, Part I and Part II, which provides short vignettes that teach children not to touch a gun in any situation and to tell a parent or other adult.

National Committee to Prevent Child Abuse (NCPCA)
332 S. Michigan Avenue, Suite 1600
Chicago, IL 60604
(312) 663-3520

This organization is a volunteer-based organization dedicated to involving all concerned citizens in actions to prevent child abuse

in all its forms, including physical abuse, emotional maltreatment, neglect, and sexual abuse. Activities include prevention
programs, public awareness, education and training, research,
and advocacy.

National Council of Churches (NCC)
Committee on Justice for Children and Their Families
475 Riverside Drive, Room 848
New York, NY 10015-0050
(212) 870-2297
Fax: (212) 870-2030

This NCC committee is just beginning an exploration of how
they can best involve the churches in their organization in efforts
to end violence in the lives of children. They recognize that while
churches decry violence, many congregations, especially those in
middle-class communities, do not recognize how closely it affects
their own children. They have created an opportunity for children in the churches they represent (mostly white, mainstream
churches) to speak out themselves. A four-question survey,
"Voices on Violence," was circulated among children and youth
ages 8 to 18 in the summer and fall of 1994 to help gather information. The committee will use results from this survey as the
basis of an essay in a 1995 pamphlet, *Violence in the Lives of Our
Children and Youth: Challenge to Churches.*

National Council of Juvenile and
Family Court Judges (NCJFCJ)
P.O. Box 8970
Reno, NV 89507
(702) 784-6012
Fax: (702) 784-6628

NCJFCJ provides direction on juvenile and family law to the nation's juvenile and family jurists. It offers continuing education to
judges, referees, probation officers, social workers, law enforcement personnel, and other juvenile justice professionals. It stays
abreast of the changing areas of the law in such areas as child
abuse and neglect, crack babies, foster care, custody issues,
school violence, gangs, and serious juvenile crime. It offers programs addressing current topics in these areas.

National Crime Prevention Council (NCPC)
700 K Street, NW, 2nd Floor
Washington, DC 20006-3817
(202) 466-6272
Fax: (202) 296-1356

NCPC is a private, nonprofit organization with a major focus on enabling people to prevent crime and build safer, more caring communities. It manages a public-service advertising campaign, provides information and referral services and technical assistance, conducts training in crime prevention skills and techniques, and conducts demonstration programs and research to discover the most effective ways to prevent crime in local communities.

Its Youth as Resources project started as a demonstration project in three Indiana cities in 1987. It is a locally based program that provides small grants for youth to design and carry out projects to meet their community's needs, and is based on the premise that young people, given the opportunity, have the desire and ability to organize and act effectively to help solve some of society's most pressing problems.

National Institute for Violence Prevention (NIVP)
One Cleveland Park
Roxbury, MA 02119
(617) 427-0692

NIVP focuses on developing expertise in violence prevention strategies among health, education, and human service professionals. Their training associates train others—including teachers, youth, public health workers, medical professionals, criminal justice workers, and social service workers—in violence prevention and anger management. Trainees learn to see violence as a public health problem, develop prevention strategies, incorporate prevention strategies in their work, and train co-workers. They also provide consultation services and technical assistance in curriculum and materials development, cultural diversity, intervention strategies for high-risk youth, research, and translation services.

National Rifle Association
Eddie Eagle Gun Safety Program
Safety and Education Division
11250 Waples Mill Road
Fairfax, VA 22030
(800) 231-0752
Fax: (703) 267-3993

The National Rifle Association developed the Eddie Eagle Program, an accident prevention program for students in preschool through sixth grade, to help prevent the death of children. Its message to kids is that if you see a gun, stop, don't touch, leave the area, and tell an adult. The program is used by schools, law enforcement agencies, and other groups concerned with the safety of children.

New Mexico Center for Dispute Resolution (NMCDR)
620 Roma NW, Suite B
Albuquerque, NM 87102
(505) 247-0571
Fax: (505) 242-5966

Established in 1982 to provide mediation services for a wide range of disputes, develop and implement innovative applications of mediation, and provide mediation and conflict resolution training to other organizations and to individuals, NMCDR is a nonprofit organization. It is nationally known for its innovative conflict resolution programs for children, youth, and families. Programs include peer mediation in schools, parent/child mediation, victim/juvenile offender mediation, mediation in juvenile corrections and residential facilities, and violence prevention skills for juvenile offenders and their parents. NMCDR also sponsors national training institutes for professionals throughout the country on topics such as school mediation, parent/child mediation, and mediation and conflict resolution for gang-involved youth. It sponsors a Violence Intervention Program along with the Juvenile Probation and Parole Office in Bernalillo County, New Mexico. The program provides a cost-effective community option for juvenile offenders likely to be incarcerated for drug-related or violent offenses, promotes public safety by providing surveillance and risk control strategies for juvenile offenders, and improves the cognitive and social skills of juvenile offenders and their parents to enhance their ability to function effectively in interpersonal relationships.

Publications: Managing Conflict: A Curriculum for Adolescents, developed in collaboration with the Youth Diagnostic and

Development Center. This is a 15-lesson curriculum designed to teach communication, problem-solving, and anger management skills. The *Training and Implementation Guide for Student Mediation in Elementary Schools* prepares elementary-school staff to implement a school-wide mediation program. It also publishes a training guide for secondary-school staff. *Mediation and Conflict Resolution for Gang-Involved Youth* is designed as a training or resource manual for those working with gang-involved youth.

Omega Boys Club
One Hallidie Plaza, Suite 701
San Francisco, CA 94102
(415) 346-1183
Fax: (415) 346-2055
This organization is for youth and young adults between the ages of 11 and 25 years and is based on the premise that it takes an entire community to raise a child. The club believes in extended family, and that nonrelated adults and youth can come together and have an impact on the issues of drugs and violence. The club's academic program prepares and assists members who are interested in pursuing a college degree. They provide non-college-bound members with verbal, academic, keyboard, and computer literacy skills to successfully enter the job market and encourage and facilitate the development of entrepreneurial capabilities. Their Peer Counseling Program works with incarcerated youth to reduce recidivism: directors, volunteers, and peer counselors hold weekly meetings with youthful offenders and act as advocates.

Omega's violence prevention effort also reaches out to the community at large. Major components include a weekly radio call-in talk show, an annual youth conference where participants seek solutions to the violence in their communities, and Street Soldier training in which members are trained to conduct violence prevention work in other communities.

Peace Resource Center
Wilmington College
Pyle Center, Box 1183
Wilmington, OH 45177
(513) 382-5338

The Peace Resource Center's primary mission is to provide resources produced by others, including conflict resolution materials, for use in schools, churches, and families. They offer a variety of materials on children and how violence impacts their lives.

Publications: Publications include *Alternatives to Violence: A Manual for Teaching Peacemaking to Youth and Adults* and *Conflict Management: A Middle School Curriculum.*

Prince William County Community Services Board
8033 Ashton Avenue, Suite 107
Manassas, VA 22110
(703) 792-7730
Fax: (703) 792-7704

The Community Services Board cosponsors and is the contact for the Turn Off the Violence campaign, which is directed toward increasing the public's awareness of violence prevention. It encourages everyone to "turn off" violent television, movies, and music and begin to choose nonviolent entertainment and nonviolent ways to reduce conflict. This campaign is a coalition of more than ten different organizations and individuals working together in a campaign to raise awareness about violence and the ways in which communities can reduce violence. The campaign identified two problem areas it wants to address: the media's negative influence on attitudes concerning the acceptability of violence, and the lack of information available to young people about positive ways to resolve conflict. People are asked to turn off violence in all its forms, including physical, sexual, domestic, verbal, family, gang, and playground violence; hate crimes; and violence in music. The campaign provides a list of positive, safe, legal, and enjoyable alternatives to violence; distributes educational materials to educators, law enforcement personnel, and youth group leaders; solicits sponsors; produces public awareness materials; operates a speakers bureau; and uses volunteers for many activities.

Program for Young Negotiators
The Consensus Building Institute, Inc.
31 Mount Auburn Street
Cambridge, MA 02138
(617) 492-1414
Fax: (617) 492-1919

This program works with educators to reduce violence among students, reduce the number of students dropping out of school, and reduce racial tensions. It teaches students to deal effectively with violence without resorting to violence themselves. The program teaches students and teachers to negotiate more effectively.

It also creates experiential teaching materials, conducts negotiation workshops, and develops specialized training programs for
schools and communities.

Resolving Conflict Creatively Program (RCCP)
Educators for Social Responsibility
163 Third Avenue, Suite 103
New York, NY 10003
(212) 387-0025
Fax: (212) 387-0510

Begun as a joint venture of the New York City Public Schools and
Educators for Social Responsibility, the RCCP is a school-based
program in conflict resolution and intergroup relations that provides a model for preventing violence and creating caring, learning communities. The program shows young people that they
have many options besides passivity or aggression in dealing
with conflict, gives them skills to make these choices, increases
their understanding and appreciation of all cultures, and shows
them that they can play a powerful role in creating a more peaceful world. In 1994, the RCCP will provide services to 4,000 teachers and 120,000 children in 250 schools nationwide.

Stand Against Violence Everywhere (SAVE)
590 E. Lockwood Avenue
St. Louis, MO 63119-3279
(314) 962-8112

The SAVE program promotes violence-free zones in schools.
Essentially, people sign a pledge to create a violence-free zone
and display a poster that declares the area a "violence-free zone."
The pledge can be displayed at school, home, or work. The
pledge emphasizes committing no violence against people, reforming any group condoning or advocating violence, encouraging peace among nations, respecting and loving the Earth and all
its creatures, speaking out against the glorification of violence in
the media and our culture, protecting victims of violence, and encouraging a commitment to nonviolent resolutions of conflict.

Toughlove International
P.O. Box 1069
Doylestown, PA 18901
(800) 333-1069

Toughlove is a crisis intervention, self-help program for families who have an out-of-control family member, often a child. It provides self-help materials to parents, children who are in trouble, and professionals involved in helping these children and families. Support groups exist throughout the United States (over 500 at this printing). A network of trained representatives serve as speakers and trainers and work with parents to help stubborn, rebellious, and abusive kids. The program emphasizes cooperation, personal initiative, avoidance of blame, and action.

Publications: Toughlove Kids Program is a structured curriculum for bringing about positive behavior change, which can be facilitated by professionals who have experience in working with out-of-control children. A self-help program is also available on audiocassette. Videotapes describing the program are available.

Violence Prevention Education Program (VPEP)
Bowie State University
MLK Building, Room 0216
Bowie, MD 20715-9465
(301) 464-7707
Fax: (301) 464-7706

VPEP is a unique community violence prevention education project implemented by Bowie State University and the W.K. Kellogg Foundation in cooperation with the Prince George's County Public Schools and the town of Glenarden, Maryland. Materials developed include a *Training and Curriculum Guide*, which provides educational activities aimed at violence prevention for children/teenagers from kindergarten through twelfth grade. These materials are culturally relevant to African-American children, but all at-risk children can benefit from these activities. Four modules are included: the parent-education module, the school-based education module, the church-based education module, and the community-based education module. Eight other states and three countries have also implemented the VPEP curriculum.

Violence Prevention Project
Department of Health and Hospitals
1010 Massachusetts Avenue, 2nd Floor
Boston, MA 02118
(617) 534-5196; Fax: (617) 534-5358

This project is a community-based primary and secondary prevention program focusing on the prevention of violence among young people. Their goals include preventing violent behavior among adolescents and the resulting medical and social hazards, providing support services for youth exhibiting violent behavior, identifying risk factors, educating the public about prevention, fostering community coalition building, advocating for stricter gun laws, and recruiting teenagers to help with outreach and training.

War Resisters League (WRL)
39 Lafayette Street
New York City, NY 10012-9911
(212) 228-0450; Fax: (212) 228-6193

WRL was founded in 1923 by opponents of the First World War. They reject the use of violence for national defense or for revolutionary change. Their philosophy is influenced by Gandhi, Thoreau, Tolstoy, Martin Luther King, Barbara Deming, and others, and like them believe that war is a crime against humanity. Their work focuses on education and action. A major component of their work is community organizing—helping people to organize in their own communities because they believe real change begins at the local, individual level.

Publications: No More War Toys is a one-hour video of a live cable call-in show first broadcast in November 1991. The show discusses the impacts of toys that encourage violence and stereotyping in our children and society and what we can do about them. *A Manual on Nonviolence and Children* contains over 100 exercises, games, and agendas designed to help children understand the value of cooperation and interdependence.

Wholistic Stress Control Institute Violence Prevention Program
3480 Greenbriar Parkway, Suite 310-B
P.O. Box 42841
Atlanta, GA 30331
(404) 344-2021

The Wholistic Stress Control Institute is a nonprofit organization that uses training programs, consulting services, and educational resources to help people develop their own resources to cope with the stress in their lives. Their "A Brother Is a Terrible Thing To Waste" violence prevention program teaches ways to prevent violence among young people through a comprehensive interactive education program using lectures, films, group discussions, and various role-playing and other exercises. The program has three components: one for teachers, administrators, and youth workers; a second for parents, guardians, and significant others; and a third for children and youth.

Women-In-Action for the Prevention of Violence and Its Causes, Inc.
112 North Queen Street
Box F
Durham, NC 27701-3715
(919) 862-1431

Women-In-Action is a multicultural organization dedicated to the prevention of all violence and its causes. Its purpose is to enhance human relations and improve the human condition by working with other community organizations to prevent the conditions that lead to violence. It is one of many agencies working with the local School Violence Task Force to introduce a conflict resolution curriculum in all grades in their schools. It is also a part of the Violence Prevention Network, a networking group of approximately 30 agencies and individuals trying to address violence in their community. Involved with the City/County Crime Prevention Task Force, they are working to get an ordinance passed banning possession of handguns and semi-automatic weapons in public places. Services they provide include support and referral services for families in crisis, life-skills seminars and workshops, and supervised activity and play areas for children of their clients.

Yale Child Study Center
Child Development and Community Policing Program
230 S. Frontage Road
P.O. Box 207900
New Haven, CT 06520-7900
(203) 785-3377
Fax: (203) 785-7611

In collaboration with the New Haven Department of Police Services, the Yale Child Study Center has developed the Child

Development and Community Policing Program. Its purpose is to facilitate the responses of police agencies and mental health professionals to lessen the impact of violence on individual children, families, and the community. The program teaches police officers how to interact with children in ways that will provide the children with a sense of security, positive role models, and positive authority. Three major components of the program include training all police recruits in the basic principles of child development, providing clinical fellowships for police field supervisors, and operating 24-hour consulting services for officers responding to incidents of violence in which children are involved.

Youth ALIVE
3012 Summit Avenue, Suite 3670
Summit Medical Center
Oakland, CA 94609
(510) 450-6225
Fax: (510) 450-6271

The mission of Youth ALIVE is to reduce violent deaths and injuries to youth, particularly firearm homicides and suicides. It emphasizes three areas to prevent the epidemic of youth violence: (1) it documents the health impact of violence at the state and local level; (2) it educates professionals, policy makers, and the media about violence and advocates for prevention strategies; and (3) it involves urban youth—those most at risk of dying—in seeking solutions. Youth ALIVE addresses violence as a public health issue in urban communities, working to keep young people alive while the root conditions of the disease of violence (social, racial, and economic disparities) are moved up on the nation's agenda. Youth ALIVE has initiated model teen violence prevention efforts in Oakland and Los Angeles. In Oakland, Teens on Target (TNT) is the first youth violence prevention advocacy program in the United States.

The work of Youth ALIVE is built on four principles: youth violence prevention must be multidisciplinary; build constituencies; mobilize those most at risk, their families, and communities; and capture media attention.

Youth Change
275 N. Third Street
Woodburn, OR 97071-4705
(800) 545-5736
(503) 982-7910

This program develops and runs workshops on troubled youth, provides consultation services, and publishes intervention lesson books on strategies to teach and counsel youth for teachers, counselors, justice personnel, and other youth workers. Workshop topics include "Powerful Techniques To Help Youth and Children Succeed," and "Breakthrough Strategies To Teach and Counsel Troubled Youth," a series of workshops that provide social, coping, and school skills and intervention to help at-risk youth. These topics include turning on the turned-off student, temper and tantrum tamers, a coping-skills sampler, learning to like the kid in the mirror, and a child's guide to surviving in a troubled family.

Publications: Temper and Tantrum Tamers, which provides 20 lesson plans on topics such as "Outside Anger That Comes to School" and "Spot Aggression Before It (or You) Strikes."

Selected Print Resources

6

Books

Juvenile and General Violence

Baker, Falcon. *Saving Our Kids from Delinquency, Drugs, and Despair.* New York: Cornelia and Michael Bessie Books, 1991. 348 pp. Notes, index. ISBN 0-06-39115-4.

Falcon Baker has over 20 years of experience in juvenile justice. He views the juvenile justice system as an outdated relic that has failed the population it was originally set up to help; he argues that the current system creates criminals rather than rehabilitating them. Proposed solutions to some of these problems are offered, including restructuring the welfare system and the public school system, early intervention, and "workfare." He suggests radically altering the juvenile justice system, with an emphasis on punishment instead of rehabilitation. A dual system of responsibility is recommended—one that forces the juvenile to assume responsibility for his actions, and one that asks society to accept responsibility for creating the conditions that lead to delinquency. Baker recommends intervening at an early age, restructuring schools, providing shelters for "throwaways" and runaways, and creating jobs, and suggests ways to win the war on drugs and put justice back in the juvenile justice system.

Carlsson-Paige, Nancy, and Diane E. Levin. *Who's Calling the Shots? How To Respond to Children's Fascination with War Play and War Toys.* Santa Cruz, CA: New Society Publishers, 1990. 188 pp. Index. ISBN 0-86571-164-X.

To help parents understand the attraction of war toys and war play to children and to discover specific ways to counteract the negative aspects and foster healthy development, Carlsson-Paige and Levin suggest practical ways for parents to create positive play experiences for their children. They discuss the importance of children's play—how children use it to work on issues important to them and to make sense of experiences they have. They believe that parents should not try to eliminate war play, in part because children need to feel they are in control of what they play and because it helps them work through all the violence to which they are exposed. Until American society changes the emphasis it places on violence, this book will help parents understand their children's interest in war play and gain some control over their children's involvement in war play.

Ewing, Charles Patrick. *When Children Kill: The Dynamics of Juvenile Homicide.* Lexington, MA: Lexington Books, 1990. 173 pp. Notes, index. ISBN 0-669-21883-9.

Charles Patrick Ewing, a clinical and forensic psychologist and attorney, studies juveniles who kill their parents or siblings, who kill while committing other crimes, gang killings, girls who kill, children under ten years of age who kill, thrill killings, cult-related killings, and murders committed by disturbed children. He estimates that in the United States each year between 1,000 and 1,500 juveniles are arrested and charged with murder or manslaughter. Legal and scientific studies are reviewed.

While society reacts with horror at all the stories in the news about children committing murder, the debate over how to handle these children (as children or adults) continues, and society's idealized concept of childhood is challenged. Ewing examines the legal system's provisions for dealing with juvenile murderers—all U.S. jurisdictions provide for prosecuting juveniles as adults under certain circumstances. Finally, he looks at the ways to reduce juvenile crime.

Greven, Philipp. *Spare the Child: The Religious Roots of Punishment and the Psychological Impact of Physical Abuse.* New York: Alfred A. Knopf, 1990. 263 pp. Notes, index. ISBN 0-394-57860-0.

Greven, a history professor, examines the history of physical punishment of children in America from both religious and secular perspectives. He looks at the physical, emotional, and psychological consequences of physical punishment and the effect of this punishment on American culture and behavior. Greven's purpose in writing this book is to help us understand some of the subtle ways a child's mind copes with the anxieties, fears, and suffering resulting from physical punishment. He shows how punishment shapes our attitudes toward authorities of all kinds. He demonstrates that physical punishment of children has resulted in our increasingly violent society (which has the highest rates of crime and murder in the Western world), our focus on defense and warfare, and the many individual maladies we suffer: anger, depression, paranoia, and family violence. He persuasively argues against physical punishment of children, urging nonviolent methods instead.

Kramer, Rita. *At Tender Age: Violent Youth and Juvenile Justice.* New York: Henry Holt and Company, 1988. 309 pp. Bibliography, index. ISBN 0-8050-0419-X.

Rita Kramer, given unprecedented access to New York City's juvenile justice system, provides us with an inside view of what juveniles encounter when they enter the juvenile justice system. She describes a system set up to deal with children who steal hubcaps and skip school, not with those who beat up the elderly, murder a playmate, or rape a neighbor. She travels from police interrogations to court hearings to probation offices to correctional facilities, relating incidents about what she sees happening to the children involved—children who are dealt with by virtue of their age, not by the seriousness of their crime.

Kramer explores the social, psychological, and political issues raised by the cases she has studied and challenges the reasons for creating the juvenile justice system. She describes a system designed to protect the child instead of the community, that emphasizes rehabilitation but provides few resources to rehabilitate, that ensures the child's rights but requires little acceptance of responsibility on the part of the child, and a process that takes so long the child does not see a connection between the crime committed and the punishment assigned.

Kvaraceus, William C. *Anxious Youth: Dynamics of Delinquency.* Columbus, OH: Charles E. Merrill Books, Inc. 1966. 247 pp. Bibliography, index. LC Catalog Number 66-14403.

This book focuses on adolescents, their anxieties and worries about growing up, and how these concerns can lead to delinquent, sometimes criminal, behavior. Kvaraceus discusses seven cultural and social factors that influence the appearance of delinquent behavior. He discusses the difference between a prank and delinquency, the psychodynamics of delinquency, means for early identification and treatment, the role of the schools in contributing to or preventing delinquency, police and community resources, and the prevention of delinquency in other countries. Hopefully, the attention that delinquency and violent behavior have received recently will help society find some answers to preventing delinquency, because children growing up today are under even more pressure and are more anxious than any earlier generation.

Magid, Ken, and Carole A. McKelvey. *High Risk: Children without a Conscience.* New York: Bantam Books, 1987. 361 pp. ISBN 0-553-34667-9.

Magid and McKelvey wrote this book for a large audience, demonstrating how babies, parenting, genetics, and crime are all intimately related. The authors believe that one of the primary reasons children become criminals having no conscience is improper bonding between the mother and the child. These children become psychopaths; they suffer from what the authors refer to as an antisocial personality disorder. Some of the causes for this improper bonding include working mothers, divorce, problems with day care, teenage pregnancies, foster care, parental absence during critical periods, infant medical problems, and child abuse and neglect. They review the literature pertaining to mother-infant bonding—how it works, warning signs that bonding is not occurring, and research into many of the causes mentioned above. Recommendations are made to solve this problem.

May, Rollo. *Power and Innocence: A Search for the Sources of Violence.* New York: W. W. Norton, 1972. 283 pp. Notes, index. ISBN 0-393-01065-1.

As a psychotherapist, Rollo May drew upon his years of experience in writing this book about impotence, violence, innocence, and power, and how we control our natural tendencies toward violence. He believes that the condition of being powerless leads to apathy, which leads to violence; he believes that many people who commit violent acts do so because they have low self-esteem, lack a positive self-image, and are trying to prove to others that they are important and significant. He believes that there are five levels of power: power to be, self-affirmation, self-assertion, aggression, and violence. How a person sees himself as an individual as well as how he sees himself in relation to the rest of the world plays a strong role in becoming violent or acting violently. May examines various types of violence and provides historical examples. He discusses ways in which society can become a less violent, more empathetic community.

Miedzian, Myriam. *Boys Will Be Boys: Breaking the Link between Masculinity and Violence.* New York: Doubleday, 1991. 337 pp. Bibliography. ISBN 0-385-23932-7.

Miedzian, with a doctorate in philosophy and a master's degree in clinical social work, applies her knowledge and analytical abilities to a study of the relationship between violence and the American male mystique. Drawing on research in psychology, sociology, sociobiology, and anthropology, Miedzian examines theories about why boys and men become violent. Her review of the research of the factors contributing to violence includes heredity, family environment, child-rearing practices, acculturation, and mass marketing. She looks at popular culture—the influences of television, movies, music, sports, and war toys—attempting to discover ways to reduce the violence in American society. Family environment and child-rearing play a crucial role in producing violent children, according to many experts, and Miedzian clearly explains why girls do not become as violent as boys. Believing that many men have the potential to be violent, she strongly recommends that society take steps to discourage violence and encourage the development of empathy and other moral and personal characteristics to reduce the incidence of violence. Providing specific recommendations for curbing violence, she describes some successful programs in home and school environments and offers innovative and workable solutions to this challenging social problem.

Mones, Paul. *When a Child Kills: Abused Children Who Kill Their Parents.* New York: Pocket Books, 1991. 361 pp. ISBN 0-671-67421-8.

Paul Mones is an attorney and children's rights advocate who defends abused children who are accused of killing their parents. He tells the stories of eight of those children in this book. He reviews the literature on child abuse, showing how these cases confront society with the contradictions and confusion about our ideas of the roles of parents and children and our attitudes toward family violence. These stories show us how the legal system deals with these cases and what happens to other friends and family members involved. Mones examines the ways in which the legal system is designed to protect abused children and how, in many cases, it fails to protect not only the children but ultimately the parents and other family members. Child abuse and other forms of family violence take a devastating toll on families and on society, and Mones provides an inside look at what happens to some of these families.

Montagu, Ashley. *The Nature of Human Aggression.* New York: Oxford University Press, 1976. 381 pp. References, index. ISBN 0-19-501822-2.

Montagu reviews the research suggesting that human beings are genetically aggressive and proposes another option: that the type of behavior a person exhibits is not due to his genes but to his life experiences and his reactions to these experiences "in interaction with those genes." He reviews the work of Konrad Lorenz, Robert Ardrey, Desmond Morris, Anthony Storr, Sigmund Freud, Charles Darwin, Erich Fromm, Sheldon and Eleanor Glueck, and others prominent in this field. He reviews the research on instinct and adaptation, cannibalism and aggression, the use of tools and weapons, cooperation, the brain and aggression, territoriality, war and violence, and the social and political consequences of believing in innate aggression. He argues that genes may interact negatively with the social environment and lead to aggressive, often violent behavior; that no one is born with aggressive, violent impulses; and that explanations for aggression and violent behavior are more complicated than many experts believe. Montagu believes that no child who is adequately loved becomes aggressive or violent; therefore, "aggression is often a signal, even at its most violent, of the need for love."

Nagler, Michael N. *America without Violence: Why Violence Persists and How You Can Stop It.* Covelo, CA: Island Press, 1982. 188 pp. Index. ISBN-0-933280-14-9.

Michael Nagler has long been involved in peace studies and is a cofounder of a center for nonviolent priorities. He asserts that most solutions to violence considered by society today are what he calls "downstream" solutions—when the bridge goes out upstream, we look for ways to fish bodies out of the river instead of going upstream to fix the bridge. We promote stiffer jail sentences, locking doors and windows, and increasing police coverage—all of which attempt to reduce violence after it has occurred instead of getting to the causes of violence and stopping it before it occurs. Nagler sees violence primarily as a disorder of human relationships, a gradual loss of respect for human life, and a feeling of alienation; the only way to reduce it is to reduce the alienation that causes it. He reviews the literature on television, movies, and sports and their contribution to youth violence. He believes television provides a strong influence on how and what children learn; it leads them to develop moral and social values that conflict with the standards of a civilized society. Going back into history, to Gandhi, Martin Luther King, and others who promoted nonviolence, he demonstrates the power of nonviolence. He provides guidelines on how families can reclaim their moral and social values and work together cooperatively in order to survive.

Peck, M. Scott. *People of the Lie: The Hope for Healing Human Evil.* New York: Simon & Schuster, 1983. 269 pp. ISBN 0-671-52816-5.

M. Scott Peck is recognized for his writings on the relationship between religion and psychology. In this book, he considers people who are evil to have a disease; it is a mental illness that should be examined just like any other mental illness. He believes that they are not crazy or demented. Instead, they project their pain onto other people, making them scapegoats. Peck argues that evil people are focused on protecting their image of themselves as perfect, always wanting to appear morally upright; they do not care about being good, they are only concerned about appearing good. This is their "lie." He discusses the psychological aspects of evil, evil in everyday life, group evil, the dangers of evil, and hope for dealing with evil through love.

Prothrow-Stith, Deborah, with Michaele Weissman. *Deadly Consequences: How Violence Is Destroying Our Teenage Population and a Plan To Begin Solving the Problem.* New York: HarperCollins, 1991. 228 pp. Index. ISBN 0-06-016344-5.

Prothrow-Stith is a physician, a former public health commissioner of Massachusetts, and a top administrator at the Harvard School of Public Health, where she has focused on developing a violence prevention curriculum for schools. Her primary theory in this book is that teenage violence is a public health problem as well as a problem for the criminal justice system. She looks particularly at adolescent violence in disadvantaged neighborhoods. In the first part of the book, she examines the causes of violence, primarily among poor, young black males, the group at highest risk for violence. She examines social, psychological, racial, cultural, and economic factors that may contribute to youth violence. Describing research she conducted at a Boston high school, she uses quotes from the students to vividly illustrate the fears, insecurities, and other emotions they experience growing up in a violent environment.

In the second part of the book, she describes ways to reduce the incidence of violence among our nation's adolescents. She details several anti-violence programs currently being offered, including her own curriculum that she began developing as a student at Harvard Medical School. Her senior project was to create a public-health intervention curriculum to help curb adolescent violence; she incorporated materials from three disciplines: criminal justice, mental health, and the biological sciences. In an appendix, she lists, by state, anti-violence and parenting programs aimed at reducing teen violence.

Reaves, John, and James B. Austin. *How To Find Help for a Troubled Kid: A Parent's Guide to Programs and Services for Adolescents.* New York: Henry Holt and Company, 1990. 376 pp. Index. ISBN 0-8050-0885-3.

This book is written for parents who are having trouble with their children and do not know where to turn for help. Reaves and Austin guide the reader through the types of available programs and services, including tutoring, alternative schools, self-help groups, boarding schools, group homes, residential treatment centers, and other alternatives to hospitalization or incarceration. The authors' purpose is to help parents learn about the range of programs and services available to them, before their children find themselves in serious trouble.

Richards, Pamela, Richard A. Berk, and Brenda Forster. *Crime as Play: Delinquency in a Middle Class Suburb.* Cambridge, MA:

Ballinger Publishing Company, 1979. 280 pp. Bibliography, index. ISBN 0-88410-798-1.

This book examines delinquency from the self-reports of middle-class adolescents. The authors began studying common assumptions about juvenile delinquency after they found that the data they had collected did not fit other theories of juvenile delinquency. The authors review the many different theories that currently exist on delinquency in general and middle-class delinquency in particular, including class theories, subcultural theories, and socialization theories. The boredom of an affluent lifestyle is the focus of most theories on middle-class delinquency. The authors present information about their study samples and data: vandalism as a leisure activity, drug use, minor theft and leisure, the leisure context of serious delinquency, and decision making.

Samenow, Stanton E. *Before It's Too Late: Why Some Kids Get into Trouble—and What Parents Can Do about It.* New York: Times Books, 1989. 225 pp. Index, notes. ISBN 0-8129-1646-8.

A clinical psychologist in private practice, coauthor with Dr. Samuel Tochelson of the three-volume *The Criminal Personality*, and author of several books, including *Inside the Criminal Mind*, Dr. Samenow spent years evaluating and counseling juvenile and adult offenders. In this book, he provides instructive insights for approaches parents can take in dealing with their antisocial, problem child. His "central premise is that children become antisocial by choice: lying, fighting, stealing, and other forms of destructive behavior are willful acts." While the environment certainly can play a role, he believes that children make choices as they respond to their environment. Parents are responsible for teaching their children right from wrong and instilling moral and ethical principles and positive values, but children choose to accept or reject these teachings.

Dr. Samenow presents information to help parents recognize signs of developing antisocial behavior patterns in their children—ways of thinking by both parents and children that can lead to antisocial behavior—and recommends ways that parents can help teach their children how to make responsible choices. He identifies seven common indications of antisocial behavior, maintains that the tendency to blame the environment is wrong, and believes that antisocial children know the difference between right and wrong, but choose to believe that the rules don't apply to them. While the decision to act responsibly lies with the child,

Dr. Samenow shows parents how they can help their children learn to make the right choices.

Schwartz, Meg, editor. ***TV & Teens: Experts Look at the Issues.*** Reading, MA: Addison-Wesley Publishing Company, 1982. 224 pp. Index. ISBN 0-201-10295-1.

Action for Children's Television (ACT) was a group formed in 1968 by a group of Boston mothers concerned about the role of television in their children's lives, especially the violence and the commercials. ACT went to educators, researchers, psychologists, medical and health practitioners, and producers of teenage programming for answers to their many questions about adolescents in society. The result is this book, edited by Meg Schwartz, which provides comprehensive research on adolescents' needs, describes what teenagers are learning from television, and provides some creative programming ideas to best meet the needs of teenagers. Chapters address young adolescents, what they focus on and what stresses they feel; the influence of television sports and television news; cable television shows; television programs developed by teenagers for teenagers; the changing roles of males and females; teenagers and the elderly; minority teens and minority role models; working and career choices; sex, sexuality, and pregnancy; alcohol and drug use and abuse; suicide and depression; advertising; and juvenile crime.

Stanton, Marietta. ***Our Children Are Dying: Recognizing the Dangers and Knowing What To Do.*** Buffalo, NY: Prometheus Books, 1990. 217 pp. Bibliography. ISBN 0-87975-609-8.

Children's deaths are caused by many things, including accidents, illnesses, child abuse, drug use, violence, and suicide. Stanton presents a comprehensive overview of the ways and reasons why children die. Her purpose is to explain these causes and help prevent future deaths, through individual efforts and community-based programs. When examining children's deaths by homicide, Stanton looks to our violent society as part of the cause, including factors such as child abuse and battered wives. She also believes low self-esteem pushes some children into committing dangerous pranks in order to gain approval from friends and peers. Often, children join gangs for the family feeling and atmosphere they can provide. She discusses current research and lists resources that are available to parents and other concerned individuals who want to help reduce the incidence of juvenile deaths.

Wilson, James Q., and Richard J. Herrnstein. *Crime and Human Nature.* New York: Simon & Schuster, 1985. 639 pp. Bibliography. ISBN 0-671-54130-7.

This book is a result of a classroom course Wilson and Herrnstein taught on the causes of crime. It provides a thorough analysis of crime and its sources. After reviewing many common theories that attempt to explain criminal behavior, they propose that each of these theories is a specific part of a more general theory. This general theory, according to the authors, assumes that there are rewards for both committing a criminal act and for not committing a criminal act. They theorize that a person is more likely to commit a crime when the reward for committing it is greater than the reward for not committing it. This assumes that whatever people choose to do, they choose it because they prefer it. Wilson and Herrnstein believe that such things as race, gender, family background, education, the availability of drugs, and the influence of television are factors that come into play when a person is confronted with a decision to commit or not commit a crime. However, they believe that most people will choose the criminal or noncriminal response depending on whether or not the reward is greater for committing or not committing the crime. They provide a comprehensive review of the literature on constitutional factors (gender, age, intelligence, personality), developmental factors (families, schools), social context (community, labor markets, television, alcohol, and heroin), and history and culture (historical trends, crime across cultures, race and crime). Their book is an excellent overview of criminal theory.

Winn, Marie. *Children without Childhood.* New York: Pantheon Books, 1981. 224 pp. Notes, index. ISBN 0-394-51136-0.

Like many other people, Marie Winn has seen a change in the behavior, language, and demeanor of American children since the 1960s, as well as a change in society's attitude toward children. Today's parents are profoundly aware that their children are exposed to, and may get involved in, a variety of dangerous, illegal, or unsuitable activities, and that they, as parents, cannot do much to keep their children from doing whatever they want. The pervasive influence of television on teenagers, the effects of peer pressure, the lack of parental supervision, and other factors have led to children growing up too fast and parents losing control over many aspects of their children's lives. Citing specific examples based on hundreds of interviews with both parents and children, Winn examines the shrinking boundaries between childhood and adulthood, the resulting decline in children's respect for parental authority and adults in general, and the once-forbidden areas that children are now allowed to explore.

————. *The Plug-in Drug: Television, Children, and the Family.* New York: Viking, 1985. 288 pp. Notes, index. ISBN 0-670-80378-2.

Marie Winn believes that we have focused too much attention on the content of television programs, especially violence in programs, instead of what she believes is the more profound impact—simply watching television and using it as a time-filler and a baby-sitter. She reviews evidence indicating that television has played a central role in the growing incidence of juvenile aggression, especially murders, rapes, and assaults committed by juveniles who have no feelings of remorse for what they have done. The simple act of watching television dulls the senses, requires no actions or thoughts on the part of the viewer, and is, in essence, a passive, one-way experience. People choose to watch action-filled, violent programs because that helps them feel somehow involved in some action themselves and compensates for the passivity of watching. Winn believes that it is this passive inactivity that dulls the senses to real events and blurs the distinction between reality and fantasy—it appears that violent children have become emotionally detached from reality and can commit unspeakable crimes with a complete absence of normal feelings. Television conditions them to relate to real people as if they were actors on a television screen. Television has also deprived children of play time, where they learn to get along with others and develop skills for coping with adult life and responsibilities, and find motivation to enjoy living. In this revised version, originally published in 1977, Winn also looks at video games and computers, the school and television, and means of controlling children's viewing hours through the use of lock boxes.

Child Abuse

Justice, Blair, and Rita Justice. *The Abusing Family.* Revised edition. New York: Plenum Press, 1990. 297 pp. Bibliography, index. ISBN 0-306-43441-5.

This book looks at whether or not children who grow up in abusing families become abusers themselves. The authors discuss attitudes and behaviors that make a home abusive and present information on what characterizes a "resilient" child—i.e., one who grows up in an abusing home but does not become abusive or violent. Some of these characteristics include the ability to not blame themselves for their beatings, to form supportive relationships outside the family, and to bring a loving adult into their lives as children. The Justices, as psychologists, describe what they do in therapy with both parents and children. They provide a conceptual framework for therapy that is derived from their model on the causes of abuse.

Miller, Alice. *For Your Own Good: Hidden Cruelty in Child-Rearing and the Roots of Violence.* Translated by Hildegarde and Hunter Hannum. New York: Farrar, Straus and Giroux, 1983. 284 pp. Bibliography. ISBN 0-374-52269-3.

This book grew out of Miller's curiosity about how a person (Hitler) could have done what he did (gassing millions of human beings), and how so many people could have believed in him without question and helped him carry out his plan. She believes that the practice of physical punishment, of beating children to make them behave, is not "for their own good" (as parents often like to say), but a cruel means of raising children, causing many problems in later life. People often beat their children because they were beaten as children and had no chance to defend themselves; when they have children, they repeat the cycle. Children can overcome many of the consequences if they are able to express their pain and anger and to react to what has happened. When they are prohibited from reacting and from expressing their feelings, they are more likely to become dangerous in later life.

————. *Thou Shalt Not Be Aware: Society's Betrayal of the Child.* Translated by Hildegarde and Hunter Hannum. New York: Meridian, 1986. Bibliography. ISBN 0-452-00929-4.

Dr. Miller, in this ground-breaking book, presents her premise that sexually abused children have obeyed the statement, "Thou shalt not be aware," believing that they are to blame for what happens to them. Freud's "drive theory" suggests that infantile sexual fantasies and conflicts create later neuroses in the adult. His Oedipal theory proposes that male children desire their mothers in a sexual way and want to get rid of their fathers so they alone can have their mothers. Dr. Miller argues that therapists have harmed those they have treated by trying to make them fit neatly into the popular theories, instead of listening to the child victims and learning from them. She believes that therapists should listen to the children and identify with them in order to understand them. Therapists must become advocates for their clients instead of representing current societal theories and values; they must not spare the parents at any cost. Therapists need to understand the ways in which sexuality is used to control or have power over those weaker in society.

Sandberg, David N. *The Child Abuse–Delinquency Connection.* Lexington, MA: Lexington Books, 1989. 165 pp. ISBN 0-669-17022-4.

David Sandberg examines the relationship between child abuse and delinquency through interviews with experts in the field of juvenile justice, including a counselor, a psychiatrist, researchers, a judge, a probation officer, a lawyer, and a victim. As these interviews demonstrate, victims of child abuse require a different approach when they are in the juvenile justice system; they often have difficulty accepting responsibility for their actions, traditional types of treatment may not meet their needs, and they do not often benefit from punishment. Sandberg became aware of the relationship between child abuse and delinquency while he was director of a residential treatment program for delinquents referred by the courts. He was appalled at the stories that those juveniles told him about maltreatment at the hands of their parents. The stories and information presented here come from experts who are on the forefront of the child abuse/delinquency field.

Straus, Murray A., Richard J. Gelles, and Suzanne Steinmetz. *Behind Closed Doors: Violence in the American Family.* Garden City, NY: Anchor Books, 1980. 301 pp. References, index. ISBN 0-385-14259-5.

This book reports the results of the first comprehensive national research conducted on family violence in America. As sociologists, the authors studied the extent and breadth of family violence and what the violence meant to those participating in it, willingly or not. They examined a variety of forms of violence, including spanking a child, which many families do not consider violent behavior. Based on over 2,000 interviews, they determined which families were violent, and then they assessed the causes of that violence. Their research shows, for the first time, the extent of violence acts toward children, including many actions that could injure, maim, or kill them. The evidence shows that how parents raise their children is the primary source of our violent society. The authors cover violence between brothers and sisters, social patterns in family violence, the social heredity of family violence, the causes of violent behavior, and ways to reduce family violence. They suggest reducing the violence-provoking stresses created by society, integrating families into community networks, changing the sexist character of family and society, and breaking the cycle of violence in the family.

Societal Causes

Dobson, James, and Gary L. Bauer. *Children at Risk: The Battle for the Hearts and Minds of Our Kids.* Dallas: Word Publishing, 1990. 291 pp. Index. ISBN 0-8499-0703-9.

Dobson and Bauer believe that America is in the middle of a second civil war: on one side are those supporting and defending traditional values, while on the other side are those supporting secular values. The authors argue that children today are exposed to a variety of influences that can lead to a moral decline; these include television, movies, alcohol, drugs, pornography, gambling, premarital sex, child abuse, and homosexuality. They describe to parents, family members, teachers, and other concerned individuals the stresses that children are exposed to, and the arenas where children are most often exposed to these factors: at school, on television, through the popular culture, in the church, and in the family environment. Dobson and Bauer discuss the role of the church in society today, prescribe values that should be taught in schools today, and suggest how to strengthen and protect the family and the sanctity of life.

Elkind, David. *The Hurried Child: Growing Up Too Fast Too Soon.* Reading, MA: Addison-Wesley Publishing Company, 1981. 210 pp. Index. ISBN 0-201-03967-2.

Elkind, as a child professional, realized that many of the children he was seeing were under too much pressure to achieve, to succeed, to please, and to be adults. These children are forced to accept and handle competently the physical, psychological, and social aspects of being adults before they acquire the necessary coping skills. They are often the troubled, sometimes violent children of today. The stresses these children face are totally overwhelming, creating confusion, illnesses, anger, and violent responses. Elkind explores the causes of these stresses as well as the results, including children who have chronic psychosomatic complaints, or who are delinquent, unhappy, depressed, violent, hyperactive, lethargic, or unmotivated. He explores how children become hurried in different environments—at home, at school, and through the media. He also describes how these children can be identified and helped.

Hamburg, David A. *Today's Children: Creating a Future for a Generation in Crisis.* New York: Times Books, 1992. 376 pp. References, index. ISBN 0-8129-1914-9.

David Hamburg, a medical doctor, president of the Carnegie Corporation of New York, and a nationally known authority on child development, analyzes changes that have occurred in the American family and the stresses they currently face. Children grow up today facing many obstacles: poverty, drug abuse, child abuse, ill health, illiteracy, prejudice, and violence at home, in school, and on the streets. Dr. Hamburg examines the causes of many of today's problems, and he presents ways in which society is responding to and resolving these problems. He discusses the changes occurring in the family structure—including working mothers, high divorce rates, teenage pregnancy, and family violence—and how these changes have impacted our children. He presents important research in changes in child development and examines innovative programs that work to ameliorate the influence of these changes.

Hayes, E. Kent. *Why Good Parents Have Bad Kids: How To Make Sure That Your Child Grows Up Right.* New York: Doubleday, 1989. 209 pp. ISBN 0-385-24352-9.

Hayes, as a child advocate and juvenile criminologist, believes that children are shaped by their environment and that parental neglect plays a major role in turning children to delinquency. Even though many parents Hayes has known appear to be "good parents," he believes they are neglecting their children in important ways, from overindulgence to lack of communication. He believes that parents need training in order to become good parents and that truly good parents know how to teach children the importance and value of delayed gratification—they must provide structure in the home; must understand their children by knowing their interests, desires, and activities; can communicate with their children; know how to discipline their children; and know how to laugh and enjoy themselves. These homes must be nurturing and not provide negative self-images. He also believes that parents must love each other or they will produce disturbed children.

Kohn, Alfie. *No Contest: The Case against Competition.* Boston: Houghton Mifflin Company, 1986. 324 pp. Index, bibliography. ISBN 0-395-39387-6.

Kohn explores the American attitudes toward competition and the reasons why most Americans believe that someone else must lose in order for them to win as he makes a case against competition. He believes that America's fondness for competition is based on four myths; these myths include the belief that competition is innate, part of our human nature, and therefore unavoidable; that competition brings out the best in everyone; that competitive events are the only way to play, to enjoy, and to have fun; and that competition builds character and makes us good people.

Kohn believes that, because many Americans believe these myths, they are perceived as uncooperative. He cites research studies demonstrating that American children are more competitive than children from other countries, and that American children learn early to compete and to be aggressive, rather than cooperative, with others. Kohn presents additional research studies that have shown that cooperative approaches to solving problems are usually much more successful than competitive approaches. He argues persuasively for a more cooperative atmosphere, citing research showing that cooperation encourages people to be happier, feel more secure, and be more productive.

Minear, Ralph E., and William Proctor. *Kids Who Have Too Much.* Nashville: Thomas Nelson Publishers, 1989. 192 pp. Notes. ISBN 0-8407-4251-7.

A noted Harvard Medical School pediatrician, Dr. Minear is seeing more children with what he terms "Rich Kids' Syndrome," defined as "children who have too much of something—whether it's pressure to perform, freedom, money, food, protection, or parental sacrifice." He estimates that one in eight American children suffers from a mental-health problem serious enough to warrant treatment. The authors ask readers to look at their own families and determine if they are giving their children too much freedom, too many material goods, too much pressure to perform, too much information, too much protection, too much independence, too much food, or too much parental sacrifice, along with too little education at home about being responsible. Children who have thus lost their moorings at home are seen as commodities as adults, are deteriorating physically, are emotionally unhealthy, and they have generally become too jaded. These children are given too much freedom without responsibility—they've been given everything except guidelines by which to live, rules of morality, and meaningful morality. The authors suggest ways to help such children develop into fully functioning adults.

Postman, Neil. *The Disappearance of Childhood.* New York: Delacorte Press, 1982. 178 pp. Index, bibliography. ISBN 0-440-01691-6.

This book explores the many ways childhood is disappearing as a crucial growing-up time for children. Postman discusses the influence of the media, especially television, and the ways in which children are now exposed to aggression and sexuality that force them to grow up too soon, to become adults before many have completed their childhood. Many of the subtle ways that society is working to destroy children and childhood are exposed. He tracks the history of childhood, how it was often seen as a necessary stage of life and, at other times, how it was seen as unnecessary. He then discusses solutions: ways in which parents can help their children overcome the influence of television, how to be able to think abstractly, and how to think for oneself.

Monographs, Articles, and Bibliographies

American Psychological Association. *Violence & Youth: Psychology's Response, Volume I: Summary Report of the American Psychological Association Commission on Violence and Youth.* Washington, DC: American Psychological Association, 1993. 96 pp.

The American Psychological Association convened the Commission on Violence and Youth in 1991 to review the vast body of literature and research on violence and youth and to use that knowledge to help solve the current problems created by violent youth. This summary report presents an overview of the causes of youth violence and suggests ways that this research can help create, evaluate, and replicate effective treatment and prevention programs. Influences reviewed here include biological factors, family and child-rearing factors, school and academic achievement, emotional and cognitive development, and the influence of social and cultural factors. Societal characteristics explored include attitudes toward violence in society, poverty and socioeconomic inequality, and prejudice and discrimination. The availability of firearms, alcohol and other drugs, gang involvement, mob violence, violence in the mass media, ethnic minority cultures, and cultural factors in preventing and treating violent youth are all examined. Characteristics of successful intervention programs are described and recommendations are made for areas of future research.

Cheatham, Annie. *Annotated Bibliography for Teaching Conflict Resolution in Schools.* Amherst, MA: National Association for Mediation in Education, 1989.

This bibliography contains over 200 entries, including books, curricula, videocassettes, and training materials for teaching conflict resolution in schools. It is divided into three sections including implementation, skill building, and related areas. The implementation sections contains materials for starting a program in schools, teaching a course in conflict resolution, and evaluating programs. The skill-building section includes teaching conflict resolution skills, such as teaching communication, problem solving, brainstorming, and evaluation skills. Materials related to conflict resolution, but more general in nature, including peace education, cooperative education, law-related education, special education in mediation, dropout prevention, and substance abuse, are found in the related-areas section.

Conflict Resolution: A Secondary School Curriculum. San Francisco: Community Board Program, 1987. 300 pp.

This curriculum has been set up to be taught as a separate unit, or it can be integrated into social studies or other subject areas. Areas emphasized include understanding conflict, styles of conflict, the communication process, how to develop effective communication skills, and a series of conflict resolution processes that can be tested. In understanding conflict, the value of conflict, use of conflict resolution in the classroom, attitudes toward conflict, the cycle of conflict, and causes and varieties of conflict are emphasized.

Styles of conflict include avoidance, confrontation, and problem solving. Discussions of communication cover reasons why communication is important in resolving conflicts; the process of communication; factors that influence communication;

the role of values, perceptions, attitudes, and styles in communication; and ways to learn how to communicate. Skills for effective communication include active listening, sending clear messages, and "I-messages." A discussion of roadblocks and other barriers to communication is also provided. Ways to resolve conflicts are discussed, including problem solving, formal negotiation, third-party processes, conciliation, mediation, and arbitration. Background information is provided in all these areas, key concepts are defined, and a series of activities are offered. This curriculum is contained in a loose-leaf binder, which makes removing and making copies of the various handouts quite easy.

Deutsch, Morton. **"Educating for a Peaceful World."** *American Psychologist* 48, no. 5 (May 1993): 510–516.

Deutsch describes actions that schools can take to encourage constructive ways of dealing with anger and conflict, as well as how to develop positive attitudes, values, and knowledge that will foster cooperation among students. He believes these programs must have four components in order to be successful, including cooperative learning, conflict resolution training, use of constructive controversy in teaching subject matters, and mediation or conflict resolution centers in schools. He discusses five important elements of cooperative learning: positive interdependence, face-to-face interaction, individual accountability, interpersonal and small-group skills, and ways of evaluating group cooperation. Deutsch emphasizes the importance of the constructive resolution of conflict. Teachers play an important role in demonstrating how to deal with conflict in their classrooms and can be instrumental in helping students understand the importance of solving conflicts peacefully. Mediation programs in the schools are effective ways of solving conflicts that require a third party for resolution.

Farrington, D. P. **"Early Predictors of Adolescent Aggression and Adult Violence."** *Violence and Victims* 4, no. 2 (1989): 79–100.

In this study, Farrington wanted to determine those factors that were believed to lead to violent behavior among young males. He conducted a longitudinal survey of 411 males ranging in age from 8 to 32 years in London to examine the relationship between adolescent aggression and later adult violence. The study spanned a period of 24 years. The boys were tested by a psychologist when they were 8, 10, and 14 years old. When they reached the ages of 16, 18, and 21, interviews were conducted at the research office.

Finally, when they reached the ages of 25 and 32, they were again interviewed. The boys' parents were also interviewed once every year while the boys were between the ages of 8 and 14 or 15. The author found that males with low incomes were more likely to behave violently as teenagers than other males (42 percent). They were also more likely to be convicted of violent crimes. Factors that often predicted adolescent violence included poor housing, large family size, parental disharmony, boys whose parents had been convicted, low verbal and low nonverbal intelligence, and boys who exhibited more daring behavior, taking more chances than other boys.

Griffin, G. W. **"Childhood Predictive Characteristics of Aggressive Adolescents."** *Exceptional Children* 54, no. 3 (November 1987): 246–252.

This study examined several childhood characteristics that were thought to predict later acts of juvenile aggression. The author studied a sample of three groups of adolescents treated in a residential program for emotionally disturbed youth. One group of 26 juveniles with serious emotional, neurological, or mental handicaps had been classified as violent and aggressive. The second group included 28 adolescents who had already completed the residential treatment program and had successfully maintained their improved behavior. The third group included 28 randomly selected adolescents who had been in the treatment program between 1970 and 1980. The author found that aggressive and violent juveniles were more likely to suffer from organic problems, including physical abnormalities, central-nervous-system problems, and developmental abnormalities; were more likely to have come from aggressive and violent families; and had already exhibited aggressive behavior and other difficulties in school. Griffin suggests that intervention strategies should be developed to identify aggressive children early in their lives so that they can be helped before they commit violent acts later in adolescence.

Kreidler, William J. *Creative Conflict Resolution: More Than 200 Activities for Keeping Peace in the Classroom.* Glenview, IL: Scott, Foresman and Company, 1984. 216 pp.

This book contains over 200 activities and exercises for teachers to use in their classrooms to encourage the use of cooperative learning to reduce the amount of conflict and violence in the classroom. Kreidler believes that school should be a place where children cooperate with each other, communicate their needs and feelings effectively, tolerate differences among each other with respect, honestly express their feelings, and resolve conflicts creatively and nonviolently. Each activity presented offers the appropriate grade level for use and lists materials required to complete the activity, procedures for conducting the exercise, and suggestions for starting discussions among the students. Fourteen reproducible worksheets and game cards are included. For use with students in kindergarten through sixth grade.

Lam, Julie A. *The School Mediation Program Evaluation Kit.* Amherst, MA: National Association for Mediation in Education, 1989. 24 pp.

This kit is an excellent guide for coordinators of school mediation programs to help them evaluate the impact of their program. Forms included in the kit are a blank monthly progress report that the project coordinators can use to gather and disseminate information and statistics about the program, a mediation contract form, a questionnaire for students/trainees in the program, a parental consent form, a parental evaluation form, an evaluation form for students/trainees, a school climate questionnaire, and a follow-up form to determine the results of mediation of a conflict. Directions are provided for filling out the various forms, their purpose, and ways to analyze the information that is gathered.

Lewis, D. O., et al. **"Biopsychosocial Characteristics of Children Who Later Murder: A Prospective Study."** *American Journal of Psychiatry* 142, no. 10 (October 1985): 1161–1167.

This research was conducted to examine the psychological, neurological, and experiential characteristics of juveniles who commit murder. A group of nine murderers and another group of 24 delinquents who had not committed a murder were studied. The authors found that all of the adolescents who had committed a murder had also committed other violent acts before the murder, including sexual assaults, robbery, assaults with a knife, choking a bird, and throwing a dog out of a window. All nine murderers had psychotic symptoms, and three had been hospitalized for psychiatric reasons. Seven had severe neurological impairment, six had had head injuries, and all had had a relative who had been hospitalized or was demonstrably psychotic. Seven had been victims of physical abuse by their parents.

National Association for Mediation in Education, Violence Prevention Packet, second edition. Amherst, MA: National Association for Mediation in Education, 1993.

This packet includes several articles providing information and resources on school violence and shows the relationship between conflict resolution and violence prevention. Subjects include preventing victimization, teaching communication skills, teaching conflict resolution in juvenile correctional facilities, implications of violence in schools for education and educators, how schools can help stem youth violence, and drug abuse and violence in rural schools. It also includes a resource list of violence prevention organizations and programs.

Pincus, J. H., and G. J. Tucker. **"Violence in Children and Adults: A Neurological View."** *American Academy of Child Psychiatry* 17, no. 2 (1978): 277–287.

This article reviews the literature on the relationship between neurological damage and violent behavior. Areas examined include animal research, episodic violence in humans, psychomotor seizures and violence, alcohol and violence, causes of violent behavior, treatment, and the prognosis for violent offenders. Animal research has indicated that changes in behavior can be traced to stimulation or destruction of specific areas of the brain. Abnormal EEGs (electrocardiograms) were found in violent young males, indicating that a large number of violent youth had some sort of brain dysfunction. Pathological intoxication, or the susceptibility to alcohol, was found in many violent adults. Several environmental and neurological factors were documented as causes of violent behavior. The authors concluded that the evidence suggesting a relationship between neurological problems and violent behavior was contradictory and suggested continuing research be conducted to determine if a relationship does exist and how strong that relationship actually is.

Prothrow-Stith, Deborah. *Violence Prevention Curriculum for Adolescents.* Newton, MA: Education Development Center, 1992.

This curriculum, including a 110-page teacher's guide, student handouts, and a teacher-training video, is based on the research of

Dr. Deborah Prothrow-Stith, a physician and public health official. Dr. Prothrow-Stith has proposed a public health approach to
preventing violence among youth. Her approach and the curriculum acknowledge anger as a normal and legitimate emotion, and
emphasize the importance of making students aware of the risk of
being involved in violent situations, discussing the possible gains
and losses of fighting, proposing alternatives to violence, providing positive ways to deal with anger, and recognizing the warning signs of a potential fight and teaching ways to resolve conflicts
without violence.

Reducing School Violence: Schools Teaching Peace. Nashville,
TN: Tennessee Education Association, and Charleston, WV: Appalachia Educational Laboratory, July 1993.

This joint study by the Tennessee Education Association (TEA) and
the Appalachia Educational Laboratory (AEL) grew out of a study
group on conflict resolution that wanted to examine current programs offering conflict resolution training and services, and create
a resource guide for teachers. This resource guide was developed to
help teachers find materials on conflict resolution that will help
them learn to resolve conflicts in the classroom. The materials provide information on the basic characteristics of conflict resolution
programs; detailed descriptions of several successful conflict resolution programs for elementary, junior, and senior high schools; an
annotated list of resources, including programs, books, curricula,
videotapes, and sources to contact for more information on training; and a bibliography.

Russell, D. H. **"Girls Who Kill."** *International Journal of Offender
Therapy and Comparative Criminology* 29, no. 2 (1985): 171–176.

This article presents information about two girls who have murdered someone. The author has studied boys who kill and found
that these boys often displayed abnormal maternal relationships
that prevented them from developing a sense of personal identity
and autonomy. The author wondered if other factors influenced
girls who committed murder—factors such as maternal depriva-
tion when they were very young and the placement of many
harsh restrictions on their behavior during adolescence. The author found that both girls were extensively controlled by their
mothers, little or no caring was provided in the family, the girls

were abused or received little or no support from family members, and they did not possess a positive sense of self. The author believes that the causes of violence and murder for girls are different than those for boys. The author recommends that more research should be conducted in this area.

"Saving Youth from Violence." *Carnegie Quarterly* 39, no. 1 (Winter 1994).

A report from the Carnegie Corporation, this issue focuses on youth violence. It discusses children as both victims and perpetrators of violent crimes, the threat and availability of guns in relation to violent youth, and the roles of family, community, and society in shaping children's behavior. Strategies to reduce violence are presented, including conflict resolution and mediation, social support and life skills training, violence prevention curricula, and ways to deal with bullies. The important role of the schools in helping parents teach their children about nonviolent behavior is emphasized. Community and youth organizations can also play a vital role in helping youth refrain from violent actions and learn to deal nonviolently with all situations.

Schmideberg, M. **"Juvenile Murderers."** *International Journal of Offender Therapy and Comparative Criminology* 17, no. 3 (1973): 240–245.

In this report, the author explores the characteristics and causes of juveniles who commit murder, the causes of youth violence, and discusses society's response to this type of violence. Schmideberg believes that because youthful violent offenders have been treated humanely by often giving them the benefit of the doubt while neglecting the victim, some of these juveniles take their offenses and punishments less seriously than they should. Many juveniles know how to get around the juvenile justice system and how to use it to their advantage. The author believes that, in order to prevent juvenile crime, society must reduce the violence shown on television, develop a conscience and sense of morality in children, treat juveniles who commit murder severely to teach them about the sanctity of life and responsibility for their actions, and instill in juveniles the belief that society does not condone violence.

Students Promoting Alternative Resolutions to Conflict Packet.
Ithaca, NY: Community Dispute Resolution Center, 1988.

The Community Dispute Resolution Center supports the Students Promoting Alternative Resolutions to Conflict program, which has put together resource materials to help create and maintain school conflict resolution programs. The center has introduced conflict resolution programs and activities to schools, and they always encourage schools to take over these programs after the initial introduction and organization. This packet of information includes three separate packets whose concerns are: how to sell mediation to a school community, steps for mediators to take for problem solving, and role-playing. The packet on how to sell mediation to a school community was developed to encourage schools to take over and operate conflict resolution programs and offers ways to set up and work with a school advisory committee. Sample agendas, suggested milestones, letters of agreement, notices to families, recruiting forms, questionnaires for teachers, permission slips, and news releases are some of the valuable types of information included. The mediator's packet offers a step-by-step approach to mediating conflict situations in the school and suggests appropriate phrases to use and questions to ask for the beginning mediator. The role-playing packet provides 13 disputes with varying degrees of difficulty. Explanations are included to help create packages for role-playing exercises.

Truscott, D. **"Intergenerational Transmission of Violent Behavior in Adolescent Males."** *Aggressive Behavior* 18, no. 5 (1992): 327–335.

In this study, the author's goal was to prove that violent behavior is transmitted from one generation to another, that the self-esteem of violent juveniles from violent homes is lower than that of other juveniles, that these juveniles have more externalizing than internalizing defenses, and that they display more psychotic behavior than both violent and nonviolent juveniles from nonviolent homes. Males in the experimental group were inpatient offenders from a treatment program at Alberta Hospital in Edmonton, Canada; a control group consisted of males in the tenth grade from a Catholic high school in Edmonton. Various psychological tests were administered to both groups. Findings supported the hypothesis that violence is transmitted from one generation to the next. Violent juveniles from violent families did display more psychotic behavior than nonviolent juveniles, but they did not have lower self-esteem or use more externalizing defenses. Violent youth who were exposed to parental violence were significantly different from those violent youth who were not exposed to parental violence and from those youth who were nonviolent. There was also a proven relationship between juvenile violence and physical and verbal abuse by the father.

Violence Prevention: A Proactive Approach. Lexington, MA: D. C. Heath and Company, 1994. 26 pp. ISBN 0-669-36103-8.

This document is a result of the collaboration of D. C. Heath and Company and the Community Board Program, located in San Francisco. As a result of evaluations of the Community Board Program's curriculum, *Conflict Resolution: A Secondary School Curriculum* (see above), evaluators found that many teachers believed that prejudice was a major factor in many of the conflicts involving students. This document offers ways to improve awareness of causes of prejudice for both teachers and students. Lessons focus on learning to become aware of conflict, attitudes toward conflict, assessing personal styles of conflict, and ways to resolve conflicts nonviolently. Student activities include role-playing activities and worksheets for identifying and observing conflicts and determining the student's conflict style. Handouts for measuring feelings, exercises in "active listening," and story scripts are also included. Student sections include material on awareness of school-based violence as well as gang, domestic, and sexual violence; personal assessment; and conflict resolution.

Alternatives to Violence

Type: VHS
Length: Two 30-min. tapes
Date: 1994
Cost: $150 (includes two 30-minute videos, one mediation curriculum with suggestions for use, lesson plans, discussion questions, role plays and an implementation plan for school mediation programs, and two sets of blackline masters for duplication)
Source: Chariot Productions
2819 3rd Street
Boulder, CO 80304
(800) 477-5128
Fax: (303) 786-9799

This two-part program and curriculum is designed to provide students with an understanding of the concepts and skills they need to resolve conflicts productively rather than violently. Students are shown the value of conflict resolution as an alternative to fighting in Part 1, which includes sections on understanding conflict, communication skills, conflict resolution, and peer mediation. Part 2 focuses on similar information for teachers, administrators, parents, and community members, and discusses the value of teaching conflict resolution to students. It also demonstrates how to develop and operate a school-based conflict resolution and mediation program. It is designed for students in sixth through twelfth grades.

Angry John

Type:	VHS
Length:	23 min.
Date:	1994
Cost:	$295
Source:	Pyramid Film and Video
	Box 1048
	Santa Monica, CA 90406-1048
	(800) 421-2304
	Fax: (213) 453-9083

Angry John is a cartoon hero who beats up his enemies. As a little boy, Cliff, is watching Angry John on television, he has his own temper tantrum and Angry John comes out of the television to encourage his destructive, angry behavior. Cliff has been having trouble at school and at home; he feels stressed, frustrated, and angry. Angry John encourages Cliff to continue his troublesome behavior, and since Cliff is the only one who can see Angry John, Cliff gets sole blame for his behavior. Finally Cliff gets into serious trouble and learns how to deal with his anger. Cliff then teaches Angry John how to manage his anger.

Debates on the effects of television violence on children have continued for many decades, and this video teaches children how to deal with their anger. It uses a negative image of a cartoon hero, meeting up with a little boy, and shows how they both learn to evaluate each conflict situation that arises and think before they act. It provides them with the tools they need to step back from conflict situations, think about their reactions, communicate their angry feelings to someone who can help, and find creative, positive ways to solve the situation.

Beyond Brochures: New Approaches to Prevention

Type:	VHS
Length:	25 min.
Date:	1987
Cost:	$65

Source: Contra Costa County Health Services Department
Prevention Program
75 Santa Barbara Road
Pleasant Hill, CA 94523
(415) 646-6511

This video presents a comprehensive model for strategies for preventing violence and is aimed primarily at health workers, although it is also valuable for social service and other community service professionals. Recognized leaders discuss how medical and other community leaders can come together on basic health issues to provide a coordinated approach to prevention. The program focuses on six levels of intervention: strengthening individual knowledge, promoting community education, educating service providers, promoting coalitions and networking, changing organizational policies, and influencing policy and legislation. Watching this video should help interested professionals better understand how to develop programs to prevent violence among youth.

Beyond Hate
Type: VHS
Length: 88 min.
Date: 1992
Cost: $76
Source: Mystic Fire Video; available from:
National Association for Mediation in Education
205 Hampshire House
Box 33635
University of Massachusetts
Amherst, MA 01003-3635
(413) 545-2462

Produced as a PBS special, and narrated by Bill Moyers, this video discusses the emotion of hate. Included are people who are filled with hate and those victimized by it—gang members, world leaders, and regular, everyday people trying to deal with the impact of hate in their lives. Organizations and individuals working to rid their environments of hate are described, showing how people can live together with tolerance and understanding. While it is often hard to understand how people can be filled with so much hate, this video helps us understand how hate can develop in an individual and what we can do to live and work together without hating each other.

Cadillac Dreams
Type: VHS
Length: 30 min.
Date: 1988
Cost: $325
Source: Pyramid Film and Video
Box 1048
Santa Monica, CA 90406-1048
(800) 421-2304
Fax: (310) 453-9083

For junior and senior high-school students, this video focuses on the discrepancies between an inner-city teenager's dreams and the reality of his daily life. It graphically depicts life on the street, with the presence of drugs and violence clearly shown. A young black man, the eldest of three brothers, dreams of inventing a way to walk on water. Instead, he turns to dealing drugs and is murdered by men to whom he owes money. The middle brother, armed with a gun, seeks to avenge his death. In a dramatic ending, he chooses not to continue his violent ways, throws away the gun, and teaches his youngest brother how to walk on water. The video can be used to stimulate discussion about choices and decision making. It provides a message of hope that students do have choices, can escape the drugs and violence found in many areas of this country today, and can be successful. It does contain explicit language.

Conflict Resolution
Type: VHS
Length: 26 min.
Date: 1992
Cost: $180
Source: Sunburst Communications; available from:
National Association for Mediation in Education
205 Hampshire House
Box 33635
University of Massachusetts
Amherst, MA 01003-3635
(413) 545-2462

This video presents students, teachers, and parents discussing ways to improve communication skills, listen more sensitively, and be more aware of other people and their feelings. It demonstrates various styles of conflict including avoidance, confrontation, and problem solving. Students are shown how to identify their own styles of fighting with each other and what they can do to minimize fights and learn to communicate with each other. The video discusses reasons why conflict occurs between people and the differences between interpersonal and group conflicts, and emphasizes the importance of communication as the primary means of resolving conflict. Produced for students in seventh through twelfth grades.

Dealing with Anger: A Violence Prevention Program for African-American Youth

Type:	VHS
Length:	Three 14–20 min. tapes
Date:	1991
Cost:	$495
Source:	American Correctional Association
	8025 Laurel Lakes Court
	Laurel, MD 20707-5075
	(800) 825-2665
	Fax: (301) 206-5061

This training program includes a leader's guide, ten sets of skill cards, and three videotapes (*Givin' It, Takin' It,* and *Workin' It Out*), to help school personnel and community leaders teach African-American youth social skills for appropriately dealing with anger. Each tape presents a conflict situation that escalates into a potentially dangerous confrontation, a skill lesson, and the same situation using a key conflict resolution skill. A training session is shown with a leader and a small group of adolescents who discuss violence in their own lives, role-play the skills taught, and give and receive feedback. This video can be an excellent tool for teachers and other professionals in helping young people learn to resolve conflicts peacefully. The program is recommended for teachers, counselors, social workers, psychologists, clergy, and anyone else who works with adolescents.

Everyday Conflicts, Creative Solutions

Type:	VHS
Length:	9 min.
Date:	1992
Cost:	$185 (includes leader's guide)

Source: Northwest Mediation Service; available from:
National Association for Mediation in Education
205 Hampshire House
Box 33635
University of Massachusetts
Amherst, MA 01003-3635
(413) 545-2462

This video trains students by providing them with the opportunity to observe and model professionally trained and coached young actors who act as conflict managers. Students are exposed to a variety of conflict management skills that include active listening, balancing power, enforcing rules, and brainstorming; they learn how to apply skills in situations involving conflict. These skills are demonstrated in ways that students can relate to, which helps them develop new, less violent ways of dealing with conflicts in their everyday lives.

An Eye for an Eye . . . Makes the Whole World Blind

Type: VHS
Length: 12 min.
Date: 1991
Cost: $25
Source: Educators for Social Responsibility
23 Garden Street
Cambridge, MA 02138
(800) 370-2515
Fax: (617) 864-5164

Students, teachers, and principals in a New York City alternative high school discuss the changes they have made since participating in the Resolving Conflict Creatively Program (RCCP). The RCCP is a school-based program in conflict resolution and intergroup relations that provides a model for preventing violence and creating caring, learning communities. The program shows young people that they have many options besides passivity or aggression in dealing with conflict, gives them skills to make these choices, increases their understanding and appreciation of all cultures, and shows them that they can play a powerful role in creating a more peaceful world. Participants explain the changes in their attitudes and behaviors and the effect this course has had on their personal relationships with each other. For students in seventh through twelfth grades.

Facing Up
Type: VHS
Length: 20 min.
Date: 1990
Cost: $195 (includes teacher's guide)
Source: Committee for Children
             172 20th Avenue
             Seattle, WA 98122
             (800) 634-4449
             Seattle area: (206) 322-5050
             Fax: (206) 322-7133

This film focuses on preventing youth violence. It illustrates the internal struggles of two boys trying to gain the skills needed to face their problems and break the cycle of violence. Brian is emotionally abused at home and acts out his anger by bullying fellow students. Josh is one of his favorite targets. Observing these skills used in a lifelike situation and then practicing the behaviors help students deal with similar peer conflicts. This video effectively addresses violence prevention at the level of the offender as well as the victim. Young people can learn from this video how to avoid conflicts, but when they occur, it shows them how to resolve their problems without resorting to violence.

Fighting Fair: Dr. Martin Luther King, Jr. for Kids
Type: VHS
Length: 18 min.
Date: 1986
Cost: $10 rental (includes teacher's guide)
Source: Wilmington College Peace Resource Center
             Pyle Center, Box 1183
             Wilmington, OH 45177
             (513) 382-5338

Showing how a coach helps children resolve a conflict during a basketball game, this video urges students to stand up for their rights using skills and education, instead of their fists, to resolve conflict. Students are shown how to fight fair and are shown how conflicts can be resolved without violence. It describes how this fits into the teachings on nonviolence by Dr. Martin Luther King, Jr., using clips from the civil rights movement and Dr. King's life and activities. Especially effective for young African Americans, this video helps all young people understand that violence is not the only way to resolve their problems.

A Fistful of Words
Type: VHS
Length: 23 min. (adult version), 13 min. (student
            version)
Date: 1990
Cost: $25 (each version)
Source: Educators for Social Responsibility
            23 Garden Street
            Cambridge, MA 02138
            (800) 370-2515
            Fax: (617) 864-5164

In the adult version, teachers, school administrators, students, and school board members describe the reasons they are so enthusiastic about using a conflict resolution curriculum in their schools. Some of the reasons are fewer incidents of aggressive and violent behavior among students, calmer classrooms, and less fear among students and teachers. In the student version, students describe how they became peer mediators and what they like about being peer mediators. A peer mediation process is acted out by some of the children. This video effectively demonstrates to students how they can take an active role in resolving conflicts peacefully.

**Friendly Creature Features: Puppet Shows
and Conflict Resolution Workshops
for Primary Grade Children**
Type: VHS
Length: 50 min.
Date: 1985
Cost: $15 guidebook and $25 video (purchase);
            $15 rental (includes guidebook)
Source: Western New York Peace Center; available from:
            Wilmington College Peace Resource Center
            Pyle Center, Box 1183
            Wilmington, OH 45177
            (513) 382-5338

The guidebook includes four plays using puppets and lesson plans for 12 workshops on conflict resolution that can be used to teach children how to resolve conflicts peacefully. The video presents the plays and teaches several songs about conflict resolution. Also included are a bibliography and a directory of relevant organizations concerning conflict resolution. For children in primary grades.

Gangs, Guns, Graffiti
Type: VHS
Length: 30 min.
Date: 1989
Cost: $325
Source: Pyramid Film and Video
             Box 1048
             Santa Monica, CA 90406-1048
             (800) 421-2304
             Fax: (213) 453-9083

Vividly demonstrating the effects of being in a gang, this video helps junior and senior high-school students understand the price they pay when they are in a gang. Interviews are conducted with gang members, victims of gang violence, and prosecutors involved in criminal proceedings against gang members. Viewers are able to see and hear firsthand what it is like to be a gang member—the widespread use of guns, the effects of drug money, and gangs' use of graffiti in their battles to win new members and expand their territory. The consequences of gang membership are vividly described. This video is an excellent training tool for anti-gang programs, parent education, law enforcement personnel, newly hired police and public-safety personnel, community workers, and teachers and school administrators.

Getting Better at Getting Along: Conflict Resolution
Type: VHS
Length: 16 min.
Date: 1992
Cost: $93.50
Source: Quest International
             537 Jones Road
             P.O. Box 566
             Granville, OH 43023
             (800) 446-2700

Skills such as listening to each other and methods for solving problems through conflict resolution are presented in this video. Students learn how to communicate with each other, listen to each other, and how to resolve their problems before they become serious or turn violent. For second- through fourth-grade students.

Getting to the Heart of It
Type: VHS
Length: NA
Date: 1994
Cost: $215.95 (includes teacher's guide)
Source: Tom Snyder Productions
            and Conflict Management Inc.; available from:
            Educators for Social Responsibility
            23 Garden Street
            Cambridge, MA 02138
            (800) 370-2515
            Fax: (617) 864-5164

Produced for middle-school students, this video will help these students resolve conflicts without violence. Using the proven techniques of Roger Fisher for negotiating solutions to conflicts, an exciting cast of characters demonstrate how they negotiate their way through compelling and realistic conflict situations. Students share in the characters' experiences, using follow-along workbooks for role-playing and discussions that teach effective new skills and vocabulary for negotiating conflicts. The program has a flexible structure, so all teachers, no matter what their teaching style, can work with the video. Includes teacher's guide, detailed lesson plans, 30 follow-along workbooks, role-playing cards, and a sample take-home video and booklet.

Identification and Prevention of Youth Violence:
A Protocol Package for Health Care Providers
Type: audio/slide
Length: NA
Date: 1992
Cost: contact the project for current cost
Source: Boston Department of Health and Hospitals
            Violence Prevention Project
            1010 Massachusetts Avenue, 2nd Floor
            Boston, MA 02118
            (617) 534-5894

This training program is designed to help health care professionals develop the skills to identify and prevent youth violence. The package consists of a provider protocol, an audio/slide presentation with a script for staff training purposes, and samples of chart decals, educational posters, and brochures. The protocol provides methods of approaching a patient and beginning a meaningful dialogue and gives suggestions for developing a resource list for referrals. Anger management and risk avoidance strategies are addressed.

JAILBRAKE: The Videotape
Type: VHS
Length: 33 min.
Date: 1990
Cost: contact the Sheriff's Department for cost
Source: Commonwealth of Massachusetts
             Suffolk County Sheriff's Department
             200 Nashua Street
             Boston, MA 02114
             (617) 725-4009

Based on an educational program implemented by the Suffolk County Sheriff's Department, this video was developed to help reduce the number of young men and women entering the criminal justice system. It vividly demonstrates to students that there is no badge of courage, no honor, no power, or no strength to doing hard time. The program and videotape focus on the realities, often harsh, of life in jail. The video centers around the experiences of four students with serious disciplinary problems who spend two days inside the Charles Street Jail in Suffolk County, Massachusetts. They experience firsthand the negative aspects of life in jail, especially the loss of control over their lives, loss of privacy, and loneliness. They discover, with astonishing clarity, that they alone are responsible for their actions and they must pay the price, which is extremely painful to them. In addition to the video, an instructor's guide contains an overview of the criminal justice system, background information about the JAILBRAKE program, discussion questions, and suggested activities.

Just the Two of Us
Type: VHS
Length: 14.5 min.
Date: 1993
Cost: $65
Source: Agency for Instructional Technology; available from:
           National Association for Mediation in Education
           205 Hampshire House, Box 33635
           University of Massachusetts
           Amherst, MA 01003-3635
           (413) 545-2462

This program teaches primary-school-age children how to solve everyday disputes. Strategies taught include active listening and talking things over. Children are portrayed in typical conflict situations, appropriate for primary-school-age children, which helps the students better understand and apply the lessons taught. Also included are sing-along songs, rap dances, animated sequences, and a fantasy sequence. Includes a teacher's lesson guide.

Juvenile Justice in the United States: A Video History
Type: VHS
Length: 24 min.
Date: 1992
Cost: $73.50
Source: American Correctional Association
8025 Laurel Lakes Court
Laurel, MD 20707-5075
(800) 825-2665
Fax: (301) 206-5061

This video documents the history of how society's attitude toward the treatment of children has changed over time. It includes attitudes during the Industrial Revolution, the beginning of advocacy for children's welfare, and the entry of Cook County, Illinois, into the history books for its juvenile justice practice, laws, and experience starting in 1899. It discusses constitutional rights given to juveniles and the reform of treatment philosophies for juveniles. This video provides an interesting and informative history of how American society has treated its children.

Kids Mediating Kids' Disputes
Type: VHS
Length: 24 min.
Date: NA
Cost: $10 rental
Source: Wilmington College Peace Resource Center
Pyle Center, Box 1183
Wilmington, OH 45177
(513) 382-5338

This video was taped at Mitchell Middle School in Wisconsin. Narrated by Suzanne Miller, a mediation consultant and trainer, a school-based mediation program is described, including how it works and how to start a program in other schools. Real-life student mediators, principals, a juvenile court judge, a police investigator, a counselor, and representatives from the Wisconsin Bar Association describe the benefits of mediation programs based on their own individual experiences. This video is an excellent tool for other schools interested in developing their own student mediation program. Developed for adult audiences.

Making a Difference
Type: VHS
Length: 26 min.
Date: 1989
Cost: $25
Source: Educators for Social Responsibility
        23 Garden Street
        Cambridge, MA 02138
        (800) 370-2515

This video, produced by the director of the Resolving Conflict Creatively Program (RCCP), examines the dramatic changes brought about in students and teachers through the use of peer mediation and conflict resolution. The RCCP is a school-based program in conflict resolution and intergroup relations that offers students a model for preventing violence and creating a positive environment for learning. The program shows young people that they have many options besides passivity or aggression in dealing with conflict, gives them skills to make these choices, increases their understanding and appreciation of all cultures, and shows them that they can play a powerful role in creating a more peaceful world.

The Morning After: A Story of Vandalism
Type: VHS
Length: 27 min.
Date: 1990
Cost: $395
Source: Pyramid Film and Video
        Box 1048
        Santa Monica, CA 90406-1048
        (800) 421-2304
        Fax: (213) 453-9083

Three students from Sibley High School in St. Paul, Minnesota, and a friend had been drinking one evening and decided to break into the high school. They stayed in the school for a few hours, crashing into doors with a vehicle they found inside the school, using blow torches on vending machines, turning on all the fire hydrants, and smashing art objects and whatever else they could find. This video blends coverage from local television news with interviews with the vandals, their parents, other students in the high school, and the judge who heard their case and sentenced them. The four student-vandals talk about their feelings after being caught, why they did it, and how they feel about their uncertain futures.

This thought-provoking video should enhance discussions of causes and solutions to problems of teen vandalism, hostility, and violence, as well as alcohol and drug use and abuse, and encourage students to think twice before they act impulsively. The perpetrators explain that they got caught up in the emotion and action of the moment and never really meant to do such extensive damage. Junior and senior high-school students, teachers and school administrators, community organizations, social service organizations, and law enforcement personnel should benefit from this video.

On Television: Teach the Children
Type: VHS
Length: 56 min.
Date: 1992
Cost: $49
Source: California Newsreel
            149 9th Street, #420
            San Francisco, CA 94103
            (415) 621-6196

This video is designed to help educators, parents, students, and others find and expose television's hidden curriculum, i.e., product marketing, sex, violence, and anti-intellectualism. Including clips from Saturday morning cartoons, sitcoms, and music videos along with commentary by critics, scholars, and network executives, the video explores the values television communicates and the role models it provides to young children. A 16-page study guide and transcript is included. It contains reports on recent research and legislation, a policy history, an action guide, and a resource list. In addition, it outlines a complete media policy module for classroom and informal study.

On Television: The Violence Factor

Type:	VHS
Length:	56 min.
Date:	1984
Cost:	$49
Source:	California Newsreel
	149 9th Street, #420
	San Francisco, CA 94103
	(415) 621-6196

This video remains one of the only documentaries to examine television violence, ask why it is so widespread, and study its impact on behavior and attitudes. Clips from action-adventure series, Saturday morning cartoons, the nightly news, and MTV are interwoven with comments by researchers, scholars, and producers. A prominent researcher, Dr. George Gerbner, reviews 30 years of research on television viewing. The video challenges the viewer to help program rather than be programmed by television. It encourages viewers, young and old, to be more selective and critical in their selection of television shows to watch, and explains how to police the violent imagery television brings into our living rooms each night.

Peacemakers of the Future

Type:	VHS
Length:	23 min.
Date:	NA
Cost:	$10 rental
Source:	Milwaukee Public Schools; available from:
	Wilmington College Peace Resource Center
	Pyle Center, Box 1183
	Wilmington, OH 45177
	(513) 382-5338

This video documents the changes that occur as a result of a mediation program instituted for elementary-school students. It follows the students as they move into middle school and then to high school. The video demonstrates the ways a mediation program can be integrated into elementary-school curricula and then how the students apply its principles. Teachers and school administrators describe the effects of peer mediation programs from their relevant experiences and perspectives.

Real Men Don't Bleed

Type: VHS
Length: 20 min.
Date: 1991
Cost: $350
Source: Coronet/MTI Film and Video
420 Academy Drive
Northbrook, IL 60062
(800) 777-8100

This video follows the experiences of Michael, a young African-American man. He is knocked out during a fight on a basketball court. While unconscious, he is visited by himself as an older man. He is shown what will happen to him if he continues to follow the violent path he is on. The video offers alternatives to the macho role that many young men believe is necessary for their success in life. The video emphasizes the importance of thinking about what to do in a conflict situation instead of reacting violently. By witnessing a "real-life" situation, students can learn what will happen to them if they resort to violence to solve their problems and receive positive reinforcement to encourage them to challenge the idea that violence is the only way to solve their problems.

Resolving Conflicts through Mediation

Type: VHS
Length: 8 min.
Date: 1990
Cost: $40
Source: Albany Dispute Mediation Program, Inc.;
available from: National Association for Mediation
in Education
205 Hampshire House
Box 33635
University of Massachusetts
Amherst, MA 01003-3635
(413) 545-2462

This film includes dramatized situations of student conflicts among students in kindergarten through sixth grade. It demonstrates how other students, acting as peer mediators, are able to resolve conflicts on the playground, at lunch, and on the school bus. It describes to teachers, students, and school administrators the value of a peer mediation program.

Teaching Students To Be Peacemakers
Type: VHS
Length: 15 min.
Date: 1991
Cost: $28.75
Source: Interaction Book Company; available from:
National Association for Mediation in Education
205 Hampshire House
Box 33635
University of Massachusetts
Amherst, MA 01003-3635
(413) 545-2462

David W. Johnson and Roger T. Johnson, well-known authorities in cooperative learning, competition, and conflict resolution, describe and demonstrate peer mediation. Produced for children in kindergarten through sixth grade, this is a companion guide to their book, *Teaching Students To Be Peacemakers.* Students learn how to use mediation to resolve conflict issues in their daily lives.

Teen: Speak Out against Violence
Type: VHS
Length: 50 min.
Date: 1990
Cost: $40
Source: Contra Costa County Health Services Department
Prevention Program
75 Santa Barbara Road
Pleasant Hill, CA 94523
(415) 646-6511

This video highlights an all-day assembly in which professionals working to prevent adolescent violence and students from numerous California high schools came together to describe and discuss the issues of adolescent violence, including dating violence. Panels were brought together to discuss related questions including the magnitude of the problem, and the responsibility of schools, parents, and youth. Students in the audience voice their concerns, describe personal accounts, and present what they feel should be done to prevent the violence. This video provides insight into how students, teachers, parents, and school administrators view violence and articulates steps that everyone can take to reduce violence in their lives.

Tough Cries
Type: VHS
Length: 25 min.
Date: 1994
Cost: $95 (includes leader's guide)
Source: The Bureau for At-Risk Youth
645 New York Avenue
Huntington, NY 11743
(800) 999-6884
Fax: (516) 673-4544

Produced for students from seventh through twelfth grades, as well as adults, this provocative video vividly demonstrates how reacting angrily and violently to a conflict situation is not an effective solution. It also demonstrates that being willing to fight in order to prove toughness, friendship, and loyalty, is not necessary for young males. Ways to resolve conflicts without violence are suggested. The video effectively shows how violence escalates and becomes increasingly difficult to end.

Violence: Inside Out
Type: VHS
Length: 60 min.
Date: 1993
Cost: $125 (includes study guide)
Source: Chariot Productions
2819 3rd Street
Boulder, CO 80304
(800) 477-5128
Fax: (303) 786-9799

This video has been produced for students from seventh through twelfth grades, as well as adults. It explores violence, how it affects our lives, and demonstrates how we can work together to prevent violence at home, at school, and in our communities. Interviewing young victims, perpetrators, and witnesses of violence from culturally diverse backgrounds, this video examines domestic abuse, sexual abuse, gang-related violence, anger, suicide, and dating violence. Suggestions are provided to students for stopping the cycle of violence; these include staying away from stressful situations, dealing with problems as they occur, being honest about their feelings, trusting their instincts, finding positive role models, staying in school, determining ways to change, choosing supportive friends, and finding new ways to express themselves through sports, art, or other activities. Its poignant interviews clearly demonstrate the pain and suffering of the victims and the price society pays for violence.

Violence Prevention Curriculum for Adolescents
Type: VHS
Length: 54 min.
Date: 1987
Cost: $150 (includes teacher's guide)
Source: Education Development Center
             55 Chapel Street
             Newton, MA 02160
             (617) 969-7100

This curriculum includes a 110-page teacher's guide (with student handouts) and a teacher-training videotape. The ten-session course addresses the growing problems of violence and homicide among adolescents and offers positive ways to deal with anger and arguments—the leading precipitants of homicide among adolescents. It is based on the research of Dr. Deborah Prothrow-Stith, a physician and public health official. Dr. Prothrow-Stith advocates for a public health approach to preventing violence among youth. The curriculum acknowledges anger as a normal and legitimate emotion, and then emphasizes the importance of helping students understand the risk of being involved in violent situations. This curriculum discusses possible gains and losses to fighting and proposes alternatives to violence, provides positive ways to deal with anger, recognizes the warning signs of a potential fight, and teaches ways to resolve conflicts without violence.

Waging Peace in Our Schools
Type: VHS
Length: 26 min.
Date: 1992
Cost: $39.95
Source: Educators for Social Responsibility
             23 Garden Street
             Cambridge, MA 02138
             (800) 370-2515
             Fax: (617) 864-5164

This video describes the components of the Resolving Conflict Creatively Program (RCCP). A school-based program in conflict resolution and intergroup relations, the RCCP offers a model for preventing violence and describes ways to create caring, learning communities. The program teaches young people that they have a variety of options to deal with conflict, gives them skills to make these choices, increases their understanding and appreciation of all cultures, and shows them that they can play a powerful role in creating a more peaceful world. This video shows how conflict resolution skills are taught and how students are involved in peer mediation. Testimonials are provided by children, teachers, parents, and administrators.

When You're Mad, Mad, Mad!: Dealing with Anger

Type:	VHS
Length:	33 min.
Date:	1991
Cost:	call or write for current cost
Source:	Sunburst Communications
	39 Washington Avenue
	P.O. Box 40
	Pleasantville, NY 10570-9971
	(800) 431-1934
	Fax: (914) 769-2109

This video, along with a teacher's guide, demonstrates to students how they can deal with their anger in a positive way. It shows students how to refrain from becoming aggressive or violent by controlling how they act. The video suggests steps students can take to learn how to cope with their angry feelings instead of resorting to violence to resolve their problems.

Index